Mundane Heterosexualities

Also by Victoria Robinson

INTRODUCING GENDER AND WOMEN'S STUDIES, 3rd edition (*with Diane Richardson*)

EVERYDAY MASCULINITIES AND SPORT: MALE IDENTITY AND THE EXTREME SPORT OF ROCK CLIMBING

Also by Jenny Hockey

EMBODYING HEALTH IDENTITIES (*with Allison James*)

SOCIAL IDENTITIES ACROSS THE LIFE COURSE (*with Allison James*)

DEATH, MEMORY AND MATERIAL CULTURE (*with Elizabeth Hallam*)

Mundane Heterosexualities

From Theory to Practices

Jenny Hockey
University of Sheffield

Angela Meah
University of Manchester

Victoria Robinson
University of Sheffield

First published 2007 by
PALGRAVE MACMILLAN
Houndmills, Basingstoke, Hampshire RG21 6XS and
175 Fifth Avenue, New York, N.Y. 10010
Companies and representatives throughout the world

PALGRAVE MACMILLAN is the global academic imprint of the Palgrave
Macmillan division of St. Martin's Press, LLC and of Palgrave Macmillan Ltd.
Macmillan® is a registered trademark in the United States, United Kingdom
and other countries. Palgrave is a registered trademark in the European
Union and other countries.

ISBN-13: 978–1–4039–9745–6 hardback
ISBN-10: 1–4039–9745–4 hardback

This book is printed on paper suitable for recycling and made from fully
managed and sustained forest sources. Logging, pulping and manufacturing
processes are expected to conform to the environmental regulations of the
country of origin.

A catalogue record for this book is available from the British Library.

Library of Congress Cataloging-in-Publication Data
Hockey, Jennifer Lorna.
    Mundane heterosexualities : from theory to practices / Jenny Hockey,
    Angela Meah, Victoria Robinson.
        p.   cm.
    Includes bibliographical references and index.
    Contents: Unmasking heterosexuality — Theories of hererosexuality
    reconsidered — A heterosexual life : agency and structure —
    Heterosexuality across the twentieth century — Getting the story straight —
    Getting it together? carnal and romantic discourses — What's sex got to do
    with it? heterosexuality as an organising principle — Nothing natural? at home
    with heterosexuality — Different heterosexualities : different histories.
    ISBN-13: 978–1–4039–9745–6 (cloth)
    ISBN-10: 1–4039–9745–4 (cloth)
    1. Heterosexuality.   2. Feminist theory.   I. Meah, Angela.   II. Robinson,
    Victoria, 1959–   III. Title.
    HQ23.H7 2007
    306.76'401—dc22   2006053250

10   9   8   7   6   5   4   3   2   1
16   15   14   13   12   11   10   09   08   07

Printed and bound in Great Britain by
Antony Rowe Ltd, Chippenham and Eastbourne

For Gladys Settle

Contents

Acknowledgements

Many people have contributed to the production of this book and the empirical project which underpins it. In particular, we would like to thank Peter Halfpenny for his support in helping us refine our initial thinking on the topic of heterosexuality. Ros Billington, Paul Blackburn, David Morgan, Julie Seymour and Amanda Wade were an exemplary Advisory Board who provided intellectual and practical support throughout the life of this project. Their enthusiasm for our work remains invaluable. David Morgan we would like to thank for his insightful comments on an earlier draft of this book. The entire project could not have been imagined, executed and completed without the guidance of Diane Richardson and Liz Stanley. Their published work and the personal commitment that, in different ways, they have shown to each of us have provided the underpinning for our investigation of this topic. We would also like to express our gratitude to the 72 women and men who so generously shared their stories with us – and who trusted us with their pain as well as their happy memories. And finally, we wish to acknowledge the insights we have gained from those who participated in our own eventful heterosexual lives across the last five years. You know who you are.

1
Unmasking Heterosexuality

This book addresses a dominant identity category – heterosexuality. It argues that although both pervasive and privileged, heterosexuality is, as Kitzinger and Wilkinson (1993: 3) suggest, a 'given', 'a silent term'. In that empirical work on heterosexuality remains limited, this chapter draws parallels with similarly dominant social identities – masculinity, able-bodiedness, whiteness. Indeed many of these mesh with heterosexuality itself, mutually reinforcing positions of power and privilege. Thus, for example, discussing gender, Kimmel and Messner (2004) argue that men are often treated as if they have no gender. Listening to a conversation between a white and a black women discussing who they saw in the mirror each morning – the white woman seeing simply a woman, the black woman seeing a *black* woman, Kimmel realised that he saw 'a human being: universally generalizable. The generic person' (Kimmel and Meissner, 2004: x). As these authors stress, 'the mechanisms that afford us privilege are very often invisible to us' (2004: x). Dyer's discussion of whiteness echoes these points:

> the position of speaking as a white person is one that white people now almost never acknowledge and this is part of the condition and power of whiteness: white people claim and achieve authority for what they say by not admitting, indeed not realizing, that for much of the time they speak only for whiteness. (1997: xiv)

While Dyer's concern was with visual representation, ours is with the *experience* – and reflections on the experience – of heterosexuality. Yet as Dyer highlights, the power of a dominant category is in part tied up with not acknowledging its specificity – or, as he says, with not 'realising it'. Similarly, Lonsdale (1990) shows how the politicising of disability has

1

problematised the taken-for-granted status of 'able-bodied', hence the term 'temporarily abled' (Whyte and Ingstad, 1995: 4) which signals its limitations. Disabled people, Lonsdale argues, find themselves unable to 'participate in the social and economic activities *which most people take for granted*' (emphasis added) (1990: 1).

Although interview data from people living heterosexual lives contribute to this book's arguments, the status of 'heterosexuality' as an unmarked category renders them far from transparent. Interviewees describe finding out about their adolescent body in relation to those of members of the 'opposite sex', growing up into relationships with differently gendered people, setting up home, having a family, losing partners through divorce or death. Like whiteness, however, heterosexuality *per se* is barely 'realised' in their accounts. It is what interviewees are telling us *about* – but without it being foregrounded, as either a concept or an identity. In that power inheres in heterosexuality, these stories therefore constitute politically mediated understandings of what it means to be heterosexual.

This volume presents our analytic understandings of heterosexuality, ones we worked hard to develop during the research process. This effort partly reflects working with data that describe something rarely articulated; and partly our embodied experiences of heterosexuality and so needing the intellectual and emotional space to think outside, as well as within, its frames of reference. In addition, however, we present our interviewees' *implicit* understandings of heterosexuality, drawn on in stories of attraction, love, sex, parenthood and family life. While these are resorted to without their heterosexual nature necessarily being 'realised', interviewees' reflexivity was noteworthy – and data show them striving to articulate a critical perspective. This chapter's title therefore describes the ongoing process of 'unmasking' that we and our interviewees undertook in investigating this category. As Mason (2002) argues, the notion of the researcher as a 'miner' who excavates hidden knowledge belies the ontological status of that knowledge; and in its place Mason highlights the co-construction of knowledge which we call the research interview.

Reflecting on heterosexuality

The project is rooted in mundane heterosexual life. Its stimulus was everyday conversations which explored the nature of heterosexual relationships and which Jenny Hockey found herself being invited into. These asked how such relationships should be conducted, what they should feel like, and what should be expected. Love, monogamy, intimacy, commitment, loss, loyalty, pleasure were issues or values which percolated this talk. Giddens (1991) argues that reflexivity is key to the post-traditional project of the self in that relationships are now 'pure' and 'uncontaminated' by agendas other than wanting to be with another individual. Reflexivity is the process through which the progress of this 'project' is monitored and involves asking whether new departures and the severance of unfruitful connections are required. Jenkins queries the notion that self-monitoring is specific to contemporary life, arguing that 'reflections upon identity are not a historical novelty' (2004: 12). Instead, he suggests, the uncertainties produced by change of all kinds stimulate such reflection – and change is not new. There are, however, changes specific to particular historical eras and Jenkins does suggest that 'the *volume* of discourse about identity has reached new magnitudes', a reflection of the fact that 'global noise and chatter about *everything* has increased with the population and sophistication of communication technologies' (2004: 11).

In thinking sociologically about the reflexive 'heterosexual' conversations which stimulated our research, we asked whether they *were* historically specific? Or whether, as Jenkins suggests, they both *are* and *are not*? By interviewing people who had grown up heterosexual during different historical eras we were asking whether reflexivity had been a constant within their experience – and, if so, whether it might take different forms at different times. This is not to say, however, that everyday 'heterosexual' conversations were investigations of heterosexuality *per se*. People may have spoken to Jenny as heterosexuals, about their relationships with members of the opposite sex, yet their identity category was never foregrounded. Instead, the assessment of relationships, behaviours and emotions, in relation to vague yet important yardsticks, was prioritised. These personal reflections continue to surface. For example, in the *Guardian* newspaper's 'Private Lives' section (25 May 2006), a 29-year-old woman described her indecision about leaving her 'loving partner' of eight years' standing, a relationship she had thought 'perfect', for a man for whom she had instantly felt 'intense desire' and, subsequently, 'deep love'. Reflecting the breakdown of a (heterosexual) metanarrative (Giddens, 1991), readers' replies ranged through condemnation of her belief in 'romantic love'; encouragement to sustain relationships with both men; and the attribution of the problem to her avoidance of grieving for her recently deceased mother.

Methodological challenges

This chapter introduces the methodology we used to investigate 'hetero-sexuality' – and highlights the perversely obscure nature of a dominant and all-pervading identity category. The question addressed here – and throughout the project – is how an identity which occupies such a status, and is therefore difficult to 'realise', can be investigated and indeed interrogated. So both theoretical perspectives on heterosexuality and the methodological challenges of working empirically with a category which has been largely the preserve of theorists are introduced here.

In addition, by engaging with heterosexuality as a dominant, pervasive and invisible social category, we begin to understand what is occurring when 'heterosexuality' becomes the implicit focus for some-times painful processes of reflexivity. Being 'everywhere and nowhere', heterosexuality resists critical reflection, yet demands conformity, a point which extends to other 'invisible' or 'unmarked' identities. For example, discussing the implications for disabled women of taken-for-granted criteria for feminine 'beauty', Lonsdale (1990) acknowledges that for all women '[t]he stereotype is usually extremely difficult to attain naturally', a 'Holy Grail of Beauty' pursued not only via cosmetics, hairdressing and dieting but also body modification through surgery. In that our data describe individuals' parallel attempts to conform to an implicit yet powerfully felt 'holy grail' of heterosexuality, they were often unsettling, if not upsetting, for Angela Meah, as she conducted the interviews. As transcripts, they can be difficult to read, even though sexual abuse and domestic violence do not predominate. Instead, the freight of intense emotional, social and economic aspirations with which heterosexuality is laden makes much of our data disturbing, as individuals describe struggles to fulfil heterosexual goals – and become reconciled to their elusiveness. Chapter 9's historical compar-isons explore this point more fully.

Naturalising heterosexuality

Dyer argues that images of whiteness are not 'raced', going on to state that 'as long as race is something only applied to non-white peoples, as long as white people are not racially seen and named, they/we func-tion as a human norm' (1997: 1). Highlighting the power of repres-enting oneself as 'just' human, he echoes Richardson's argument that 'heterosexuality's naturalization means that it is rarely acknowledged as a sexuality, as a sexual category or identification' (1996: 13). This means that heterosexuals are a *socially* inscribed class, whereas lesbians and gay men are a *sexually* inscribed grouping – a point Dyer echoes when he stresses that only black and Asian people are raced. White people, he says, represent themselves simply as 'the *human* race' (emphasis added) (1997: 3). With respect to able-bodiedness, Morris similarly argues that it is defined by the *lack* of physical and learning 'impairment', suggesting that '[j]ust as beauty – and goodness – are defined by the absence of disability, so ugliness – and evil – are defined by its presence' (1991: 93).

Arguably, therefore, silence and invisibility are key to claiming and maintaining a dominant social identity which allows the individual to speak from a naturalised, universal position. And in attributing racial-ised and sexualised or disabled identities only to individuals whose skin colour, sexual practice or mind/body differs from those of a dominant category, the normativity of white heterosexuality is absolved from scrutiny, explanation, condemnation or tolerance. By contrast, JoAnne Rome, born without a left hand or arm below the elbow, describes being stared at by able-bodied people. 'I owed an explanation to whomever demanded one ... "What happened to your arm?" was not a question that I could choose to answer or not ... the world made it clear that I owed them an explanation' (cited in Morris, 1991: 28). Representa-tions of an 'unmarked' category such as white, however, show it to be 'without properties, unmarked, universal, just human' (Dyer, 1997: 38). With reference to heterosexuality, Richardson similarly describes it as 'the assumed bedrock of social relations' (1996: 3). In following Carby (cited in Dyer, 1997: 3), therefore, who refers to the task of making visible 'the (white) point in space from which we tend to identify differ-ence', we too aim to expose a dominant social category to scrutiny and explanation. In writing from a feminist perspective, we may wish to 'condemn' some aspects of heterosexuality. Equally, as feminists, we acknowledge women's and men's agency within heterosexual relation-ships, a position which allows a critical stance towards the universality – and associated homogeneity – attributed to heterosexuality.

These features of heterosexuality – its claims to homogeneity and universality – are key to the book. Dyer (1997) describes 'white' people implicitly assuming an authoritative voice grounded in a view of them-selves as 'just people'. As such the category 'whiteness' shares features of another dominant social category: masculinity. Whitehead, for example, cites John Stuart Mill's injunction: 'Think what it is to a boy, to grow up to manhood in the belief that without any merit or exertion of his own ... his is by right the superior of all and every one of an entire half of the human race' (cited in Whitehead, 2002: 1). Brittan (2001) uses the term 'masculinism' to describe the trans-historical ascendancy of men over women, one which transcends variation in styles of masculinity. As Haywood and Mac An Ghaill describe, '[m]asculinism is an ideology that stresses the natural and inherently superior position of males, while serving to justify the oppression and subjugation of females. The ideology of males being naturally more powerful, competent and fundamentally different from females is one that can be located in various historical periods' (2003: 10).

Via identities and ideologies such as these, intra-categorical differences tend to be subordinated to other kinds of difference: for example, between white and non-white, able-bodied and disabled or male and female. With respect to sexuality, for example, differences between heterosexual and lesbian or gay individuals are emphasised. So, as Chapter 2 exemplifies, within the history of feminist theorising around sexual identities the 'gay/straight' divide occupies a pole position, so obscuring less apparent differences *within* sexual identity categories; for example, those based on gender, race, age or class. This downplaying of difference and highlighting of homogeneity arguably sustains private concerns as to how an individual might judge their own experience against an apparently unitary category: heterosexuality – hence the painful reflections which pervade both everyday conversation and research interviews.

Butler (1990, 1993) discusses the processes through which such forms of social difference are *made* to disappear – so lending heterosexuality a naturalised, homogenised status. For her heterosexuality is 'always in the process of being constructed . . . through repeated performances that imitate its own idealizations and norms and thereby produce the effect of being natural' (cited in Richardson, 1996: 5). Thus, heterosexuality involves living up to a particular idealisation, a perspective which makes our interviewees' private struggles unsurprising. Given our own heterosexual experience, a sometimes painful identification with their mundane difficulties becomes inevitable.

Butler's perspective is echoed in VanEvery's (1996) account of the production of *gender*. Just as heterosexuality is seen as an innate, bodily propensity to desire and to bond with someone of the opposite sex, so gender is commonly conceptualised as 'a property of individuals wholly separable from the social practices' (1996: 45). When gender is used as a variable, therefore, in seeking to make sense of how something like housework is organised, authors neglect to recognise that domestic labour produces not only hot dinners and clean clothes, but also *gender* itself. So gender is not external to housework, a body-based characteristic which directs individuals to a particular kind of work, any more than heterosexuality is a biological 'drive' towards particular sexual encounters and reproductive strategies. Instead, the concept of 'accountability' helps explain how:

> a person engaged in virtually any activity may be held accountable for performance of that activity as a woman or a man . . . to 'do' gender is not always to live up to normative conceptions of femininity or masculinity; it is to engage in behaviour at the risk of gender assessment. (West and Zimmerman, cited in VanEvery, 1996: 46)

This notion of the 'risk of gender assessment' is addressed in subsequent chapters which explore interviewees' parallel sense of failing to live up to hegemonic heterosexuality via both the *content* of their talk and its style and use of language.

Whither heterosexuality?

The theoretical perspectives we used demanded a quite specific methodology, in terms of both who we interviewed and how we made sense of their data. Whilst demographic data suggest radical change in the patterning of gender relationships since the 1900s, heterosexuality itself has received little empirical attention. Given its inaccessibility to conscious reflection, this gap is unsurprising.

In the parallel example of whiteness, Dyer (1997: 23) describes the notion of 'spirit', or 'get up and go', thought to characterise being white, an embodied spirit which can 'master and transcend the white body'. Differerentiating white from non-white bodies, the 'spirit' immanent within white flesh has empowered colonisers, rulers and administrators for centuries, furnishing all white people with 'an invisible weightless knapsack of special provisions, assurances, tools, maps, guides, codebooks, passports, visas, clothes, compass, emergency gear and blank cheques' (McIntosh, cited in Dyer, 1997: 9). However, despite its material outcomes, investigating this 'unrealised' category is far from straightforward. As noted, Dyer's concern is the *representation* rather than experience of whiteness and he describes the white body displaying 'spirit' in its appearance, posture and functioning: 'A hard, lean body, a dieted or trained one, an upright, shoulders back, unrelaxed posture, tight rather than loose movement, tidiness in domestic arrangements and eating manners, privacy in relation to bowels, abstinence or at any rate planning in relation to appetites, all of these are the ways the white body and its handling display the fact of the spirit within' (1997: 23–4).

While these observable attributes are critical to whiteness as a privileged identity category, they do not reveal the nature of white subjectivities. And the same applies to able-bodiedness and masculinity. While people who are disabled have provided vivid, theoretically informed accounts of their experience (see Murphy, 1987; Morris, 1991), what it means to be able-bodied is less easily articulated. Delineating men's experience of masculinity is also, arguably, challenging and, in a discussion of how this area might be researched, Haywood and Mac An Ghaill point out that when interviewer and the interviewee are both men, whatever their differences of class or ethnicity, they will have 'access to the experience of being men, a shared knowledge that is often worked through traditional male relationships deriving from fraternity' (2003: 109). As a result it may be difficult to 'make strange' and so interrogate the category of masculinity. Hay and Mac An Ghaill (2003: 109) cite Hearn's suggestion that psychoanalytic interviews, a focus on men in subordinated positions, and the use of triangulation can help overcome this problem.

These then are the methodological challenges we faced. As noted, making sense of our data required considerable reflexivity in order to generate sufficient distance from our material. Accounting for the practice(s) of heterosexuality is therefore complex, for as Bourdieu argues, 'the scheme (or principle) immanent in practice ... should be called implicit rather than unconscious, simply to indicate that it exists in a practical state in agents' practice and not in their consciousness, or rather their discourse' (1977: 27). So if being heterosexual is immanent in practice, how can it be explored, particularly by women with their own heterosexual experience? Using the example of the intense 'reculturation' which Goffman (1961) describes as the purpose of 'total institutions', Bourdieu notes the centrality of 'insignificant details of dress, bearing, physical and verbal manners' (1997: 94) to culture and identity. These, he argues, reflect the entrusting to the body of 'the fundamental principles of the arbitrary content of culture' (1977: 94), so making them 'beyond the grasp of consciousness, and hence (they) cannot be touched by voluntary, deliberate transformation, cannot even be made explicit; nothing seems more ineffable, more incommunicable, more inimitable, and, therefore, more precious, than ... values given body' (1977: 94). While Goffman's work concerns extreme situations, it nonetheless highlights the *relative* inaccessibility of that which is learned in an embodied sense. Heterosexuality's embodied pervasiveness therefore constitutes a methodological challenge which we addressed partly by encouraging interviewees to reflect critically upon their heterosexual subjectivity. Nonetheless, interviewees' assumption of shared hetero-sexual understandings on the part of the interviewer was something requiring sustained attention. None of this makes heterosexuality readily amenable to empirical investigation then.

From theory to method

These theoretical orientations highlight our concerns with the entire cultural, social and intersubjective environment which surrounds appar-ently straightforward identity claims such as 'I am heterosexual'. They are both contextualised and developed in Chapter 2's critical review of feminist work in this area. Here, however, we trace their method-ological implications, suggesting that the following perspectives have helped overcome these difficulties: (1) the notion of heterosexuality as a residual category; and (2) the notion of heterosexuality as an organising principle.

Heterosexuality as a residual category

Jenkins describes social identity – or identification – as the outcome of an interaction between the way we experience ourselves and how others perceive us: 'the internal-external dialectic of identification' (2004: 18). So if we feel drawn to, or desiring of someone of the opposite sex, and if others note this, then claiming that 'I am heterosexual' is unlikely to be challenged, either by others, or indeed ourselves. But is this the end of the heterosexual story? Or indeed the nub of what we are invest-igating? As Chapter 2 shows, feminist theorising has described how the authenticity of a statement such as 'I am heterosexual' comes into being. It argues that an entire system of social organisation can be embodied in private moments of physical and emotional longing, or in the public interlocking of male and female hands. Once unpacked, however, as VanEvery argues, 'heterosexuality is about much more than sexual desire and sexual acts' (1996: 52). Noting the relational dimension of heterosexual practice, she argues that 'a particular type of hetero-sexual relationship is hegemonic in Western societies: lifelong, mono-gamous, cohabiting relationships, legally sanctioned through marriage and producing children' (1996: 52). To convincingly utter the statement 'I am heterosexual' therefore begins to look rather more demanding. As an identity, for example, heterosexuality can be 'spoiled' (Goffman, 1968), through emotions, experiences, language and behaviour which whilst indicating a broadly sexual orientation towards someone of a different gender, still fail, markedly, to reproduce hegemonic heterosexuality.

So if heterosexuality is not simply a set of sexual desires and practices, we can make some sense of it by listening to what had 'gone wrong' for our interviewees and their families. These data pointed towards the boundaries of hegemonic heterosexuality – that is to say, heterosexuality conceived of as 'natural', universal and internally undifferentiated. We were therefore attentive to the *limits* of an identity category which is popularly represented as 'only natural', as the normal process of human maturation, desire, bonding and reproduction. Observing that, for our interviewees, heterosexuality had 'limits', that it could somehow 'fail', affirmed our initial theoretical stance. Were heterosexuality simply the living out of natural drives or inclinations, it would reproduce itself relatively effortlessly, requiring no 'work', simply the avoidance of transgressions or inadequacies.

However, as Chapter 6 demonstrates, our interviewees' everyday lives could involve silences, exclusions or contradictions. Growing up heterosexual, for example, was primarily a matter of being told what *not* to do, whether hair-washing whilst menstruating, having contact with members of the opposite sex whose relatives had given birth 'illegitimately', or kissing someone in public whilst drunk. *Being* heterosexual, however, remained mysterious. Both older women and men and young adults described the absence of information about the physical and emotional aspects of heterosexual relationships – or indeed heterosexual desire (see Chapter 8). For our interviewees and their families, therefore, 'being' heterosexual equated to 'doing what comes naturally' – and so could be left unsaid. What *could* be articulated, however, was how individuals might transgress, or digress from its boundaries. When recalling how relatives who had failed to conform to the requirements of heterosexuality were ostracised, and their inadequacies and transgressions never mentioned, interviewees revealed the nature of heterosexuality by virtue of what it was *not*, or not meant to be. Our empirical approach to this category therefore developed by focusing on heterosexuality's shadow self, on those 'heterosexual' identities, experiences or practices which were somehow failed, fearful or discrediting. Rather than assuming that what was not appropriately 'heterosexual', was by definition gay, lesbian or bisexual, we encountered a system of patriarchal power which implicitly exhorted conformity to a quite specific, *institutionalised* form of heterosexuality (Jackson, 1996: 30).

Does this argument that heterosexuality is achieved rather than innate undermine its parallels with 'whiteness'? Skin colour, regardless its meaning, is surely a given? While feminist authors have challenged 'compulsory heterosexuality' (Rich, 1980), is being black or white not a fixed property of the body? To answer yes to this is to naturalise racial identities and to normalise whiteness, along with heterosexuality. As Dyer exemplifies, whiteness includes *and* excludes certain categories of people, '[t]he Irish, Mexicans, Jews and people of mixed race' (1997: 19), depending upon historical contingencies. Moreover, it can incorporate shifting internal hierarchies with 'the Anglo-Saxons, Germans and Scandinavians usually providing the apex of whiteness under British imperialism, US development and Nazism' (Dyer, 1997: 19). So just as the apparently straightforward materialities of the body remain vulnerable to different classificatory processes, so the contours of heterosexuality have markedly excluding qualities which can spoil the heterosexual identities of those who, for example, are young but without opposite sex partners, either short or long term; are heterosexually partnered and celibate; have never been romantically in love; do not cohabit with an opposite sex partner; have chosen to remain childless; avoid penetrative sex. And while this list might summarise contemporary criteria for disqualification, historically the boundaries of heterosexuality have undergone many changes, hence the ostracism of older female interviewees if they, or a member of their family, had borne children without being married, or to a partner who was married to someone else. Thus while heterosexuality's boundaries are mutable, *describing* its hegemonic form remained perennially difficult. If adolescent girls are no longer told not to wash their hair whilst menstruating, embodied heterosexual practices such as holding hands or bringing home a flower given by a boyfriend could still attract unwelcome parental teasing. So that which is marginal to, or risky about hegemonic heterosexuality may shift across time – and this means that listening carefully to the 'private troubles' of heterosexual people can throw light on the ongoing reproduction and reinvention of heterosexuality, even though 'doing' and 'being' heterosexual are far less easy to articulate. And this brings us to our second theoretical premise.

Heterosexuality as an organising principle

As discussed, parallels between heterosexuality, whiteness, ablebodiedness and masculinity lie in their respective normativity, their universality, and their status as unmarked categories. Also instructive is Dyer's reference to the drawing and redrawing of the lines of ethnic difference, depending upon historically located political contingencies. He says, for example, that 'whiteness has been enormously, often terrifyingly effective in unifying coalitions of disparate groups of people. It has generally been much more successful than class in uniting people across national cultural differences and against their best interests' (1997: 19). Thus, a perspective on identities which *appears* limited to skin colour or sexual orientation, in practice informs social and political organisation more broadly. Both the reproduction of heterosexuality and the reproduction of particular kinds of bodies, then, are goals rendered both implicit and inevitable in that they constitute the hidden organising principle of everyday life.

This is an important insight. Questioning 'naturalised' accounts of heterosexual desire and practice, evokes the puzzle of why and how heterosexuality remains so pervasive. If, as interviewees described, a heterosexual practice such as marriage *does* require effort, vigilance and single-mindedness, how can we equate these demands with something which 'comes naturally' – and, perhaps more pertinently, why do individuals persist in claiming identities, and engaging in practices which are heterosexual? For example, *The Bankruptcy of Marriage*, published in 1929, surveyed rising divorce rates and family breakdowns and concluded that marriage had had its day (cited in Morrison, 2002: 2). Over seventy years later, in 2002, the *Guardian* asked 'Why do we do it?' and in response Blake Morrison cited legal advantages, long-term physical and emotional comfort and security, a chance to buy a new outfit for the wedding, a belief that children should be born to married parents, and love, as reasons. However, for almost all these rationales, he provides counter-evidence which highlighted their fragility. Provocatively, Kitzinger and Wilkinson (1993) argue that heterosexual women incur ills ranging from the burden of an unequal division of domestic labour, through to poverty, coercive penetrative sex, madness, violence and abuse. Rich (1980) proposed that women were neither innately heterosexual, nor heterosexual through choice. Instead, it was 'something which had to be imposed, managed, organized, propagandised, and maintained by force' (cited in Kitzinger and Wilkinson, 1993: 3). The conspiratorial flavour of her words arguably belies the more subtle, yet pervasive processes evident within our data. While interviewees may not have articulated what heterosexuality *was*, instead describing what it was *not*, they did recount everyday lives organised according to implicit heterosexual principles. And it is our recognition of heterosexuality's role as a key organising principle within everyday life which led to our concern with 'mundane heterosexualities' as a fruitful means of moving from 'theory' to 'practices'. Starting from what people said about their everyday lives – from managing menstruation to struggling with disappointment, from finding a home to going weak-kneed at a first kiss – we not only asked how women and men came to be sexual and marital partners, but also how heterosexuality might operate, as a system of power relations which pervaded the organisation of everyday life. Drawing on Bourdieu's argument that 'the fundamental principles of the arbitrary content of culture' (1977: 94) acquire robustness through their inaccessibility to consciousness, we focused on their location within everyday life.

This analytic perspective led us to existing work on everyday life within the social sciences: for example, Smith's *The Everyday World as Problematic* (1987); Mackay's *Consumption and Everyday Life* (1997); and Nettleton and Watson's *The Body in Everyday Life* (1998). Its roots lie in an earlier sociological tradition which defines social reality as 'a process constantly reconstructed through the everyday action of individuals' (Swingewood, 1991: 268). The work of Schutz ([1932] 1972), for example, exemplifies trends towards social action theory stimulated by tensions between concepts of subject and structure, voluntarism and determinism within classical sociology. Meaning, as generated through social interaction, as inter-subjective, is core to Schutz's notion of the culture of the life-world, a stock of shared or sedimented knowledge which derives from individual experience – and is drawn upon in everyday social encounters. This privileging of the ordinary, as a way of making sense of the social, characterises an approach which is evident in Mackay's (1997) work on consumption. He says a focus on everyday life 'means that we are less concerned with the powerful and that which is recorded and codified, and more concerned with the unpredictable, the improvised and with the routine activities and control of ordinary people as they go about their day-to-day lives' (1997: 7). With respect to heterosexuality, then, the domain of mundane improvisation and routine has been selected in order to make sense of its capacity to demand conformity, whilst remaining unremarked. As Chapter 2 describes, social policy is critically underpinned by heterosexist assumptions and only recent feminist scholarship has made this manifest. Alongside social policy's more codified representations of heterosexuality, our exploration shows the same institution reproduced, negotiated and resisted within the ordinary world of family life. Thus, the notion of everyday life is 'characterised by small, local communities, with close and emotional ties, connectedness between people, caring, spontaneity, immediacy, participation and collaboration' (Mackay, 1997: 7). This contrasts with state bureaucracy and market relations. However, while we focus on 'emotional ties' and 'connectedness between people', we do not see everyday life as separate from wider systems of regulation. Rather, to understand heterosexuality as a social institution which pervades *all* aspects of society, we explore its entrenchment within routine bodily and emotional experiences such as 'having a girlfriend' or 'being a wife'. This resonates with Smith's (1987) arguments for a feminist standpoint grounded in the everyday world of women's lives. While our concern with relations between women and men leads us to include men's everyday standpoint, our approach nonetheless reflects Smith's view that: 'From within its (the ruling apparatus) textual modes the embodied subject and the everyday world are present only as object and never as subject's standpoint' (1987: 108–9). Thus, she goes on, 'the grounding of an abstracted conceptual organisation of ruling comes into view as a product in and of the everyday world' (1987: 109).

Chapter 7 develops these theoretical perspectives by discussing ruptures within the heterosexual relationships of family and coupledom – in contrast with Chapter 6 which examines their *stability* as, in part, an outcome of silencing and sequestration. When it comes to unmasking heterosexuality, then, such points of rupture demand our attention. As Mies argued, 'Only when there is a rupture in the "normal" life of a woman – a crisis such as a divorce, the end of a relationship, etc. – is there a chance for her to become conscious of her true condition' (1983: 125). Mies' notion that 'as long as normalcy is not disrupted they are not able to admit even to themselves that these relationships are oppressive or exploitative' (1983: 125) belies the experiences of some of our interviewees who did experience moments which prompted profound changes within those lives. Indeed, as Highmore argues, the exceptional is 'there to be found at the heart of the everyday' (2002: 3) – and he uses the example of Conan Doyle's fictional character Sherlock Holmes to show that understanding the mysterious and the bizarre involves scrutinising the everyday for that is precisely its site. This paradox at the heart of the mundane is addressed throughout this book. In 'making strange' the everyday in order to understand it we make it more governable but also more alien.

Rather than being 'imposed' or 'maintained by force', then, mundane heterosexualities inform the organisation of public and private space, the hierarchisation of 'special' moments, of bodily responses or intuitions, the timetabling of life course events and the domestic division of emotional labour. Heterosexuality, as 'institution, practice, experience and identity' (Jackson, 1996: 30), is produced out of the performance of other things, while interviewees were metaphorically 'looking elsewhere'. So, for example, 36-year-old Alison Innes, now separated from the father of her children and living in social housing in Hull, described how '*lovely*' it was, having a boyfriend for the first time. When explaining this she recalled '*having somebody*', '*just going to his house*', '*starting to go out in pubs on nights*'. In forming her first heterosexual relationship then, we can see its role as the organising principle of her *social* rather than sexual life. The coupledom towards which these social activities were assumed to lead was represented by his parents, the established couple providing a focus for the young people's nights out: '*His parents used to have a (group)*', recalled Alison, '*so we used to go, with nights out, we used to go with them a lot, to wherever the band, group was playing.*' After eighteen months the question '*shall we get engaged?*' emerged with apparent predictability, alongside practical activities such as: '*saving up for things in the house, and we got lots of furniture and bits and bobs like that*'. The social activities Alison described are entirely everyday in nature and indeed having someone simply '*being my boyfriend sort of thing*' led her to '*feeling a bit special about that*' (emphasis added), rather than him. The taken-for-granted nature of this heterosexual trajectory fuels its capacity to shape these young people's passage through the life course. Only after the engagement did Alison find that, '*one day I just sort of thought, this is getting boring and I just didn't want to spend my life doing this all the time, so just finished*'.

These data show heterosexuality exceeding the categories of sexuality to the extent that 'constructed notions of sexual behaviour and sexual identity have become primary organising categories for many key aspects of social life including but not limited to marriage, family, politics, religion, work, and education' (Ingraham, 2005: 2). Unremarkable practices such as first going out to pubs at night and saving for furniture emerge as crucial to heterosexuality's pervasiveness, revealing its embeddedness within everyday life. For these reasons, then, the institution of heterosexuality can be difficult to reflect upon and somehow 'do differently'.

Matters of methodology

The two perspectives outlined above show how we worked with our data, attending to what interviewees described as problematic, disappointing or shocking – but also exploring the fine grain of everyday lives organised according to heterosexual principles. Via accounts of the mundane, but also the extraordinary experiences of everyday life, we were able to work empirically. We now consider the implications of these theoretical orientations for the collection of data and for the overall design of the study.

If heterosexuality is rarely exposed for scrutiny, what we asked about were institutions more familiar to interviewees, those they had experienced directly and may have reflected upon more deliberately: marriage and family life. Though these well-researched social arrangements were our *empirical* concern, therefore, the institution of heterosexuality was our *analytic* focus. As VanEvery argues, 'the hegemonic form of heterosexuality is marriage' (1996: 40) and for this reason, it plays a central role within our data – even though many interviewees were not married when we spoke to them. This empirical/analytic distinction is developed in subsequent chapters where the related point is made that heterosexuality is not just about something we call 'sex'. Yet 'sex' is prominent if not dominant within our data. How do we reconcile this apparent disparity? Again, while our approach to analysis is informed by a relatively extensive body of feminist theory – and a small range of empirical studies (for example, VanEvery, 1995; Wilkinson and Kitzinger, 1993) – our data gathering was guided by a different principle – popular understandings of the concept of heterosexuality. And these were grounded in notions of sexual maturation and practice, the bodily and emotional dimensions of creating particular relationships between women and men. Not only everyday life, then, but sex itself is organised around particular values and assumptions which we call heterosexuality (see Jackson and Scott, 2004b). If heterosexuality is about more than simply sex, 'sex' *per se* embraces more than just cross-gender fucking, no matter how emotionally and physically satisfying that might turn out to be.

In addition to the content of interviews, there are questions about the historical prevalence of *reflection* upon aspects of experience which could be seen as heterosexuality manifested, if not made overt; for example, coupledom, marriage, monogamy, love. To address these questions we interviewed people from different age cohorts. In exploring similar issues with each one, we aimed to find out if not only their experience, but also its *significance* for them varied. This comparative material potentially revealed how an implicit commitment to a heterosexual identity might have changed historically.

While our data show heterosexuality permeating all aspects of everyday life, we nonetheless located our study within the dynamics of intra- and cross-generational family life. Though schooling, religious practice, social policy, health care and the media are all implicated in the reproduction of heterosexuality, it was the *making* of heterosexual relationships and their achievement through 'family practices' (Morgan,

1996), which particularly interested us. And as Morgan notes: 'It is impossible to write or think about family without also thinking about gender' (1996: 81). In other words, our aim was to get as close as possible to the living out of heterosexuality across generations and across the individual life course. This allowed us to get at its reproduction within the home, as children grew up, and at the reproduction or renegotiation of children's early familial environments as they themselves formed and sustained heterosexual relationships. So we not only sought to understand how the institution might have changed across the twentieth century. We also concerned ourselves with the ways in which the living out of heterosexuality might change as individuals grew up and grew older.

In sum, we investigated the processes of intra-familial, cross-generational cultural transmission which enabled the reproduction of heterosexual lifestyles and identities. We were interested in the possibility that heterosexuality now encompassed more diverse options than previously – and we wanted to know whether possible changes were felt as empowering or a source of risk and uncertainty. In addition we asked how femininities and masculinities might have changed across time (see Weeks, 1989; Connell, 2005: 185–203), and how any changes might relate to the institution of heterosexuality. In that reflection upon experience was a core interest, a life history approach revealed the emotional narratives drawn upon by our interviewees.

Located in East Yorkshire, our study worked in depth with male and female representatives of three generations within twenty extended families and was designed to access the experiences of partners at every stage of the life course. However, although the heterosexual principle of coupledom might characterise the institution as idealised, it corresponded poorly with everyday lives shaped by divorce, separation and widowhood. Moreover, topics such as sexuality, marriage and parenting proved highly sensitive, a finding which evidences the heavy freight of aspirations which the institution of heterosexuality bears. Recruitment was therefore an ongoing challenge throughout the project, given the siting of our work within the extended family. The willingness of one member of a couple or a family to participate was not necessarily matched by their father or mother, their husband or children. As one potential participant of the middle generation said: 'No, I don't want you talking to my mother. She thought I was doing loads of bad things when I was young, but I wasn't.'

We made contact with families through a variety of locations: the East Yorkshire Federation Women's Institute Conference, local press and

radio, mailings and visits to local voluntary organisations, email advert-
ising among staff and students at Hull University, and a display stand
on campus. Responses were initially limited with women of the middle
generation our typical initial point of contact, something we go on to
explore in Chapter 3. To expand recruitment we also conducted six
focus groups within existing local organisations: a church group and an
Adult Education group gave access to middle-class participants, while
two day centre groups, a women's group and a young men's group drew
working-class participants. Four groups were single sex, with two made
up of older adults, one of older men and one of younger men. Access
to data was enabled by a quiz comprising statements about marriage,
divorce and sex made by people of different ages and at different periods
of the twentieth century. Asked to guess who said what and when, focus
group participants were then encouraged to review their assumptions
about marital and sexual mores among different age cohorts and to begin
exploring their own experiences and attitudes. Given that the project
sought to fill gaps in the empirical bases of feminist theories of heterosexuality, this method allowed more theoretically derived research questions to be refined (Hockey et al., 2002).

Among the twenty-two families who we eventually worked with, six
were from rural locations in the East Yorkshire Wolds and sixteen from
urban environments, predominantly the city of Hull. Five families were
unequivocally 'middle class', the rest having a more working-class background. Since class variation tends to occur across successive generations, it is difficult to unambiguously assign an extended family to a
particular class location. As already indicated, only three couples were
interviewed and indeed only 48 per cent of participants were either
married (40 per cent) or cohabiting (8 per cent). This left 37 per cent not
currently in relationships, most of whom were widowed, slightly fewer
remaining single and a small proportion who were divorced. Fifteen per
cent of the total were in non-cohabiting relationships and 21 per cent
had been divorced at some point. Had we made married or cohabiting
couples our primary focus for data gathering, our access to innovative
interpretations of heterosexuality might have been restricted, divorce
and bereavement constituting ruptures which could expose the best and
the worst aspects of a heterosexual relationship.

Linked with the difficulty of accessing couples was an imbalance
between women and men, men making up only 17 per cent of our
sample: a preponderance of female respondents which points towards
women's roles as self-defined guardians of their families' emotional lives.
Towards the end of the project we were able to recruit more men and

once rapport had been established these men helped recruit other male contacts and so produced our final number.

Chapter 3 offers a reflexive account of the process of interviewing but here we provide an overview of how these interviews were designed and conducted. Using a biographical approach, we began by asking participants to contextualise their childhood before exploring how they found out about sexuality and relationships. Successive questions followed the chronology of the life course and we encouraged participants not to move forwards until discussion of a particular period of the life course had been exhausted. This strategy meant that all key transitions were discussed as fully as the participant felt able to (or was prepared to) – and often provided accounts of transitions which focused on the private or domestic, rather than public or institutional sphere. In addition, rather than offering a generalised overview of their life course, participants were encouraged to recall one period at a time, an approach which yielded fine-grain accounts of long-distant events. These showed the institution of heterosexuality being reproduced within everyday life, via sensory or embodied memories of wedding bouquets, items of clothing, meals consumed. Finally, participants were asked to reflect upon the heterosexual lives of other family members and to review their experience in its entirety. Interview questions explored participants' most positive and negative experiences, and what they felt contributed most to the making of 'successful' heterosexual relationships.

Though recruitment of extended families remained a challenge throughout, interviewing did yield extensive data, deriving from between one and five hours of discussion with each respondent. Focus group data complemented this. However, the project did not aim to provide an empirically generalisable account of beliefs and practices among different age cohorts in East Yorkshire. Instead, its *theoretically* generalisable data allow key explanatory factors and elements (Mason, 1996: 154) to be teased out via cross-generational analysis. By accumulating individual and familial heterosexual life histories (see Chapter 3), we thus made the processes and negotiations which constitute heterosexuality among women and men of different generations available for scrutiny.

Conclusion

Having outlined the relationship between our theoretical standpoint and our methodology in this chapter, Chapter 2 provides an overview of feminist theorising around heterosexuality, not only tracing its historical development but also noting its absence from academic work which nonetheless addresses many of heterosexuality's key institutions. In setting out the theoretical perspectives which are key to the project described here, it provides a basis for Chapter 3's more expansive methodological discussion which draws on the example of an extended life history. Chapter 4 then reviews existing work on the history of institutions such as marriage and the family, on sexuality and on identities such as femininity and masculinity, highlighting their implications for a contemporary study of heterosexuality. The theoretical perspectives presented in Chapter 2 are developed in Chapters 5 and 6 which introduce our analysis of data through a discussion of narratives of heterosexuality. A concern with the heterosexual imaginary is explored through a discussion of language, focusing particularly on how gender identities and emotional and bodily experiences might be separated out in the ways in which heterosexuality is narrated. Everyday life therefore remains core to discussion and is pursued in Chapter 7 where heterosexuality's scope as an organising principle is scrutinised in depth. In Chapter 8 we address the question of how heterosexuality's narratives are materialised in the living out of everyday heterosexuality. Here the relationship between home, family and sex provides a focus. Chapter 9 returns us to the question of heterosexuality's mutability – or stability – over time, focusing particularly on interviewees' reflections on how their experience matches their understandings of 'romance', 'love', 'sex', 'marriage' and 'family life'. Finally, our conclusion reiterates the book's commitment to an empirical investigation of mundane heterosexualities as a way of both drawing upon and contributing to feminist theory in this area. In addition, it highlights its contribution to sociological debates around structure and agency and the relationship between historical and biographical time.

This chapter, then, argues that the concept of heterosexuality, as an identity category, achieves dominance by virtue of its invisibility and, like whiteness, able-bodiedness and masculinity, is unmarked. It is precisely its taken-for-grantedness which constitutes a barrier to reflexivity on the part of everyday people living out their heterosexual lives. This has implications for researchers wanting to explore the meanings of 'heterosexuality' for individuals, their partners and families. How can we ask people who would identify as heterosexual about how they perceive themselves as conforming to, resisting or failing to live up to dominant expectations of heterosexuality? Such questions have, until now, been addressed primarily by theorists and, as this volume shows, many interviewees struggled to think critically and reflexively about their lives.

Indeed – for the most part – our interviewees had simply gone about the business of growing up and growing old, this process being orchestrated by a succession of events which they had perceived as marking their status as 'heterosexual'. Learning about the 'birds and the bees', first crushes, courtship, first sex, cohabitation, parenting, marriage, separation and bereavement – and not necessarily in that order – can therefore be seen as implicit within the process that constitutes 'heterosexuality'.

What this volume therefore presents is a reflection on the methods by which we engaged interviewees in critical reflection upon the nature of heterosexual subjectivity and the experiences – both theirs and those of other family members – through which this is constituted. However, our interviews revealed, the pervasiveness of hegemonic heterosexuality as a normative category is such that our interviewees often assumed that the interviewer would be able to identify with a shared experience of heterosexuality. Yet, as our data show, heterosexuality – while a dominant category – is not homogeneous. Across the sample, within families and within individual life stories, there are examples of not only conformity and reproduction, but also resistance and a failure to live up to hegemonic heterosexuality. Our challenge has been to reflect upon, explicate and make sense of these patterns while remaining mindful of the omissions and silences, the untold stories, the experiences which people did not – for whatever reason – want to own up to in an interview. The chapters which follow explore how – both theoretically and methodologically – we have met these challenges.

2
Theories of Heterosexuality Reconsidered

Richardson (1996) notes that within social and political theory there has, in the past, been little attention given to theorising heterosexuality. This is despite the fact that heterosexuality itself is very much embedded in accounts of social and political participation, our understandings of self and the world we inhabit. She further argues, as already noted, that the conceptual frameworks we use to theorise relationships between human beings tend to be reliant upon a naturalised notion of heterosexuality. In later work (2000), she goes on to argue that this area is potentially one of the most important developments within the theorising of sexuality itself, and in social and political theory more broadly. This is because it not only opens up new discussions around family relationships, for example, but also illuminates conceptual dichotomies such as the public and private distinction. The findings from the study we present here, and our subsequent theorising, contribute to, and open up, these new debates.

As Chapter 1 stated, Jackson describes heterosexuality as 'institution, practice, experience and identity' (1996: 30). In that chapter we began to address issues around all four of these aspects of heterosexuality from feminist and sociological perspectives. Jackson (1999) argues that the question of identity, especially a lesbian political identity, has been much debated in feminism. Yet heterosexuality has not been similarly theorised. Despite many women deriving their identities from being wives, mothers and girlfriends, for example, most women do not think of themselves as having a 'heterosexual identity'. As this chapter reveals, however, such theorising is now taking place and feminists, in partic- ular, have started to develop ideas around the theoretical and personal implications of 'admitting' to a heterosexual identity. Richardson (2000) also argues that feminists and other proponents of queer theory have now begun interrogating the way that institutionalised heterosexuality encodes and structures everyday life – and the lived, everyday experiences of heterosexuality are central to this endeavour. Further, the notion of 'practices' is useful in allowing us to theorise heterosexuality in terms of both structure and agency. Finally, as Chapters 5 and 6 demonstrate, such approaches allow us to engage with the discourses and narratives through which 'practices' come to be interpreted and so constitute particular *experiences* of heterosexuality.

The following chapters therefore address all four of these constituent parts, examining the ways in which our interviewees' practices and experiences serve to produce their heterosexual identity. But it is the notion of heterosexuality as institution we want to focus on here, given that such a lens allows us to look historically at how heterosexuality as a concept has been theorised within, and outside, of feminism, something already introduced in Chapter 1. This allows us to define and conceptualise how we are using the term 'heterosexuality' in our study. Taking account of changes in outward forms of heterosexual relationships during this period (see Chapter 4), it also considers social science's efforts to theorise the relationship between people's outer and inner emotional lives. In so doing, we elaborate on Chapter 1's introduction to issues of masculinity by charting how it has started to be theorised in relation to the emotions. We also highlight the recent theoretical move from 'heterosexuality' in the singular, to 'heterosexualities' in the plural, as this is central to our theoretical framework for the project.

Lastly, it is important to briefly define some key terms around heterosexuality, to give our subsequent discussions of heterosexuality coherence and to explain how such terms have been used within feminist theory more generally. 'Heteronormativity', therefore, refers to how the normative status of heterosexuality is institutionalised and legitimated through institutions such as the family and through discourse, rendering other sexualities abnormal and deviant. For example, Richardson (2000) explores this concept in relation to issues around HIV and AIDS, where, in debates surrounding health education campaigns, heterosexuality has been constructed as exempt from the need to change, particularly in relation to heterosexual males who, in the past, have been represented as safe in such campaigns, at risk simply from deviant women. In this way a 'hegemonic heterosexuality' becomes both established and the norm, with alternative heterosexual practices, such as non-monogamy for example, being seen as 'other' and abnormal when compared with dominant manifestations of heterosexuality, such as state-sanctioned marriage between heterosexuals. VanEvery's empirical research on anti-sexist living arrangements (1995) exposes the extent to which gender identities and heterosexual identities are interwoven even among participants who were actively striving to achieve alternative forms of living and 'refusing to be a wife'. For VanEvery, recognising the hegemonic character of heterosexuality as an organising principle enables a discussion of a set of assumptions about heterosexual life which are 'socially ascendant' (Connell, 1987, cited in VanEvery 1996: 40) and which become part of the popular psyche, informing young people's expectations of how their relationships should be, and providing a framework for older people to reflect upon and evaluate their relationships. As Connell (1987) observes, such hegemony or social ascendancy extends into the organisation of private life and cultural forces (1987: 184). Related to this discussion of hegemonic heterosexuality is the concept of a 'heterosexual imaginary'. Ingraham refers to this as a way of thinking which 'conceals the operation of heterosexuality in structuring gender and closes off any critical analysis of heterosexuality as an organising institution' (1996: 169). Debates around these established concepts are ongoing. For example, Jackson (2006) utilises Seidman's (2005) discussion of hierarchies of good citizenship and respectability within heterosexual relationships, which are seen to be established through traditional gender arrangements and lifelong monogamy, to argue for a need to rethink the concept of heteronormativity. This, she asserts, is: 'in terms of *what* is subject to regulation on both sides of the normatively prescribed boundaries of heterosexuality: both sexuality *and* gender' (Jackson, 2006: 105). She concludes that as well as not being able to regard gender, sexuality and heterosexuality as the same phenomenon, which map onto each other neatly, there are also aspects of these which are not reducible to the heteronormative. Further, to enable the concept of heteronormativity to have more critical purchase, it needs to be thought of 'as defining normative ways of life as well as normative sexuality' (2006: 117). By recognising these complexities, she argues, we avoid both seeing heteronormativity as so fluid it can be 'easily unsettled', and a return to seeing it as monolithic and, therefore, entrenched (see also Jackson, 2005). In the next section, we look at some of the consequences of this monolithic tendency within some feminist theories.

Heterosexuality as institution

In considering the ways in which heterosexuality has been theorised as an institution, we begin by noting its role in shoring up the centrality of gender difference as an essential property of women and men. This theoretical assumption underpins thinking about heterosexuality as a concept, one which is then institutionalised in medicine or the family, for example. So while heterosexuality has often been treated as if it were a monolithic institution, a foregrounding of its homogeneity is paradoxical, since the concept is implicitly premised on the notion of gender difference, on a hierarchical opposition between masculinity and femininity. Richardson (1996), for example, argues that heterosexual desire *presupposes* difference and indeed the history of the western body shows gendered difference being produced with increasing intensity from the beginning of the nineteenth century onwards (see Martin, 1987; Laqueur, 1987), a process which served to generate the male sexualised body and the female reproductive body. The complementarity of these bodies, each providing what the other lacks, echoes the Platonic notion of heterosexual union as the final discovery of our one and only 'other half' from whom we were sliced, like the two halves of a flat fish, before our birth (Rosen, 1968). By comparison with the gendered bodies of the nineteenth century, however, medical illustrations from the late sixteenth and early seventeenth century demonstrate how similarities between women's and men's bodies were produced, through representations of the womb which, to twenty-first-century eyes, evoke the penis (see Martin, 1987). In the case of an organ such as the anus, which is common to both women and men, Richardson argues that its inability to display 'difference' in part leads to it being relegated to an inferior position, often encoded, if seen as sexual, as the surrogate vagina of a gay man (1996: 6). This view of gender as intrinsically a matter of difference, one which stimulates a naturalised desire for the opposite sex, renders it invisible within the apparently homogeneous human experience of heterosexuality. Like class, age or ethnicity, gendered difference disappears as a focus for any kind of scrutiny.

That the historical and cross-cultural variability of gender differences is obscured within the naturalising processes of living out heterosexuality is unsurprising, given its 'invisibility' (Holland et al., 1996: 144), as Chapter 1 argued. In other words, heterosexuality does not have the status of a chosen identity, instead representing the unremarkable outcome of a 'natural' process of growing up to feel desire for the opposite sex, and of fulfilling that desire via long-term cohabitation/marriage/family life.

Moreover, we argue that institutionalised heterosexuality frames all sexualities. Richardson (1996), for example, cites the heterosexist assumption that lesbians adopt the gendered roles of butch or femme.

On the aspect of work, Jackson argues that 'heterosexuality itself is not merely a sexual institution: it is founded as much on men's access to women's unpaid work as on their sexual access to our bodies' (1996: 36) (see also Jackson, 2006). Further, Richardson (1996) argues that hetero-sexuality is institutionalised as a particular form of practice and within the relationships that constitute family structure and identity. As well, across the areas of sexuality, work and family as defined by Richardson and Jackson above, in addition to other aspects such as educational practices, the experience of institutionalised heterosexuality is also seen to be informed by, and, in turn, informs our constructions of race and class. Moreover, Holland et al. state: 'Becoming heterosexual occurs at differing levels of social activity, from the most grounded meeting of bodies to the most abstracted level of institutionalisation' (2002: 327).

These contemporary perspectives do need to be located within their broader historical context, one we elaborate upon in Chapter 4. However, before critically exploring feminist debates on heterosexuality from the 1970s onwards and examining their key role within the empir-ical project we are presenting, this chapter asks the revealing question 'who cares about heterosexuality?'

Heterosexuality and the social sciences

Within social and political theory as *traditionally* conceived, there has arguably been little attention given to the theorising of heterosexu-ality. It is rarely acknowledged, let alone problematised (Richardson, 1996). So to address the question: 'who cares about heterosexuality?' we need first to consider how heterosexuality has been conceptual-ised in more general theoretical debates. These include the sociology of the family, family policy and marital therapy literature. As noted in Chapter 1, it is a particular type of heterosexual relationship that has hegemony in western societies: one that is lifelong and monogamous. Further, it is the norm that these are cohabiting relationships which are legally sanctioned through marriage and having children. While it is precisely this type of relationship which has formed the corner-stone of academic work on the family, it is primarily in the case of gay or lesbian families that silence has been broken around the issue of heterosexuality. As VanEvery argues, 'there is a vast sociological liter-ature on households, family and marriage ... which rarely explicitly problematises heterosexuality, despite the fact that most research in these areas is on heterosexual couples' (1996: 40). Overall, then, it could be argued that work in these areas has not been centrally concerned, or even concerned at all with heterosexuality, as either institution or experience. If attention has been paid, it has been found wanting in terms of any rigorous examination of either heterosexual practices or theoretical assumptions about heterosexuality. For example, as Jackson and Scott (2004b) argue, while heterosexual sex is viewed as the corner-stone of coupledom, its supposedly transcendental qualities remove it as a focus for the sociology of everyday life. As such, therefore, they call for 'a more critical view of the special status it has acquired in common-sense, popular and academic discourse in order to investigate it in the same way as we would any other aspect of everyday social life' (2004b: 244). Contradictorily, however, sexual practice, particularly that of men, is viewed simply as a natural function which requires scrutiny only when it 'goes wrong'. And this naturalisation of 'sex' then extends itself into an under-theorised notion of heterosexuality as some kind of human 'norm'.

If we turn to the social policy literature, we find that, as Cara-bine (1996) argues, sexuality has been either invisible or ignored until recently, both within the academic discipline and in policy-making itself. Indeed, Carabine (1996) points out that although social policy has become a focus for the politics of sexuality, a site where diverse issues and 'truths' about sexuality are debated, for example, in relation to single motherhood and teenage pregnancy, little attention has been given to theorising heterosexuality *per se*. This has meant that social policy perspectives on the family have been presented in an unproblematic and universalistic way. Carabine (1996) cites numerous studies of the family, in both mainstream accounts (see for instance Mishra, 1981 and Walker, 1983) and feminist accounts (for example, MacLean and Groves, 1991 and Hallet, 1995) which either omit discussion of heterosexuality at all, or make assumptions about heterosexuality which reinforce the universality of the institution, and so have normalising effects. What both sociology and social policy have in common as fields of enquiry is the tendency to see heterosexuality in monolithic terms. Though Carabine acknowledges that feminists have long been concerned with issues of sexuality, both in theory and practice, for example campaigns and analyses around abortion, sexual violence, reproduction and porno-graphy, where feminist social policy has focused on sexuality, attention has mainly been paid to heterosexual family norms. She does, however, assert that there are exceptions to this, and new work is challenging such heterosexual assumptions.

The aim of this chapter is therefore to show how our empirically based project is both informed by, but also reinvigorates, feminist theorising around heterosexuality. We therefore begin by locating our work in relation to ongoing historically located debates within social policy about how gendered identities, marriage and the family have changed across the period covered by our interviewees. As we then argue, a broad, contemporary view of these changes reveals the emergence of new family forms (Silva and Smart, 1999) or what might be termed the 'democratisation' of the interpersonal domain (Weeks et al., 1999: 85). While these issues have been attended to in contemporary debates in sociology and social policy, the ways in which they represent changes within heterosexuality itself is a question we engage with throughout the book, via the empirical data generated through our project.

Any acknowledgement of those changes potentially allows us to ask new questions around heterosexuality from diverse viewpoints. However, as noted, it is the emergence of new family forms grounded in same-sex relationships which has provided the starting point within much of the recent literature. For instance, Weeks et al. (1999) have demonstrated that it is only via heterosexual, rather than gay or lesbian relationships, that 'real' families can be seen to be reproduced. Another emergent issue is the spatiality of non-heterosexual relationships, as evidenced in the work of social geographers who have examined the experiences of lesbians, gays and bisexuals in relation to everyday space, including the private sphere (Adler and Brenner, 1992; Bell, 1992; Valentine, 1993; Namaste, 1996). Moreover, new research is taking place on gay and lesbian marriages and the significance of legitimating same-sex relationships (Shipman and Smart, 2007), on lesbian motherhood and relationships in lesbian parent families (Gabb, 2005; Malone and Cleary, 2002), on the changing politics of sexuality in the context of new forms of social governance associated with neoliberalism in relation to lesbian and gay lives (Richardson, 2004) and on transgender practices of partnering and parenting (Hines, 2006). In light of the growth of studies such as these, one premise for our study was a sense that we now know more about the narratives of lesbian and gay identities within relationships which do not conform to prevailing norms (see Weeks et al., 1999 and Dunne, 1999), than we do about heterosexual lives. This issue is taken up in more detail later on in this chapter – and in Chapter 7.

The development of new family forms such as these calls attention to claims that the late twentieth century has seen the democratisation of the personal domain. Arguably this has produced shifts in the way family and relationships have been theorised in terms of intimacy and the emotions, yet while the practical and economic dimensions of heterosexual relationships have been prioritised within sociological studies of marriage and the family (VanEvery, 1996: 40), the emotional experience of heterosexuality still remains opaque (Jackson, 1999). Nonetheless, work is starting to emerge on these aspects of heterosexuality; for example, Johnson and Lawler (2005) present arguments surrounding the interaction of romantic love and class in heterosexual relationships and Johnson (2005) addresses debates around heterosexuality as identity and practice in relation to love relationships. In contrast with psychologists and psychiatrists for whom the psyche has been a privileged domain, sociologists have concerned themselves more with the social construction of *theories* of emotion. This tendency is being readdressed more recently in some of the literature. For example, Lupton in *The Emotional Self* (1998) explores the cultural discourses of emotion which see men's and women's affective lives as different and looks at the new models of masculinity that men have adopted. Later in this chapter, we discuss some of the implications of ignoring men and masculinities in relation to intimacy, the emotions and heterosexuality.

Giddens (1992) has maintained that the coming together of diverse social processes has brought about radical shifts in intimate relations, including those between couples and within families. As noted in Chapter 1, the notion that the self now constitutes a 'reflexive project' is key to these arguments. This, in Giddens' view, enables more democratic relations in the private sphere. However, alongside the critique that Giddens ignores the reflexivity of much earlier generations (Jenkins 2004), feminists have problematised his broad brush approaches to gender relations (Jamieson, 1998). In the analysis of our data we develop these critiques through more empirically grounded perspectives.

Against the background of shifting couples and familial relationships, Lewis and Kiernan (1996) point out that the increasing separation of sex, marriage and parenthood has led to new understandings of the idea of 'family' and an associated blurring of traditional conceptual boundaries. Beck and Beck-Gernsheim (1995) and Macionis and Plummer (2002) also indicate that less than a quarter of households in the UK include a traditional family, of married or cohabiting parents with dependent children. Within this context, the project's starting point was evidence which *suggested* increasing reflexivity around heterosexual social arrangements such as the family and marriage (Jagger and Wright, 1998; Silva and Smart, 1999). This raised further questions as to whether public policy initiatives designed to shore up traditional family values (Land, 1999), plus private uncertainties about the living out of heterosexual social arrangements, were a product of social change such as the weakening of stigma around cohabitation, lone parenthood and divorce, and new gendered patterns of paid employment.

Below, we raise the question as to whether heterosexual social arrangements and gendered identities were more taken for granted during the first half of the twentieth century. Equally, as Chapter 1 points out, contemporary marriage remains robust as a heterosexual social arrangement. For example, though there has been a long-term decline from the peak number of 480 285 marriages in 1972, marriages increased for the third successive year in England, Wales, Scotland and Northern Ireland in 2004. Also, in 2004, 49 540 marriages were remarriages for both parties, accounting for 18 per cent of all marriages (National Statistics Online, 2006a). This suggests the persistence of powerful biases in its favour. And it is this perennial conundrum, posed by evidence of both significant changes and robust continuities within the institution of heterosexuality, that we address in the project, through the analysis of the data and in the book's individual chapters.

Feminist theorising on heterosexuality

We now move on to trace the theoretical as well as empirical roots of the project presented here. Its distinctiveness reflects the diversity of the authors' existing research in the separate fields of heterosexuality and masculinity (Robinson, 1996, 1997, 2003, 2004, 2008, forthcoming), ageing and the life course (Hockey and James, 1993, 2003), and feminist epistemology (Meah, 2001). This unique combination of perspectives has allowed the investigation of heterogeneous heterosexual identities, as well as an emphasis on methodological reflexivity, and brought a historical approach to the diversity of heterosexual practices. But what underpins these areas and brings together these separate fields is a concern with feminist theory, especially in relation to heterosexuality.

While we have argued for the relative invisibility of theorising around heterosexuality within sociology and social policy, it is nonetheless the case that alongside feminist social policy, both feminist theorists *and* activists have highlighted heterosexuality's role in reproducing women's subordination through a focus on a diversity of issues such as domestic violence, child abuse, representations of sexuality, sexual relationships and practices, domestic life and the labour contract in marriage amongst other issues (see for instance: Bunch, 1975; Rich, 1980; Dworkin, 1981, 1987; Mackinnon, 1982, 1996; Jones, 1985; Walby, 1990; Delphy and Leonard, 1992; Wittig, 1992; VanEvery, 1995, 1996; Richardson, 1996, 1997; Jackson, 1997; Maynard and Winn, 1997). We can see this as a response to policy analysts' arguments that the breakdown of marital and cohabiting arrangements and the rise in lone parent households represent a social problem (Land, 1999). Indeed politicians on the right and the left have called for a return to 'traditional' family values. Though contradictory, both positions appeal to a monolithic model of the heterosexual relationship we have already discussed. Whilst on the one hand heterosexuality is critiqued by feminists for disadvantaging women in the interests of patriarchal society, on the other it it is thought of as the cornerstone of a status quo where social reproduction is taken care of within the privatised setting of the family. Neither position acknowledges the range of experiences encompassed within heterosexuality, nor do they identify the ways in which individuals resist, renegotiate or reproduce gendered relationships which unfold within 'the framework of a dominant, institutionalised "compulsory" heterosexuality' (Robinson, 1997: 143). So, along with the disciplinary areas identified above, feminist theory, too, can at times be seen to replicate the tendency to represent and critique heterosexuality in monolithic terms.

However, if we put feminism's theoretical critiques in a post-1970s historical context, we find a greater diversity of viewpoints. Rather than stereotyping feminist positions on the subject of heterosexuality, we need to recognise the intense debate and disagreement to which the topic has been subjected amongst them. As Jackson (1999) notes when referring to 1970s feminism and heterosexuality debates, current critical analyses of heterosexuality are not new and, moreover, though much feminist work of that time failed to sufficiently problematise heterosexuality, '[n]onetheless, there was work at this time which provided an implicit critique of heterosexuality and laid foundations for more radical questioning' (Jackson, 1999: 4) (see also Jackson and Scott, 1996, for a discussion of wider debates around sexuality).This insight into feminist theorising points to the need to appreciate the diversity of conceptualisations of heterosexuality, both within and between different theoretical positions.

To complicate things further, not all contemporary feminists share the same view of past theorising and where it can lead us. Rather differently, therefore, Smart (1996), asks whether we can extract discussions of heterosexuality from the framework constructed by feminists in the 1970s and, though avoiding feminist stereotypes of earlier positions, still argues that we need to move beyond old debates and positions. She concludes that unless we find new ways of speaking about *heterosexualities*, and of appreciating differences of meaning and experiences, then feminist theories 'will remain strangely repressed on a most important aspect of the lives of many women' (1996: 177).

In an account of (hetero) sex, for example, Smart seeks a way of grasping the notion that 'heterosexuality may be many things', whilst retaining the recognition that 'at times we need to collectivize this diversity (for example, whilst recognizing heterosexual privilege and its naturalization)' (1996: 170). She goes on argue, however, that 'there can be multiple meanings (although not any old random meanings) attached to different sexualities at the same time' (1996: 167), enjoining us to 'retain a politics and pleasure in more fragmented heterosexualities' (1996: 174). What Smart contests then is a tendency to treat heterosexuality as a homogeneous institution within which the agency of women and men appears not to exist, either theoretically or empirically.

However, we need to bear in mind that a linear position on the emergence of theorising on heterosexuality, which sees all past accounts as monolithic and in denial of any scope for agency, which views any attempts to revise or challenge heterosexual relationships as at best misguided and at worst futile, does injustice to some of those earlier accounts. While we have limited evidence as to how a 'compulsory' institution is actually reconstructed and practised, a circumstance which testifies to the power of heteronormativity, simply to view heterosexuality as monolithic and inflexible amounts to political nihilism (Davis, 1991: 82). Indeed, it is fair to say, as Richardson (2000) points out, that the re-emergence of debates on heterosexuality in the 1990s, as well as re-examining 'old' questions, also introduced a new focus on sexual experience and practice (particularly sexual pleasure and desire), both as critique and defence. However, she asserts that others have been more concerned with 'theorising the ways in which heterosexuality is institutionalised in society, how this is implicated in women's subordination and how heterosexuality as social practice constitutes gender (see for example: Carabine, 1996; Richardson, 1996; VanEvery, 1996)' (2000: 22). In recent years, the development of queer theory within the academy, out of lesbian and gay studies, has also begun to question the normativity of heterosexuality. Some feminists have drawn upon these developments when attempting to explore heterosexuality, including Butler's work (1990, 1993, 1997) and the theorisation of heterosexuality and its relationship to lesbian identity in particular. As Chapter 1 noted, for Butler, heterosexuality is always in the process of construction through repeat performances which have the effect of naturalising it. It has been questioned how useful queer ideas on heterosexuality are outside of theorising lesbian and gay identities. For example, Seidman (2005) argues that within queer, the consequences of a normative heterosexuality on heterosexuals has not been an issue. However, Richardson et al. (2006) argue that feminist and queer accounts overlap, and both positions therefore question the privileging of heterosexuality on a number of levels.

To address the issues raised so far we need to consider debates around structure and agency. Davis (1991), for example, takes issue with 'feminist common sense' which, in her view, 'both traditionally and in the present, tends to treat power within gender relations as basic-ally top-down and repressive. Women are regarded as the inevitable victims of male supremacy, helpless and hapless at the hands of the evil-intentioned, omnipotent male' (1991: 79). Interrogating (hetero)sex, Smart (1996) also argues that feminists have inadvertently augmented male power by over-inflating the penis. She asks, 'must we simply reas-sert that all heterosexual sex is oppression?' (1996: 161–2). Such critiques of monolithic, top-down repressive gender power remind us of the diversity of heterosexualities which women and men inhabit; *and* the agency of women (and men) within institutionalised heterosexuality. Failure to acknowledge this reduces all women to a single position: that of 'cultural dupe' (Jackson, 1999), or 'dope' (Davis, 1991: 80). Davis calls for a theory of gendered power which allows us 'to reinstate women to the position of agency without falling into the concomitant stance of blaming them for social inequalities' (1991: 82). Mann and Roseneil (1999) also highlight the agency of women who are often seen to be structurally dispossessed by conditions of poverty and disadvantage. In their view, 'there are women living in situations of structural poverty who are exercising agency and consciously deciding to have children without depending on a male partner. In this sense they are undoubtedly reflexively constructing their own "life narratives"' (1999: 113). This evidence suggests that women may choose to opt out of the institu-tion of heterosexuality, but the question does remain as to whether new heterosexual forms of relationship are emerging and as a site for women's agency.

Parallel debates within the sociology of ageing throw light on how the relationship between structure and agency may be understood. Bury (1995) points out dangers in 'structured dependency' theory, a political economy of the life course which privileges exclusion from paid work as the basis for older adults' relatively low social status. Introduced as a corrective to biologically based views of ageing which privileged indi-vidual adjustment to 'inevitable' decline, structured dependency theory, like early second-wave feminism, highlighted structural features of older adults' oppressive conditions. In both cases, however, the relationship between structure and agency needs to be addressed, for as Bury says, it is 'important in developing a perspective on ageing, since it challenges the portrayal of older people (especially women) as passive victims of circumstance' (1995: 16). Wray also argues that within the gerontological literature 'there has been a tendency to overemphasise the effects of structural disadvantages and overlook the power of women to resist and transform social structures' (2003: 512). The more micro-level life course approach which Bury advocates also has problems, however – ranging from proselytising injunctions to age 'positively', to the postmodern critique of life course stages which argues for new benefits of consumerism and 'choice'. Nonetheless, the life course perspective which we use here does consider how wider historical changes mesh with the individual biographies which form our core data.

The issue of agency is also explored in a collection of essays which represent the heterosexuality debate in feminism over more than a decade ago. This was published in the journal *Feminism and Psychology*, in 1992. Indeed, it was being asked to contribute to a further collection of connected essays in 1993 which inspired Victoria Robinson's theoretical interest in heterosexuality. The editors of this first collection, Kitzinger and Wilkinson, argued that '[h]eterosexuality has largely been untheorized within both feminism and psychology. Feminist theory tends to assume heterosexuality as a given, developing analyses with women's (and men's) heterosexuality as a taken for granted, but never explicitly addressed, substrate' (Kitzinger and Wilkinson, 1993: 1). Much debate ensued, some of which accused the editors of framing the discussion in terms of patriarchal and negative aspects of heterosexuality, whilst at the same time denying any agency or pleasure on women's part. However, referring to the heterosexual women who 'wrote of "being" heterosexual in *Heterosexuality: a Feminism and Psychology Reader* (Wilkinson and Kitzinger, 1993)', Smart points out that '[w]e can certainly see radically different heterosexual identities emerging in which these women are far from being the dupes of patriarchy, are far from homophobic, are far from accepting male sexual dominance, and are far from seeking their own missing penises as Freud would have us do. Some of them also seem to be having a good time even if they feel they should do so quietly' (1996: 177).

Central to Victoria's contribution to this volume (Robinson, 1993), was the argument that the institution of heterosexuality needs to be separated out from the experience of different women and consideration given to the diverse ways in which heterosexual relationships are lived out, for example through non-monogamous practices. An updated collection by *Feminism and Psychology* was published in 2003. It addresses feminism and marriage, and shows how thinking about heterosexuality has changed within feminism. In the early stages of our empirical study, caution was expressed by some reviewers about what appeared to be our conflation of heterosexuality with marriage. However, as VanEvery (1996) notes, marriage epitomises the hegemonic character of hetero-sexuality. In the 2003 *Feminism and Psychology* collection, heterosexual feminists were asked how they now conceptualised the institution and practice of marriage which earlier feminists had seen as being promoted by the Church and State, and had critiqued as the outcome of discourses of love and romance which masked women's position as economically dependent within marriage. The editors, Finlay and Clarke, sought to broaden the feminist discussion on marriage by bringing the personal and political perspectives and experiences of heterosexual feminists (and their male partners) to the debate. They sum up the contributions by arguing that they are not a simple celebration of marriage: 'Rather, they indicate the struggles that married feminists undergo in choosing to participate in an institution that is both the heart of heterosexual priv-ilege and the heart of heterosexual women's, lesbians and gay men's oppression' (2003: 417–18). However, they also felt that not all the ques-tions they posed to contributors were fully analysed. These included not reflecting on the challenges that lesbians and gay men offer to conven-tional marriage and institutionalised heterosexuality, for instance.

Alongside heterosexual women's struggles with heterosexual arrange-ments there have also been calls by some lesbian feminists to be able to marry and have the same citizenship rights as heterosexuals. This recent debate has caused heated discussion, both in academia and the media. Richardson (2004) utilises the concept of citizenship to explore lesbian and gay demands to equal rights of citizenship on the grounds of being the 'same' as heterosexuals. She argues that access to this new citizenship status is seen to be in the context of public recognition of a normative ('good gay') couple relationship (see also *Feminism and Psychology*, 14, 1, 2004, for diverse views on this issue). However, although this work has emerged more than ten years *later*, certain issues are still being taken for granted and so remain unexamined. For example, the largely unproblem-atised hegemonic position of monogamy within heterosexual relation-ships reveals that certain issues are still not debated, or even acknowledged (see Robinson, 1997, 2003 and Jackson and Scott, 2004a).

Additionally, Richardson notes that 'the experience of institutional-ised heterosexuality is also informed by, and informs, constructions of race and class' (1996: 2). However, citing theorists such as bell hooks (1989), she argues that there has, for example, been little public discussion of race and sexuality. Sexuality, when it is theoretically connected to race, is often seen in terms of hypersexuality, where black women and men are viewed as oversexed (heterosexuals). Richardson (2000) goes on to argue that, though there is a growing (largely North American) literature on how race, class and ethnicity interact with sexuality for lesbians and gay men (for instance, Moraga and Anzaldua, 1981 and Penelope, 1994), there has been relatively little on heterosexuality. As with race and ethnicity then, we need to still look at how sexuality, and indeed, heterosexuality mesh with class in relation to identities, relationships and practices. (Though for work on class see Skeggs (1997) for discussion on sexual working-class women and the intense feelings they can provoke in the popular consciousness, in comparison to middle-class women; Lawler (2005) and Taylor (2005a) on intersections of class and sexuality; Taylor (2005b) on sexuality, working-class lesbians and post-school transitions and (forthcoming, 2007) on working-class lesbian lives.)

Further, to avoid seeing women (and men) as cultural dupes in relation to heterosexuality, we need to reconceptualise agency in new and different ways with regard to heterosexual relationships. Whether this is in relation to issues of race and ethnicity as outlined above, or in the context of the variables of class, age and geography, which we highlight in the following chapters, it is an agency which needs to be seen and conceptualised in terms of people's everyday life and experience. Thus, in our interviewees' frequent experiences of incompatibilities between everyday and hegemonic heterosexuality, we gain insight into how the profile of heterosexuality has shifted. Where once domestic violence and forced sex were silenced, cohabitation, divorce and lone parenthood considered taboo and there existed social expectations regarding the household division of labour, age at marriage and family size, these have been replaced or incorporated within heterosexuality such that cohabitation, lone parenthood and divorce no longer carry the stigma they once had; couples marry later – if at all – and choose to be childfree, while implementing less demarcated domestic roles (see for example Robinson, 1997, 2003; VanEvery, 1995).

With a focus on agency, then, this section has reviewed the diversity of political orientations and theoretical perspectives which constitute the growing body of feminist scholarship around heterosexuality. With this in mind we now turn to a more historical perspective, one which we argue can give valuable insight into both the barriers and the scope for change within the institution of heterosexuality.

A cross-generational perspective: new questions from distant voices

The cross-generational material presented in this volume *in part* reinforces a feminist legacy which views heterosexuality largely as a constraining and compulsory institution (Rich, 1980). However, we are concerned to engage more critically and reflexively with these data. For example, while heterosexually rooted social 'categories' such as boyfriend and girlfriend, engagement, living together, marriage, wife, husband, partner, love and sex do seem to have enjoyed a relatively extensive shelf life, detailed historical evidence shows heterosexuality as a mutable social institution. Those categories which appear to be constitutive of heterosexuality cannot be seen to simply exercise a determining influence upon the individuals who inhabit or enact them. In order to develop insight into heterosexuality's capacity for fluidity and dynamism, historical evidence that its material context – possessions, places, practices and indeed the body – has changed as a site of intimacy and distance is important. Life-course transitions such as pregnancy and childbirth, entry to or exit from employment, divorce, and calendrical transitions, such as birthdays and anniversaries, provide useful filters or lenses through which to explore heterosexual relationships. These events form part of how the life course is structured, and yet are also aspects of how individuals experience and negotiate their own biographies. Social structure, in Rapport's view, 'depends on the continuing, conscious, concerned activity of different individuals to intend, produce and sustain it' (1993: 41). Importantly, as he goes on to argue, 'social structure does not inexorably give rise to homogeneity, stability, consistency or communication. As a discursive idiom, a fiction, it is always subject to creative interpretation, to individual manipulation and re-rendering' (1993: 41–2). Following this line of argument, heterosexuality can therefore be seen as a social institution which, whilst powerful and apparently enduring, in fact persists as a result of a plurality of practices on the part of women and men. It is these practices which constitute the 'cultural transmission' of heterosexuality. However, this term, in itself, implies a uni-directional handover of some kind of baton of social mores. In so doing, it neglects the capacity of children and young people to influence the lifestyles of older generations (James, 1999). If we wish to make sense of the diversity of patterns and proliferation of gendered identities which have come into being contemporarily, we therefore need to provide a more complex and inclusive account of belief and practice across the twentieth and twenty-first centuries.

In seeking to fulfil this objective, it is important to ask about the extent to which the family has been a key site within which hetero-sexuality is reproduced, resisted or renegotiated. In other words are we seeing changes in the institution of the family or in the institution of heterosexuality? Linked with this are questions about the implications for the women and men involved. Though authors such as Rapport (1993) stress the intrinsic creativity of the individual who animates cultural scripts according to their personal agendas, other theorists such as Giddens (1992), highlight the 'riskiness' which comes with the post-traditional loss of consistent metanarratives. With regard to heterosexu-ality and, indeed, established family forms, it is therefore important to ask whether these now encompass more diverse options than previously (see Jagger and Wright, 1998) and if so, whether they bring the bene-fits of personal choice and empowerment, or the dangers of risk and uncertainty. Rapport cites Leach's view of human beings as 'criminals by instinct', agents who actively resist 'the dominion of present struc-tures' and so restore culture's vitality (1993: 36). By contrast, Giddens (1992) highlights the ontological insecurity of individuals who, in post-traditional western societies, lack the cultural resources to integrate the external world into a personal narrative of self-identity.

The evidence presented in Chapter 4 points towards considerable change in the outward form of heterosexual relationships across the twentieth century. However, this does not necessarily indicate any corresponding internal shifts. Contemporary feminist theorists such as Hawkes (1996), for example, assert that heterosexual practice has remained resilient to change, persisting even within liberalising sexual discourses under the guise of new lifestyle 'choices' for women. Feminist critiques also identify the prevailing belief in the 'naturalness' of hetero-sexuality as an important reason why outdated, oppressive beliefs and practices persist. When social institutions are seen as the outcome of 'natural drives', resistance to change is harder to overcome (Hawkes, 1996: 138; VanEvery, 1996: 48). Further, it has been argued that tradi-tional forms of masculinity and femininity are reproduced within heterosexual relationships. Holland et al. (1996), for example, in their study of young women's and men's sexuality in the contexts of AIDS, considered accounts of first heterosexual experiences and concluded that: 'We are arguing that heterosexuality is not a balanced (or even unbalanced) institutionalisation of masculinity-and-femininity, it is masculinity' (1996: 145). Their work showed young women to be under pressure to conform to models of adult heterosexuality which in fact helped shore up hegemonic masculinity. Our study acknowledges such pressures but also emphasises the interactive and negotiated nature of the structure of heterosexuality and individual agency. Jackson and Scott (1996) also contribute to these debates by concluding that women and men learn to be sexual in different and gendered ways, which can lead to confusion and deception in heterosexual sexual relationships.

These authors make sexuality and sexual practice their primary focus, yet as Jackson (1996, 1999) also points out, heterosexuality is not just a sexual institution, it also permeates the way we organise and experience other institutions, such as the world of work. VanEvery similarly views heterosexuality as an institution rather than a sexual preference (1996: 48), one which is haunted by traditional models of marriage and the family which legitimise women's economic dependency and unequal burden of care work. For example, in Hakim's (1996) view, not only are 50 per cent of British women living in heterosexual family arrangements and organising their lives according to the modern family division of labour, but they have made this their lifestyle by choice. These women, she argues, have resiliently maintained their twin orientations towards parenthood and labour force participation, opting for a paid work timetable which is subordinate to and shaped by the lifestyle of children and partners. Their male partners meanwhile continue to live out the post-war male breadwinner role, only one in 50 men in employment with two dependent children opting to work part-time (Burgess, 1997: 145). Such data evidence the endurance of heterosexuality as an institution and its continuing resistance to change. However, they also indicate that it is by looking closely at the life course and both women and men's experiences within it of the family, housework and paid work, as well as areas such as people's sexual and emotional lives, that we can start to unravel the complex relationship of structure and agency.

Data such as these indicate persistent patterns of inequality and economic dependency within marriage, yet there exists little by way of a history of mentalities within twentieth-century couple relationships (see Dallos and Dallos, 1997; Cline, 1998; Jamieson, 1998). Nonetheless, the meaning of concepts such as intimacy, autonomy, commitment, monogamy, faithfulness and privacy, which can reveal the cultural shifts in the living out of heterosexual relationships across the century, merit close consideration as evidenced, for example, in the work of Duncombe and Marsden (1993, 1996). Arguably, however, social scientists have been deterred from investigating the mental and emotional lives of society's members by a spurious opposition between the 'inner' and 'outer' person. Reinforced by the disciplinary boundaries between, for example, psychology and sociology, sociologists and anthropologists feel constrained to limit themselves to the 'outer life of overt behaviours' (Cohen and Rapport, 1995: 4), whilst aware that these cannot be read as simple mirrors of the individual's agendas and priorities. When it comes to examining heterosexual relationships, this misleading separation between behaviour and affect is likely to reinforce what Simpson (1998) describes as the difference between actual social relationships and people's conceptions of them. Researching post-divorce families, he argues that although individuals may be out of sight for interviewees, they were not out of mind (1998: 129). Yet these 'imagined' relationships are often relegated to psychologists and psychoanalysts, charged with the task of elucidating the 'inner' world. Given that heterosexuality is often represented as an exclusive social formation of two bounded individuals, a feature which has attracted strong feminist criticism (Rosa, 1994; Robinson, 1997), to make the canonical 'pair-bond' a boundary to our field of study inhibits proper accounts of the imagined world of relationships through which the particular identities of both the individual and their partner are constituted. As Carrithers observes, 'we cannot know ourselves except by knowing ourselves in relation to others' (cited in Simpson, 1998: 128). For Simpson therefore, 'the imagined world itself is populated with characters "felt to be there" and which continually splice into the real world' (1998: 129). The more emotional, intimate aspects of heterosexuality thus require urgent investigation by sociologists tuned to the intersubjective nature of social institutions such as 'family', 'coupledom' or 'marriage'.

An example of work which attempts to bridge 'inner' and 'outer' worlds is Dallos and Dallos' (1997) use of feminist perspectives to examine intimate relationships. Seeking to understand what they describe as a sexual cycle of male demand–female reluctance, they critique the individualising orientation of many therapies and instead cite structurally located ideological and material-based inequalities between women and men. The difficulty with this kind of approach is that its attempt to defuse individualised blame can produce impoverished accounts of agency. Women's sexual withdrawal from men, for example, is described as 'rarely a deliberate strategy, rather it is a desperate reaction which is often associated with misery and negative consequences' (1997: 1). Thus, while Dallos and Dallos refuse the notion that structural factors determine people's actions, they still see individual problems as a reflection of an external world which acts upon the individual, rather than a cultural milieu within which they participate.

The relationship between 'inner' and 'outer' worlds is also a focus for sociologist Jamieson who provides a critical account of the notion that intimacy is 'at the centre of meaningful personal life in contemporary societies' (1998: 1). As she points out, knowledge of another person's 'inner' world has not everywhere and at all times been seen as a basic human need, a point we develop in Chapters 4 and 9. While Dallos and Dallos operate from the premise that a lack of sexual intimacy is likely to be a source of distress for couples, Jamieson's sociological gaze makes the public stories about how human beings should relate to one another her primary focus. In her view individuals are increasingly influenced by such discourses in a world where private life has become open to public scrutiny. What is less evident in the empirical work she reviews is the quality of emotional experience. When it comes to couples' relationships, the emphasis falls mainly on sex and housework and one is left feeling that there must be more to life than these two activities in the households which sociologists explore.

What we have argued, therefore, is that commonsense assumptions about the divisions between 'inner' and 'outer' worlds and the separation of the bonded pair from any 'supporting cast' tend to be unthinkingly reflected in research methodologies. Similarly, popular, gendered assumptions about 'men's emotional inarticulacy' (Rutherford, 1992: 11; Lupton, 1998: 105–36) are reflected in the lack of sociological attention to the emotional dimensions of men's experiences of heterosexuality. Masculinity is now seen as 'troubled', men losing their traditional occupational structures and therefore a 'breadwinner' role within households (Connell, 1995). Theorists such as Seidler (1989, 1992) have stressed that men have had to deal with the consequences of their emotional alienation from themselves, and highlighted their painful struggle for a suitable 'emotional language'. The 'wounded' emotionally inarticulate male may now be asked to take more emotional responsibility for himself and others, but despite this, there are authors who feel that: 'Men's deafening silence about their own sexuality as opposed to the objects of their desire continues' (Middleton, 1992: 126). The problem too is that men can emphasise the 'male wounded psyche' at the expense of analysing male power and privilege (Robinson, 1996).

Nonetheless, we must recognise that theorists such as Connell (2000) have recently argued that a consideration of emotional relations in the context of masculinity are fundamental new directions in theory and research, something we consider further in Chapter 9. This mirrors the recent interest in emotion in social theory more generally and the insights of feminism in connecting heterosexuality to men's position of social dominance. In addition, some theorists are critical of the idea or existence of a 'masculinity crisis' asserted by feminist authors such as Horrocks (1994), or indeed the extent to which men might change because of such a crisis. For instance, McMahon (1999) asks why, despite the apparent feminisation of men in the public sphere, are gender relations so resistant to change, despite general enthusiasm for such a shift? He concludes that women continue to care for men, both in body and soul, and that the rhetoric that men have fundamentally changed is much exaggerated. In sum, we are arguing that what is needed now is empirical evidence which details that change (or lack of it) in relation to the supposedly natural, intimate and hidden character of heterosexual relationships.

This point does, however, raise the associated question of how we might go about conducting an analysis of material relating to emotional experience and the ways in which individuals might reflect upon that experience, particularly men. Ingraham (1999: 12) suggests that we *can* explore the ways in which both women and men make sense of their emotional experience and how these relate to the 'continual state of crisis and contradiction' of heterosexuality as historical and material conditions shift and change. This can be achieved, for example, by examining cultural manifestations such as films like *Four Weddings and a Funeral, The Crying Game, The Bird Cage* and *The Wedding Banquet*. She also goes on to say that creating an illusory heterosexuality through the romantic 'heterosexual imaginary' prevents us from seeing how institutionalised heterosexuality works to organise gender, whilst at the same time preserving racial, class and sexual hierarchies. But though empirical data are scant, there are nonetheless persuasive arguments to suggest that it is by actively participating in these narratives or scripts that women and men develop a sense of who they are and what their relationships should be like (Jackson, 1999: 106–7). Indeed, as Rapport (1993) argues, we need to recognise not only that individuals author their own lives, but also that they engage in the continuous rewriting of new or amended narratives, reflexively reformulating their own, intimate environments.

As Chapter 5 details, an important aspect of this kind of enquiry is the question of the narratives of self through which individuals sustain romantic love and heterosexual commitment (Jackson, 1999). Feminist debates on love and romance have slowly developed, having been neglected within previous feminist accounts. Early feminist attention was directed to the continual allure of romantic fiction for many women. Cultural definitions of romance were seen on one level to perpetuate gender stereotypes of women's concern with emotional issues, as well as showing women subordinate to men both emotionally and financially within heterosexual marriage. As Marshment (1997) notes, however, other feminists have stressed alternative interpretations of how romance made the erotic available for women, albeit always in an unproblematised heterosexual context. As Jackson (1999) charts, we need a feminist analysis of love and romance, to see how love is made sense of as an emotion and to see how romantic desires are culturally constructed. For such constructions, she argues, are framed within a heterosexual and patriarchal social and cultural order, impinging too on those who resist compulsory heterosexuality.

Feminist theorising has raised pressing questions about the relationship between changing femininities and masculinities and the 'decision' to form heterosexual relationships. It asks whether new gender identities produce different patterns of relationships, which in turn become sites of change where new masculinities and femininities are reinvented or stabilised (Smart, 1996). Smart has argued that debates about heterosexuality often negate the positive experiences of relationships between women and men, promoting celibacy or lesbianism as flawless alternatives. This perspective rests upon a monolithic model of 'the heterosexual relationship', one which, in her view, urgently needs supplanting by the notion of 'heterosexualities', which represents more egalitarian relationships between women and men and the site of new gendered identities.

Conclusion

In conclusion to this chapter we sum up the factors which underpin the distinctiveness of our project on heterosexuality. They include a commitment to fleshing out feminist and other theories with empirical evidence of everyday lived lives, a focus on the diversity of experiences of heterosexuality – including attention paid to men and masculinities – as well as to women and femininity, a detailed account of the proliferation of heterosexualities, rather than a monolithic heterosexuality, and a focus on older women and men who have been neglected in feminist accounts. Whilst the social sciences, especially sociology, are characterised by empirical work, sexuality, especially heterosexuality, has not been central to their theoretical agenda. Although feminist theories have indeed problematised heterosexuality, the lack of empirical evidence undermines the capacity of debates to fruitfully progress.

Out of this study, new theoretical agendas have emerged which we will go on to look at in the rest of this volume. These include the question of how to take (feminist) political agendas forward without depoliticising them; for example, by acknowledging different women's attempts at self-definition through their attempts to democratise heterosexual relationships, and, whilst acknowledging the pervasiveness of patriarchy, the issue of how to do this in ways which respond to women's and men's various experiences. There is also the question of how to make sense of the relationship between heteronormative structures and personal agency – and, in Chapter 3, we situate ourselves as 'younger' feminists who are trying to make sense of an older women's life and the historical contingency of her choices. In so doing we ask how to address agency and the constraints on agency which women and men face. To provide a nuanced interpretation of how the older woman in question fulfilled a traditional role within a male breadwinner family and undertook extended emotional labour on behalf of her mother, her husband, her daughter and grand-daughter, we require a theoretical framework which allows us to understand it as something more complex than just 'collusion' (Smart, 1996). And lastly, there is the issue of how to incorporate and theorise both diversity and commonality in the analysis of the wealth of heterosexual relationships and identities which we have investigated.

It is encouraging to recognise the growth of other feminist work which is starting to engage with the complexity of theorising 'heterosexualities'. For instance, McNulty's (2003, 2004) work on teenage pregnancies and inter-generational transmission of belief systems around sexuality, engages some of the issues we have highlighted here. It is, however, the scale of our project which makes us the first major, qualitative study of heterosexuality across the generations, and as such, we are uniquely poised to take forward these new theoretical agendas.

3
A Heterosexual Life: Agency and Structure

The previous chapters described the theoretical and methodological evolution of our empirical study, detailing how it was conceptualised in terms of existing debates about sexuality in which heterosexuality is presented as an 'unmarked', taken-for-granted category of analysis, and a system of relations, assumed by many feminists, to have historically privileged men. The starting point for our study was to move beyond feminist assumptions about the inevitability of women's subordination to men through heterosexual relationships. The aim was to test feminist assumptions about gender relations and heterosexuality against the experiences of women and men living out heterosexuality on a daily basis. Through our data, we present the limitations of arguments premised upon top-down, repressive patriarchal power, highlighting the diversity of heterosexualities which women and men inhabit; *and* the agency of women (and men) within institutionalised heterosexuality.

Drawn from life history interviews with 72 individuals across three generations in 22 families, the data on which this book is based are complex and multi-layered, presenting experiences which span a 75-year age gap, along with differences of wealth, social status and gender. Interviews had a variety of locations: the department in which two of the authors were based, farms in the picturesque Yorkshire Wolds and homes on sprawling social housing estates. Wherever the participants chose to be interviewed, the common denominator was the interviewer: Angela Meah. In principle, using only one interviewer helped sustain a consistent approach across the interviews and facilitated an overview of the data. However, as feminist researchers, we are mindful of the research interview as a social situation in which both interviewee and interviewer participate as social beings, bringing to it their own identities, experiences and stereotypical assumptions about the other.

These were the means through which the social encounter of the interview was both negotiated and interpreted. What is revealed about a
participant's perceptions of their heterosexual identity during the social
context of a research interview is intersubjective (Schutz, 1973) and
influenced by the use of life history method, the context and location of
the interview, who else was in the vicinity at the time and the particular
identities of the interviewer and the interviewee.

Participants were aged from 15 to 90, and included 60 women and 12
men. All were white. The interviewer, Angela, a woman of mixed ethnic
origins, was – at that time – aged 29. These reflections upon fieldwork
emphasise that the interview is not simply a snapshot of a moment in
time, but a social process which is subject to interpretation and reinter-
pretation after the event. What we present throughout this book are not,
therefore, straightforward accounts of different people's life stories, but
the socially mediated outcomes of encounters between individuals from
different backgrounds and with different agendas. Empirical knowledge,
we argue, must be seen as the product of intersubjective social processes
(despite the use of a common topic guide by a sole interviewer).

Drawing upon a single case study (see Hockey et al., 2004) and
building upon the discussions of agency in the previous chapter, this
chapter will highlight some of the methodological dilemmas presented
for feminist praxis when we explore the interview as a social event.
What we examine is the negotiated relationship between a historical past
reconstructed in a contemporary interview involving two people who
may share certain similarities, but where there also exist differences. How
these factors intersect in the research interview and contribute to the
social production of knowledge, as Schutz (1973) has highlighted, is our
central concern here. Thus we explore what Fawcett and Hearn (2004)
describe as the possibilities and challenges of carrying out research
when the interviewer may have no direct experience of the social divisions and oppressions experienced by those she is interviewing, but
also – conversely – the research implications of doing research, specifically semi-structured, life history interviews, when the interviewer is *not*
'other' to the people whom she is interviewing.

Informed by a feminist research practice which is concerned with the
negotiation of relationships in interviews, our methodology and analysis
have been driven by concerns such as: reflexivity, non-exploitative inter-
view/interviewee relationships, attention to hierarchical power relations
and the empowering of the interviewee by giving them a 'voice' within
the research (Oakley, 1981; Thomson and Scott, 1990; Cotterill, 1992;
Holland and Ramazanoglu, 1994; Lee, 1997; Meadows, 1997; Purwar,

1997; Stanley, 1997; Mauthner and Doucet, 2003; Fawcett and Hearn, 2004). In addition, we give consideration to the personal consequences of the research for the researcher (Brannen, 1988; Kelly 1988; Holland and Ramazanoglu, 1994). However, as Strathern (1987) observes, the 'voices' that are contained within our research accounts are *representations*. She reminds us that 'what "our" representations of others mean must depend in part on what "their" representations mean to them' (1987: 23). Smith similarly points out that the ontological ground of a non-exploitative sociology must be 'people's actual practices and activities as they are co-ordinated and co-ordered' (1990: 7). In order to achieve this, our research places itself within a feminist tradition of exploring the *researcher's* hidden and unvoiced cultural agenda and assumptions and their impact on both the conduct of the interview and subsequent interpretation of the data. Reflexivity, therefore, becomes a resource, not a problem (see for example, Seller, 1994; Davies, 1999). In summary, we would argue that our observations and judgements about heterosexuality are products of the context within which the knowledge was produced. As Maynard (1994) points out, interviewees' accounts of their lives are culturally embedded, and the act of speaking about their life is to culturally and discursively constitute it. The researcher herself is implicated in this process.

While we have been concerned with placing the standpoint of the subject at the centre of the research, and have sought to empower participants by enabling them to define their own realities, rather than imposing one on them, Marsden (2004) points out that since the division of domestic and emotional labour, sex and power (amongst other things) have become more accepted areas for research in family and kinship relationships, these then call '[f]or a more challenging, but intrusive and potentially destructive methodology' (Marsden, 2004: 70). Ethical debates about the possibility of carrying out genuinely non-exploitative qualitative feminist research are not new (see Stacey, 1988, 1994; Cotterill, 1992; Wheatley, 1994) and given the size of the data set, it was inevitable that the interviewer would encounter a range of sensibilities, stumble upon skeletons and ask participants to peek inside 'Pandora's box'. Some individuals disclosed experiences of date and marital rape, domestic violence, emotional abuse, rejection, betrayal, same-sex experimentation and experiences and feelings which they claimed they had never shared before. What we have, therefore, are reflections upon events which may have taken place up to 80 years earlier and reveal both mundane discrepancies between participants' expectations and experiences of hegemonic heterosexuality, as well as more extreme experiences. Like Mauthner and Doucet (2003) we realise that 'subject accounts are not completely transparent', but there is nevertheless 'a relationship between people's ambiguous representations and their experiences' (Hollway and Jefferson, 2000, cited in Mauthner and Doucet, 2003: 423). The problem of disentangling and interpreting the many levels of representation is an analytic one; but our initial concern was with persuading participants to share these with the interviewer in the first instance.

The researcher's initial task, then, was to engender trust and confidence and to establish rapport with 72 very different people, whose expectations of the research interview varied considerably. These included older women who anticipated companionable talk about their lives with someone outside their family; people coerced into taking part by more enthusiastic family members without knowing what to expect; interviewees who expected to discuss family geneology and others – of all ages – who were apprehensive or had been primed by other family members. Given the heterogeneity of the sample how, then, does the researcher decide how to direct the interview to engender trust and rapport and, ultimately, elicit frank responses from her interviewees without causing harm or offence?

In most cases, access had been arranged via the principal contact who, it emerged, had sometimes *told* their family members they were going to take part in the study, rather than asking them. At the point at which direct phone contact was made, participants may have felt unable to withdraw and so Angela had to manage the possibility of interviewees who were ill-informed or unwilling, assuaging anxieties and anticipating unvoiced concerns or misgivings. With only their tone of voice and perhaps limited information from other family members (such as *'oh yes, mum is VERY proper'*) as clues to how she and the interview topics would be received, Angela felt the need to reinvent herself for every interview, depending on the age and social class of the interviewee. Though apparently calculated, Goffman reminds us that '[i]nformation about the individual helps to define the situation, enabling others to know in advance what he will expect of them and what they will expect of him' (1959: 1). Angela therefore gleaned insights as to what type of 'character' awaited her from conversations with the primary contact and other family members, and from the environments that she entered, orchestrating her performance and interpreting the 'sign vehicles' (Goffman, 1959: 1) or visual and interpersonal clues provided by each player on the scene.

In *The Presentation of Self in Everyday Life,* Goffman (1959) observes that there are two types of communication: expressions which are given and those which are given off. Of the two, he places greater emphasis on the latter since it concerns more 'theatrical' forms of indirect communication conveyed through the contextual and less rehearsed elements of the performance. If we examine the minutiae of the 'scene', Angela's 'costume' and 'performance' were therefore very different when visiting older women of all social classes: 'softening' the harshness of her skinhead haircut by wearing a blouse, jacket and make-up, rather than the casual, 'urban' and androgynous look she generally preferred (and tended to maintain for most other interviews). Her 'character' and 'performance' were therefore very different when entering chintzy sitting rooms, adorned with several generations of family photos, some- times religious icons, and often pro-royalist memorabilia, where she might sometimes be treated to afternoon tea and biscuits: carefully laid out treats.

While her process of 'impression management' was premeditated, it also flowed in both directions. More than once, Angela noted someone's embarrassment when she insisted on helping carry the tea things at the end of the interview since this meant leaving from the spotless, front-of- stage sitting rooms where interviews generally took place. Participants would become flustered when she followed them into the kitchen, unin- tentionally intruding on the 'backstage' areas that she had not been meant to see, where tea trays had sometimes already been laid out. There were comments about *'the mess'* and how the kitchen needed modern- ising. One woman in her mid-60s explained that she had got her best china out, anticipating an interviewer of her own age.

Such experiences contrast with interviews among people from other generations. These seemed less 'staged', Angela arriving as the parti- cipant tidied up after lunch or dinner, still in their work 'costume', children and partners remaining on the scene and passing through from time to time. These were informal, apparently everyday scenes. Sometimes the participant smoked, asking Angela if she minded, and drinks were consumed from mugs while the interview took place at the kitchen table or with the interviewee's feet up on the sofa in the living room, relaxed and surrounded by the family's everyday clutter. Some- times other people could be heard creeping about the house to avoid disturbing the interview.

Subsequent reflections and analysis also revealed less than subtle differences in the 'script' for interviews of different ages and social class. This was particularly evident in how discussions about sex were framed and the language drawn upon by Angela. Although heterosexuality, as an analytic category, transcends the simply sexual, for our participants 'sex' was an empirical category which framed their understanding of the meaning of 'heterosexuality'. As stressed in Chapter 5, work on sexuality by key British feminists addresses the lack of appropriate language for women in particular to convey the subtleties, complexities and ambivalences of sexual desires and practices. The work of Meadows (1997) with mid-life women, and Holland and Ramazanoglu (1994) and Holland et al. (1998) with young women, shows women drawing upon either medicalised models, derogatory terms or innuendo. Given these limitations, how can the interviewer manage discussions with women and men that explore sexual experiences which occurred during historical periods when sexual mores and social attitudes towards sexuality and sexual mobility were markedly different?

Our interviews encompass the post-First World War era, the Second World War and the post-war decades. These were revealed by the Little Kinsey studies (see Stanley, 1995) and Humphries (1988) to be periods in which pre-marital sexual activity was common, but frowned upon. As Chapter 4 details, our interviewees describe how women were shamed when evidence of their 'mistakes' came to light through 'out of wedlock' birth. There were also stories from the 1960s and 1970s which reflect a period marked by the liberalisation of sex and its uncoupling from marriage, facilitated by the advent of the contraceptive pill. And there were experiences from the 1980s onwards, during which the 'free love' associated with the previous decades has been replaced with concerns about sexually transmitted diseases and HIV/AIDS.

As Chapter 1 indicates, six focus group discussions took place in an effort to sensitise the researchers to the way in which participants of different ages might respond to discussions about different manifestations of heterosexuality. These involved mainly older participants, although one group was with young men. Discussions with older people highlighted contradictions in terms of the sexual behaviour – reluctantly acknowledged – of certain *'bad eggs'* among their contemporaries during their youth, and their criticism of *'certain categories'* of young people today, among whom it is perceived to be *'just sex, sex, sex, willy nilly'*. Discomfort in speaking publicly about the transgression of sexual mores amongst their contemporaries was clear, leading Angela to broach the subject of sex with sensitivity in individual interviews, taking care over her choice of language (the issue of sex and language is discussed in more detail in Chapter 6). This appeared to be confirmed further during the course of her first interview with an older person, whose case study is discussed later in this chapter. Jean Brown, the interviewee, pointed out: *'We didn't have sex, we made love, you know, these days it's all sex, sex, sex, in't it . . . but my generation looked at it more as making love, you know.'* From this we might deduce that the language in which discussions about sex are framed is intimately linked to how the 'act' itself was and is perceived by the participant.

Drawing on arguments made by sexuality researchers, such as Holland and Ramazanoglu (1994) and Wight (1994), who suggest that interviewers need to pick up on the language through which interviewees represent 'sex' in the interview, Angela adapted her approach to each interviewee as the script unfolded. However, as pointed out earlier, interviewees were engaged in a process of impression management just as much as our interviewer. For example, whilst interviewing a young man aged 20, she sensed an awkwardness around the terms he used to describe where he had *'groped'* women: *'buttocks'* and *'breasts'*. Noting Holland and Ramazanoglu's (1994) observation that young participants may be reluctant to use slang without the interviewer's permission, she responded to his implicit requests for reassurance by telling him to use the same language that he would amongst his friends. At this point he revealed that his mother had warned him to *'keep it clean'*.

While permission-giving opened up this particular interview, there are clearly methodological implications when the interviewer directs her interviewees to the kinds of language they should use. We need to consider how it might enable but also constrain the actual interview and influence the information elicited. At one level, an active stance can yield rich data; this was particularly the case among some mid-life and younger women. However, on another level, the tentative approach used with older participants raises questions as to whether it reflects an assumption that older people would have no access to the 'crude' language available to younger people, or a concern not to cause offence with respect to their age. Similar assumptions about gender and social class also influenced the way interviews were directed and, subsequently, how they were analysed.

While issues of language are explored in greater depth in Chapter 6, this chapter offers reflection upon one interview, highlighting the extent to which the intersection of the identities of the researcher and interviewee produces socially situated knowledge. Further, it shows how the different identities and biographies of the members of a research team who were born in different decades, yet who share feminism and heterosexuality, impacts upon their subsequent analysis of data. For this purpose, we use the example of Angela's interview with Jean Brown.

Negotiating identities and interpreting knowledge

Jean Brown was born in Lancashire in 1928 and grew up during the Second World War. She offered her life history alongside that of her daughter and grand-daughter. Now widowed, Jean married Harry in 1949 and her daughter (the principal contact) and grandchildren currently live in East Yorkshire, though Jean herself has remained in Lancashire. The interview was significant in that it was the first to be carried out with someone of the oldest generation and was viewed by Angela as an opportunity to gauge how older participants would respond to intimate questions about their personal lives.

If we see Jean's life history as an example of how heterosexuality was understood and experienced between the two world wars, as well as an older widow's reflections on her earlier, married life, then we also need to explore how her story was produced through her engagement with Angela. In other words, we need to ask how their commonalities and differences may have enabled certain dimensions of heterosexuality to be highlighted while others were downplayed. For example, Jean and Angela share the same social class and regional identity, being born within fifteen miles of each other. Yet they differ markedly in age, educational background and ethnicity. While Jean was 74 at the time of interview and has always lived and worked in the same area, Angela was 29 and has three higher degrees, her PhD involving fieldwork carried out whilst alone in difficult conditions in South Africa. Both women have experienced heterosexual relationships, but how they engage with the conditions of heterosexuality is profoundly influenced by both the commonalities and the differences between them.

The question for us, as twenty-first-century feminist academics, is how we might interpret the gendered life histories of women, such as Jean, born between the two world wars. And what light might their narratives shed on the question of women's agency within the context of 'institutionalised heterosexuality' (VanEvery, 1996)? As we note in Chapter 1, in asking this question, we draw on Jackson's (1996) view of heterosexuality as more than merely sex. It is this broader notion of the interconnectedness of many domains of life – paid employment, family life, domestic and emotional labour, sexual practice – at the site of heterosexuality, which underpins this chapter. We are therefore contemplating lives which took shape around 70 years ago, but do so using political and intellectual resources developed and refined only during the last 30, running the risk of imposing theories which were inappropriate at that particular moment in time. As authors, our own ages now range between the early 30s and 60. To some extent, therefore, we must acknowledge an age-based distance which might parallel a political distance from the gendered values which informed older women's upbringing. Yet given the spread of our own ages, this chapter is not simply a young woman's investigation of chronological and age-cohort distance, of the older woman as 'other'. Nonetheless, the interview data to be discussed here were produced via an interaction between women of *different* ages, one being 45 years older than the other. As noted, many factors divide them, yet they share important commonalities, but would their commonalities be sufficient to over-ride the differences, or even be available for use in creatively producing an open and nuanced account of one older woman's experience of heterosexuality? It is also noteworthy that the data themselves were produced at a particular moment within the history of heterosexuality and this, too, informs the processes of their production.

The life story of Jean, the older woman, conforms to the profile of traditional or hegemonic heterosexuality, containing few surprises for the reader with a similar background, or with female relatives and friends from Jean's age-cohort. Should Jean's 'traditional' heterosexual history therefore be viewed simply as the outcome of a set of patriarchal relationships and practices oriented towards her family's well-being, rather than her own? As Chapter 2 highlights, engaging critically with feminist and social gerontology debates around the notion of agency means addressing the question of whether Jean nonetheless demonstrates 'a creative capacity that is irreducible to structural conditions' (Wray, 2003: 514).

As Chapter 2 notes, in an account of (hetero)sex, Smart argues that 'heterosexuality may be many things', even though 'at times we need to collectivise this diversity (for example when recognising heterosexual privilege and its naturalisation)' (1996: 170). With respect to sexual knowledge, Jean grew up within institutionalised silences and omissions – indeed the implicit injunctions to passivity, characteristic of women's lives before the Second World War. Yet she spoke directly about her sexual history and the pleasure she found and took within it. Unlike those women, described by Smart (1996), who felt obliged to enjoy their sexuality 'quietly' (1996: 177), Jean succeeded in evading this pressure. Not only did she describe her sexual experience openly when interviewed, but she said: *'there was no, not sort of forbidden territory, no barriers, really'*; *'I'd walk about with underwear on, you know, and things like that . . . '* and she says that her children's questions about sex were answered *'honestly and straightforwardly'*.

Ingrisch highlights the way Women's Studies has largely confined itself to 'the contradictions between women's socially prescribed roles and the reality of their daily lives' among women *under 60* (1995: 42). Using a life history approach which attends to gender and is relevant for micro-level data such as Jean's, Ingrisch brings older women out of the margins, giving them a voice 'through their life histories' (1995: 42). Using a grounded theory approach, she attempts to 'reconstruct the informal logic of life' (Lipp, 1988, cited in Ingrisch, 1995: 43). Her work can be compared with a 'positive ageing' approach to women's later lives which suggests they might challenge and resist gender roles which were 'barely questioned in young adulthood' (Ginn and Arber, 1995: 8). While certain categories of older women access the education, independence and good health which encourage the reinvention of gendered identities in later life, the wider scope of a life history approach provides a more subtle way of interpreting an entire heterosexual life course such as Jean's. Rather than approaching her apparently 'empowered' testimony as an eventual reinvention of her gendered identity *in the present,* we focus on that more extended trajectory of her life course and consider the nature of her agency across the whole series of discursive practices which have constituted her heterosexual history. Thus, for example, although Jean adhered to a traditional gendered division of labour until her fifties, she retained her office job, becoming sole breadwinner when her husband, Harry, was made redundant at 58. While she insisted on a corresponding reversal of domestic labour, she took responsibility for his contribution, orchestrating his involvement to help him overcome the depression of job loss. She says: *'And so I went and did this job, I used to leave him a list every day, things to shop, and I never let him do a big shop. I made him go out every day and buy a bit of something, so that got him out of the house, you know.'* Jean's heterosexual life history, therefore, reveals considerable subtlety in the overlap between conformity and reinvention, the relationship between the two shifting across the time of Jean's life with Harry. Indeed, her account of, and reflections on a lifetime's heterosexual experience, provide data which resonate with Brah's (1996) perspective on the relationship between experience, subjectivity and agency. In Brah's view, 'to think of experience and subject formation as processes is to reformulate the question of agency' (1996: 117). Rather than conceiving of the 'I' which takes action as a 'unified, fixed, already existing entit(y)' (1996: 117), Brah draws attention to contradictory, inevitably incomplete processes of identity formation within which agency manifests itself.

Growing up heterosexual

As we begin to read the interview, cohort difference is evident and Angela clearly approaches the encounter with age-based assumptions: she does not take it for granted that someone of Jean's age will articulate details of more private or emotional aspects of her experience. With only a brief phone-call as prior contact, Angela has to rely on the 'sign vehicles' provided by Jean when she arrived at her home and goes through the informed consent procedure, explaining the study and what the interview will entail. Seated in the living room of her terraced home, Jean's behaviour was formal and business-like. There was little small-talk and Jean clearly wanted to get straight on with the interview. Dressed in a smart skirt and open necked blouse, revealing a gold crucifix around her neck, Jean sat upright and apparently confident, perched on the edge of her sofa; to Angela, she was a picture of moral conservatism. Since this was the first of her interviews with older respondents, Angela was conscious of her nervousness in the face of what appeared to be a formidable woman, and her opening question, Jean's age, reveals her sense of caution: *'Can I ask first, if it's not too personal a question, what year were you born?'*

Jean's response to Angela's questions about her childhood was direct and her recollections vivid, unlike some women who were often vague and embarrassed about being asked questions about how they found out about such things as periods. When it comes to sexual and reproductive knowledge, Jean highlights the chronological distance between them – and their possible lack of a common language – for example: *'. . . they didn't call it periods in my day, you were "unwell" '.* Although Jean claimed not to have asked Diane, her daughter, what had taken place during her earlier interview, Angela felt that Jean knew exactly what she was going to ask and understood why we were interested in such questions, pre-empting many of the issues that we wanted to cover. At the precise point at which Angela was wrestling with how to ask her about her early sexual experiences, unprompted and with a twinkle in her eye, Jean said: *' . . . We weren't all virgins that walked down the aisle'.* To which Angela responded: *'I'm glad you brought that up . . . '* After this, the social encounter between the two women seems less 'tense' and Jean went on to present extremely vivid recollections of her premarital sexual experience. Nonetheless, how Jean's age and sexual experience might intersect remains uneasy territory for Angela who later asks: *'Now you might tell me to mind my own business here, what was the sex like as you got older?'* What is evident, however, is that despite *differences* in the ways in which sexual and reproductive knowledge might be articulated, the two women speak about it with similar directness. Via the following data we seek to disentangle the continuities and the changes which both unite and separate them during the social encounter of the interview in an interactive process.

We begin by noting how Jean's subjectivity develops within a culture implicitly organised according to heterosexual principles. However, we then identify aspects of her life history which suggest a position of sustained resistance to such frameworks. Finally we turn to data which attest to Jean's capacity to direct the course of events within her own life, yet with the apparent outcome of reproducing institutionalised heterosexuality. It is particularly via these final data that we attend to the complexities of agency as a life-long process through which Jean inhabits the categories of heterosexuality.

Across the data set older people reported silences regarding the acquisition of sexual knowledge among older people – and Jean too said that little explicit sexual and reproductive knowledge was made available within the family as she grew up. Interestingly, this was an experience which the mid-life women shared with their older counterparts. As Jean said, '. . . *there wasn't an awful lot of discussion. You were expected to know really.*' This 'omission' can be construed as an aspect of Jean's socialisation into heterosexuality. Of her mother she says: '*all I can remember her saying is that, [SIGH] you had to keep yourself, that was my mother's thing, "Keep yourself clean". You had to keep yourself clean.*' Along with this threat of female 'dirtiness' came the danger of washing your hair whilst menstruating – a contradiction in terms – yet one which signalled unspecified risks associated with growing up female. Among her peers, however, this process was marked by pairing off with boys, a necessary prerequisite for any kind of social status. When she went behind the bike sheds with Arthur Bradshaw at the age of 12, the exchange involved simply a kiss on the lips and an invitation to the cinema which her parents would forbid. Yet Jean felt like '*Cock of the North*' because '*he was a real bonny lad, he was, and all the girls liked him, everybody talked to him*', '*he was absolutely gorgeous*'. Already, therefore, she experienced heterosexuality as contradictory, both 'unspeakable' and a marker of social status.

That heterosexuality might frame her developing subjectivity was something she experienced not just within the family and peer group, but also at an institutional level: for example, in the double seats for 'courting couples' at the cinema. This more macro-level example of everyday life being organised according to heterosexual principles had a temporal as well as spatial dimension. Double seats were given up on marriage, the intimacies of a darkened cinema giving way to those of the bedroom. Indeed, the 'fixed abode' of the marital home was prefigured in the way these seats were allocated: as Jean said: *'ours were 17 and 19 and if ever we went, you know, these were our seats'*. Heterosexuality's spatially marked trajectory was thus segmented into temporally bounded stages: 'courting' led on to 'marriage', 'the hegemonic form of heterosexuality' (VanEvery 1996: 40).

Women's agency, however, was expressed in their recollections of this highly 'structured' marker of heterosexual status. Like women from all three age cohorts, Jean's memory of her wedding in 1949, over 50 years earlier, is richly textured: the toastmaster's red jacket; her white chiffon velvet dress; the 25 carnations which made up her bouquet; the potato pies her mother made for the reception. History and biography intersect as Jean acknowledges the constraints of that post-war era and how they were nonetheless partially overcome at her wedding: *'we had some belting wedding presents and that kind of thing, and went to Fleetwood [LAUGHS], fabulous Fleetwood'*. She goes on: *'we didn't have a fabulous spread, it was ham and something, but in those days it was very good'*. Heterosexuality also provided the organising principle for the gifts given to guests: quarter-pound boxes of Black Magic and Cadbury's Milk Tray chocolates for every *'lady'* and *'each man got a cigar'*. Moreover, the public nature of this transition to heterosexual coupledom is evident in its 'performative' aspects: Jean recalls the vicar's wife, a former student at RADA, telling her: ' *"I shall be sat at the back and I hope to hear every word".'*

Growing up heterosexual led to a traditional domestic division of labour on marriage: Jean would ensure that tea was on the table for Harry, particularly when he felt left out after the birth of their daughter. They passed on a model of family life which restricted sexual expression to within its confines, warning their daughter not to *'let them down'* by becoming pregnant and exposing them to gossip. As Harry's parents aged, Jean cared for them, organising her paid employment around her domestic role, Harry taking on the male breadwinner role. When Harry died at 63, Jean spent months in a daze, struggling to believe what had happened. She said she still thought of herself as Harry's wife, and couldn't imagine being with anybody else. For the rest of her life, we can speculate, Jean will continue to identify as the heterosexual partner of the young man she met when she was 15.

Threaded through Jean's account, however, is evidence of her reflexivity, of an alternative perspective which allowed her to view these conditions critically. For example, she flouted the unexplained injunction against washing her hair whilst menstruating; she suspected the playground stories of how babies *'popped out'* of the *'brown line down your stomach'* and *'then it sort of sealed up'*. Of this she says: *'I used to think, it's a funny how-do-you-do this'*, then asking a friend's mother, since her own mother *'hadn't got the words'*.

Having countered the 'ignorance' engendered among young women by actively seeking out this knowledge, she was better placed to make sense of sounds coming from her parents' bedroom. Indeed, her resistance to the implicit injunction to navigate a particular route into heterosexuality (with no explicit knowledge of its bodily implications) did not stop here. In her parents' bedroom she discovered their copy of Marie Stopes' *Married Love,* helped herself to its contents and, indeed, read it with Harry, then her boyfriend. Of this episode, she said: *'I think that was an absolute marvellous help.'* When they put theory into practice, she was 16 and a half. Their sexual relationship developed in both their homes, whilst their parents were out, a decision Jean made on the basis of her own experience: *'I enjoyed it too much to feel guilty'*, she said.

Jean's most valued memories were of her wedding and the birth of her children, yet despite her lack of higher education, when she and her peers were all having babies she *'got to the stage when I wanted conversation that didn't dwell on babies'*. And although her married life with Harry seemed to mesh seamlessly with the requirements of hegemonic heterosexuality, Jean deliberately ensured that she always had *'a life apart from him'*: flower arranging for the local church; pottery classes; Girl Guide leadership; Sunday School teaching; committee work. Harry's redundancy at 58 *'shattered'* him. He coped *'very badly, very badly'*, Jean said, *'he was ill with that, he'd always been the bread-winner'*. When she was offered full-time work, Jean went to Harry and said *' "from now on, I'm the breadwinner, so you can take over all my jobs [. . .] including the cooking . . . and it's not demeaning" '*.

On the basis of these data, can we conceptualise Jean as an agent of change, working across the currents of hegemonic heterosexuality? What is the status of her refusal of its limitations? Jean is also profoundly committed to a traditional form of heterosexuality, reproducing rather than just resisting its patterning of everyday life. In these final extracts from Jean's data we critically consider the assumption that as a patriarchal institution, heterosexuality denies women agency, rendering them passive within a particular set of ideological and material conditions. These are data which cannot easily be interpreted as 'resistance', yet which reveal a woman for whom heterosexuality is a self-directed system of thought and practice.

As already noted, Jean readily recalls the materialities of her wedding. As a key heterosexual 'moment', it figures alongside descriptions of her first kiss with Arthur Bradshaw; first sex, lying in the grass on a summer Sunday teatime; her first home in *'a little two-up and two-down cottage'*; and years later, discovering her husband *'stone cold'* in their bed after his brain haemorrhage. These transitional moments in Jean's heterosexual life reflect the traditional structures which inform the lives of many women and men, both then and now. First sex, for example, she describes almost as an inevitability: *'we'd gone down to the common and that, I mean, loads of other people went as well, and we were down there, and, you know, afterwards, lying down in the grass, and got kissing, and went a little bit further, and a bit further and, then it happened [SIGH]'*. When Angela puts to Jean the late twentieth-century perception of a sexually innocent older generation for whom pre-marital sex was *'not the done thing'*, Jean response is, *'it was actually, but people didn't talk about it, I mean, it happened, with most of my friends, but you didn't talk about it, you didn't brag about it, like they do now'*. Yet Jean's account suggests that she was empowered with the resources to direct her sexual practice according to her own wishes. Thus, for example, although her immediate response to this *'spontaneous'* first sex was: ' *"oh God, what if I have a baby?!" '*, she dealt with her anxiety promptly: *'after that he, we never did without, um, durex'*.

Indeed, when Jean met Harry she was only 15. He was 19, which did not go down *'terribly well'* with her mother. Jean, however, reminded her parents that whilst there was an age difference, at least his family was local and known to her own – which would not have been the case if, like all her friends, she had gone off to the local dancehall and found boyfriends among the solders, sailors and airmen who frequented it. Having secured parental consent through this rhetorical strategy, Jean and Harry began courting, yet, as Jean said, over time *'he started . . . taking me for granted, and I had no intention of being taken for granted'*. Taking control of the situation, she told him: *'I wanted a break, and, I made an excuse of another lad, but he were nothing.'* She maintained her position of strength for three months until Harry's mother asked her to take him back because he was *'crying and upset and not eating, and his life were at an end and all this, that and the other'*. Jean took him back and *'he never ever took me for granted afterwards'*. Their long marriage was, therefore, on the terms chosen by Jean. Not only did Jean find a house for them, but she talked her father into agreeing a wedding date prior to the official age of consent. Before the birth of their daughter, Jean and Harry shared the housework, though Jean took responsibility for its organisation, preparing the tea which he would cook on his return home. Indeed when Angela asked Jean whether she felt their relationship changed after marriage, she said *'Yeah, I think, I felt a bit more responsibility, yeah, I felt a bit more responsible for one another, really.'* This taking of responsibility is evident in much of Jean's data. For example, after difficulties with breast-feeding her first child, she resisted hospital birth for her second, taking note of the doctor's criticism of its quality of care. Finding a midwife from among her local contacts, she managed to secure a home birth for her second child.

As Jean and Harry's parental roles developed, this challenged their status as a heterosexual couple. Jean was quick to modify her possessive attitude to their daughter and actively ensure the involvement of both Harry and the extended family. After she caught herself just about to tell her mother-in-law not to pick up their daughter, she describes reflecting: ' *"She just doesn't belong to you", you know, and from then on, I was sort of very, very careful, and as Harry walked through the door, you know, I'd pick her up and give him, where before, I'd sort of, I'd held onto her.'* When the stitching she received after the birth compromised their sexual relationship, she again actively sought out medical advice and with Harry's patience, was determined to gradually retrieve the pleasure she valued so much.

Harry's support at this time was something she not only appreciated but also committed herself to reciprocating when he lost confidence in himself after redundancy. Thus, she deliberately chose not to take the initiative sexually: *'particularly during that period when he, things were a bit rough for him, I never, ever made any overtures, because I didn't want him to feel, if he couldn't, he was a failure'.* Clearly there are complex processes at work here as Jean actively adopts a 'passive' role, one aimed at helping rescue Harry's masculine identity.

As noted above, Jean also organised the breadwinner role reversal in such a way as to provide Harry with support during his depression. In fact, emotional labour characterises much of Jean's data. She reflects actively on the nature of relationships between different family members, on her family members' motivations and agenda, always with the aim of overcoming differences and making up for inadequacies. In addition she provides emotional support for a grandchild with serious mental health problems. At various points she provides evidence that her family see her as someone with strength and a capacity for independence. Her daughter rarely *'puts her foot down'* on Jean's behalf, conscious that Jean is more than able to defend herself when necessary; and Harry, she says, hoped not to survive her since he felt he would not cope alone as well as she would. She recalls his words after the sudden death of a work colleague: ' *"I don't want be left on my own, Jean will cope a lot better than I will"*, he said, *"but not yet"*. But you see, six months later, you know, he'd gone.'

When Angela asked Jean what advice she would pass on to her grand-children about the ingredients of a successful relationship, Jean identi-fied *'hard work'* and *'tolerance'*, as well as *'love'*. In the data with which we have completed this chapter, there is considerable evidence of Jean's 'hard work', particularly in orchestrating the emotional lives of her family's members. While this 'labour' is one characteristically under-taken by women, when viewed within this body of empirical data, it becomes evident that, like the women Jackson (1999) identifies as pursuing 'love' with realistic ambitions, Jean too feels empowered to realise her vision of heterosexual family life. Rather than entering into relations of dependency which would locate a male partner as the source of its fulfilment, Jean herself is the agent through which that life is brought into being.

Conclusion

While Rich (1980) has characterised heterosexuality as intrinsically about the absence of choice for women, VanEvery's account (1996) of the lives of women who challenge hegemonic constructions of hetero-sexuality and gender whilst still identifying as heterosexual and/or enga-ging in heterosexual sex raises the question of women's *choice*. In the data presented here we have used a life course approach both to gather and to interpret what was said. This means that the context within which we consider our material extends not only temporally, but also at a theoretical level in that it has both macro- as well as micro-level reson-ances. Therefore, if we place Jean's busy engagement with the conditions of her own heterosexual life in the broader context of data pertaining to a spread of topics, stretching across a 70-year period, we can see that her 'engagement' stands alongside positions of resistance. As described, she refused to remain ignorant of sexual knowledge, engineered her parents' approval of an older boyfriend and her early marriage to him, purpose-fully took on the breadwinner role in later life, maintained separate leisure interests and actively managed her husband's depression. Yet in doing heterosexuality 'her way', Jean also tailored her paid employment to the demands of her family and undertook extensive emotional labour on their behalf.

As our data indicate, the institution of heterosexuality profoundly shaped Jean's earlier life; and in terms of her future identity, she cannot envisage herself as anything other than Harry's wife. Yet when we consider heterosexuality as practice and as experience, Jean's life history indicates that within these two areas, she not only exercised considerable agency, but also reflected extensively upon how her practice might shape her experience of heterosexuality. These are the data which our life history approach allowed us to access (Alasuutari, 1995: 50). While we may separate out heterosexuality into its constituent elements, as Jackson (1996) does, it remains important to recognise the interrelationship between these different aspects and acknowledge the way practice and experience themselves produce an institution and an identity we recognise as 'heterosexual'. In that Jean chose what she would *not* accept, we need to recognise, as contemporary feminists, that there are important forms of agency at work in her choices of what she desires and *will* work hard for. As feminists reflecting back upon the research interview, we are confronted with the paradox that while on the one hand Jean's life story appears to confirm traditional stereotypes of how hegemonic heterosexuality was lived out in the early twentieth century, our choice of methods has made visible the complexity and subtleties within Jean's experiences. More than that, not only has her engagement in the interview process provided Jean with an opportunity to reflect upon the conditions of her own heterosexual life, but it has also forced us to reflexively question many of the normative assumptions that have been made regarding the absence of agency and choice among women of Jean's age cohort. What we were able to learn from Jean at a very early stage in the research is that what we think we know of the past may not always compare with the lived reality. Moreover, by using empowering strategies in both the conduct and the analysis of the interviews, which highlight a complex interweaving of historical and biographical time, we have been able to present a more nuanced account of our participants' experiences.

Thinking through Jean's reflections allows us to start to reconceptualise the feminist debates around heterosexuality through an appreciation of the subtleties and nuances of her changing everyday situation. Discussion has sometimes appeared polarised. Some arguments have tended to see heterosexuality as a monolithic category denying women's agency. Others have defended heterosexual pleasures or have argued that women can and do find pleasure in heterosexual relationships – end of story. Smart's reading of different women's accounts of heterosexuality reveals both an ambivalent relationship to institutional/traditional heterosexuality and a fluid identity which 'refuses to be trapped by a crudely defined notion of heterosexual identity (Smart, 1996: 176). Jean's narrative shows how women can negotiate heterosexuality in a relationship which many would see as mundane or ordinary, and though power is operating in her relationship with her husband, it emerges as fluid, negotiable and changeable. How this validation of women speaking about heterosexuality, in all its contradictions, could inform a feminist politics is worthy of much further consideration. A recognition of different (heterosexual) experiences allows for a more inclusive feminist politics which may speak to a wider group of women than previously. This also allows for a more comprehensive theory of sexuality in general, and as Richardson (2000) argues, is potentially one of the most important current developments with which to inform social and political theory more broadly.

4
Heterosexuality Across the Twentieth Century

In seeking to get at how the practice of heterosexuality might change – and the implications of particular changes for the institution itself – a cross-generational approach provides comparative material with which to work. As Foucault argues, the past is of interest not simply for itself, but in its capacity to provide us with a history of the present (cited in Weeks, 2000: 118). In addition, however, cross-generational material allows work on heterosexuality to contribute to a feminist theorisation of gender and *ageing*. As Arber and Ginn (1995) argued, feminism has not prioritised ageing as a basis from which to theorise difference. Historical time, then, constitutes a core feature throughout this book, along with biographical time representing a key contextual variable within the heterosexual lives discussed here – as already demonstrated in the case of Jean Brown (Chapter 3). Thus we highlight the critical periods against which participants mapped their biographies, the two often being intricately interwoven. As Morgan notes in describing the particular slant he has given to the concept of 'practices', these 'constitute major links between history and biography ... are historically constituted and the linkages and tensions or contradictions between practices are historically shaped. At the same time practices are woven into and constituted from elements of individual biographies' (1996: 190).

We begin by reiterating that although we have argued that 'heterosexuality' is about more than simply sexual practices, 'sex' was often the lens through which participants themselves understood and interpreted their identities as 'heterosexual' men and women. In response, this chapter highlights those historical changes within hegemonic heterosexuality which pertain to discussion of sex and sexuality within our data. What this chapter provides, then, is an *overview* of the key historical moments which, our data suggest, have impacted upon participants' lives. Although we offer a broader historical perspective, however, we also interweave accounts constructed from the perspective of individuals who lived through them. Our concern with interviewees' recollections of various moments in history and their experiences of these events means that memory emerges as an important consideration, since what our participants told us represents the past as refracted through the beliefs and values of the present. Indeed, it is a *relational* past. As Jackson points out: 'rather than the past (or childhood) determining the present (or adulthood), the present significantly shapes the past in that we are constantly reconstructing memories and our understanding of who and what we are through the stories we tell to ourselves and others' (1999: 24). The present, reflexive self – as she envisages it – is not, however, an essential or pre-social 'I'; rather it is constituted through cultural resources which are historically specific. As women and men review their heterosexual lives, therefore, they are reflecting upon their experiences through the cultural resource of heterosexuality itself. Yet this does not imply a self-sealed circularity since, as Jackson says, the self 'is not a fixed structure but is always "in process" by virtue of its constant reflexivity' (1995: 24). So our data testify to the memories of particular women and men – yet, as Misztal stresses, 'individual remembering takes place in the social context – it is prompted by social cues, employed for social purposes, ruled and ordered by socially structured norms and patterns, and therefore contains much that is social' (2003: 5). Uncoupled from both objectivist and subjectivist positions, remembering, 'while far from being absolutely objective, nonetheless transcends our subjectivity and is shared by others around us' (Zerubavel, 1997 cited in Misztal, 2003: 6). Of the social *acquisition* of memory, Smart (2006) points out that although memories are personal, the social context in which they are produced also implies that they are value-laden. She also observes that – as our data evidence – families provide an important context in which memories are created, and also forgotten.

The recollections we present here speak to age-based, generationally located identities as much as they illuminate the historically specific experience of the past. How these personal testimonies might relate to official histories is, however, far from straightforward. As Steedman argues '[p]ersonal interpretations of past time – the stories that people tell themselves in order to explain how they got to the places they currently inhabit – are often in deep and ambiguous conflict with the official interpretive devices of a culture' (1986: 6). Thus when Steedman seeks to make sense of her 'working-class childhood', she finds the analytic devices of patriarchy and social class difficult to operationalise and offers her complex (auto)biographical account as a challenge to the 'psychological simplicity in the lives lived out in Hoggart's endless streets of little houses' (1986: 7).

What follows exemplifies the overlapping lenses we have used to interpret our data. At one level, structural accounts of social history and change which have emerged over the last century or so have been important. Yet these are overlaid with nuanced and sometimes competing biographical accounts of lived experience during the periods described. In addition, the account we present reflects our theoretical concerns with heterosexuality as an institution and its mutability across the last three age cohorts. What emerges is a picture of social history in which marriage – the hegemonic form of heterosexuality – has undergone an ideological transformation from an 'institution' to a relationship (Morgan, 1991), and within which the family – the key site through which heterosexuality is both maintained and resisted – has undergone significant change. It is this complex collage of viewpoints which we will now deconstruct, comparing and contrasting public discourses with private experience.

The Victorian legacy of the family

As noted in Chapter 2, Jamieson (1998) has documented the history of the family, arguing that intimacy has made the family-based household its core. Where once community, neighbours, friends and wider kinship networks featured significantly in people's lives, rendering privacy in short supply, and where relationships were marked by social distance between the generations and genders (1998: 17), industrialisation/modernity and the steady march towards the 'post-modern' period has brought a shift towards a household-centred existence, in which the home has increasingly represented a private sanctuary. This private domain of the family-household, then, has become characterised by intimacy; that is, close association and privileged knowledge, empathy, understanding and love and care (Jamieson 1998: 18). In short, marriage and parenthood increased in emotional intensity and the home has emerged as the principal site in which heterosexuality was/is (re)produced. However, if we focus specifically on what Jamieson refers to as the post-modern period, two competing stories emerge, one inherently more optimistic than the other. First, 'family' is seen to have lost its centrality, being replaced by an emphasis on the 'good relationship', one characterised by 'disclosing intimacy', mutuality, equality, deep knowledge and understanding (1998: 19). Within such arrangements, relationships are recognised as being more fragile, but potentially more mutually satisfying and need not be located solely within the context of the nuclear family. This 'transformation of intimacy', as Giddens (1992) describes it, is premised upon a wholesale democratisation of the interpersonal domain, involving a transactional negotiation of personal ties by equals (Giddens 1992: 3). By contrast, however, proponents of a second, pessimistic evaluation of post-modernism identify the decline of intimacy as mass-consumerism promotes a self-obsessive, self-isolating individualism incapable of sustaining anything other than transitory, fragmented relationships (Jamieson 1998: 19).

The fragility associated with the type of relationships which have emerged since the 1960s, and the more individualistic approach to personal happiness upon which they are based, has also bred nostalgia for the traditional family form associated with the nineteenth and early twentieth centuries. Members of the oldest cohort of participants frequently lamented the way things *'were different when we were young'*. They were similarly critical of the *'immature'* obsession with wanting to know everything that your partner is thinking and the contemporary emphasis on sex – epitomised in their assertion that *'we didn't have sex; we made love'* . This led to frequent desires for a return to 'Victorian values'.

However, there is extensive evidence that the realities of Victorian family life and the sexual double standard belie contemporary assumptions about a pervasive commitment to 'moral', 'decent' behaviour within this period. Indeed, there existed significant discrepancies between public values and private practice (Jamieson 1998: 21), the paradox of the Victorian era being one of rigid Puritanism *and* moral hypocrisy (Weeks 1989: 19). Thus we find sexual abstinence outside monogamous marriage being exhorted alongside flourishing prostitution and pornography. Nonetheless, collective social memory preserves the public image of the Victorian family as an ideal, one which played an important role in the surveillance of sexual behaviour, and made marriage a gateway to respectability and stability. The sanctioned boundaries of marriage kept separate the virtuous, bourgeois 'angel in the house' from her working-class foil: the 'fallen' woman, from whose clutches the middle-class, bourgeois male had to be kept. Weeks (1989) also notes how notions of respect and propriety restricted individuals to sex within their own class. Unlike post-modern relationships, sexual anxieties were subordinated to familial and social concerns and we are presented with an image of 'two separate races confronting each other over the marriage bed' (Weeks 1989: 39).

Jamieson, in turn, describes idealised visions of middle-class femininity and masculinity: *she* is the good woman, pure in thought and deed, sexually innocent on marriage, accepting of sex as a conjugal duty hereafter. Her role was to aid her good middle-class husband to struggle manfully against his sexual instincts, facilitating his moral salvation and helping him to triumph over his baser nature which otherwise would be tested by dangerous and polluting working-class female sexuality (1998: 22). Clearly, therefore, social rules in relation to the nature and location of sexual practice and what was/not permissible were integral to conceptions of heterosexuality at that time – and indeed the whole notion of a distinctive heterosexuality has been traced to this period within Foucault's work (1987).

Between the wars

Accounts of how marriage, as heterosexuality's 'safe haven', was represented and lived out within the nineteenth century provide the context for the period immediately after the First World War when the lives of some our participants were about to begin. When we listen to the now distant voices of women from the early twentieth century, their very different experience immediately underlines heterosexuality's *heterogeneity* as an institution. Indeed, what they have to say enables us to address questions about how change has come to take place. Demographically, heterosexual relationships underwent radical shifts from the 1920s onwards. During the period immediately after the First World War, an unequal sex ratio gave women less chance than men of finding a marriage partner, an opportunity they only regained after the Second World War (Elliot, 1991).

The notion that heterosexuality is a static category is therefore belied by evidence of striking changes within the social arrangements through which it is manifested. And statistical evidence can be set alongside the oral history record of women's lives during this period. Thus, for example, women surveyed by the Women's Health Enquiry Committee in the early 1930s described how marriage involved giving up their paid work. This practice served to 'make it impossible to maintain after marriage the standard (often low enough) of health and well-being which was possible to them as unmarried working girls' (Spring Rice, 1939: 26). One of the Committee's sample of 1250 women described the constraining effects of embedded beliefs about married women and domestic work at that time:

I believe that one of the biggest difficulties our mothers have is our husbands do not realise we ever need any leisure time. My life for many years consisted of being penned in a kitchen 9 feet square, every fourteen months a baby ... So many of our men think we should not go out until the children are grown up. We do not want to be neglecting the home but we do feel we like a little look around the shops, or if we go to the clinic we can just have a few minutes ... It isn't the men are unkind. It is the old idea we should always be at home. (Spring Rice, 1939: 94)

Such sources are suggestive, even though, as argued above, they do not grant us unmediated access to women's lives 70 years ago. While Jackson (1995) and Misztal (2003) highlight the role of present-day social and personal concerns in shaping personal recollections of the past, so Finch and Summerfield (1999) stress the ideological agendas of the academic accounts through which women's voices are filtered.

Giles (1995) contributes to our understanding of gender relations during this period by drawing on interviews with women born between 1895 and 1922 to illustrate the effects of an anti-heroic and anti-romantic post-war social climate. She argues that, '[m]asculine heroism and feminine fragility were re-written after the war in terms that, at least on the surface, attempted to minimise sexual difference' (1995: 21). Thus, she cites the cheerful housewife who avoided 'the excesses of passion, intensity or yearning desire' in a masculinised spirit of robustness and common-sense; and the 'little man' who was 'content with his garden, home and domestic ideals' (1995: 21). Prime Minister, Stanley Baldwin, she argues, 'offered a "feminised" form of private life to men psychologically exhausted by the demands of imperialist masculinity' (1995: 21).

Though the downplaying of sexual difference can be seen as linked with the notion of 'companionate marriage', cited in the official and semi-official literature of the 1920s as the desirable form of family-based heterosexuality (Finch and Summerfield, 1999), it is not evident in the 1930s survey which Spring Rice reports (1939). As Finch and Summerfield (1999) argue, it was only with post-First World War concerns to stabilise the family that 'companionship' took hold as an ideal type model, but even then notions of 'partnership' and 'equality' were as likely to mean the 'teamwork' of matched but demarcated roles, as the more blurred distinctions of 'sharing'. Finch and Summerfield also highlight the post-war emphasis on sexual pleasure as one of the keys to marital stability. They note, however, the parallel anxiety that 'pleasurable sex was not stopping at the marriage bed and that the emphasis on it would in fact undermine the stability of marriage' (1999: 17).

While the First World War disrupted both prevailing belief systems and the marriage prospects of a whole cohort of women, a focus on companionship and mutuality within marriage was paralleled by moral panic about sexual promiscuity during the 'Roaring Twenties' and the emerging emancipation of middle-class women. Humphries (1988) argues that young people growing up during this period were expected to respect adult authority and family ties, to conform to traditional gendered roles, and at least to be mindful of an injunction against pre-marital sex (1988: 9). And Plummer (1995) compares the contemporary growth of sexual storytelling (see also Chapter 6) with the persistence of taboos around sexuality between the wars. Weeks shares this view, citing the *Evening News* in 1920: 'There are certain forms of crime prosecutions which are never reported in the newspapers and of which most decent women are ignorant and would prefer to remain ignorant' (1989: 200). Mutual sexual pleasure within companionate marriage therefore seemed to go hand in hand with 'a fear of going too far' which persisted into the late 1930s (Weeks, 1989: 205). The magazine *Home Chat* responded thus to a reader's enquiry: 'I am sorry I cannot answer so intimate a question through these columns and I am rather amazed at your ignorance about the facts of life. Ask an older friend to tell you' (Weeks, 1989: 206).

Evidence from a middle-class focus group discussion confirms a public story of the denial of sexual activity outside the respectable confines of marriage. When asked to respond to a series of quotes from young women in different historical periods who had been pressured into sex by their boyfriends, the response from participants was contradictory. A number of women insisted that these comments were '*very modern*'. However, a woman in her 90s pointed out almost inaudibly: '*No, not necessarily, no. It's always happened, but it wasn't broadcast.*' As we illustrate in Chapter 3, Jean Brown's account of her own youth confirms that this was, indeed, the case, but many focus group participants still differenti-ated between the young people of *their* youth and those of today, whom they associated with late night TV programmes depicting young people who '*just go out to get sex on holiday*'. Presented with this perspective, Angela reminded the group of her reading of the Little Kinsey Studies (Stanley, 1995), which contains an account of young people heading off to Blackpool when the mills were closed, for the same purpose. One of Kinsey's participants describes the sight of en masse furtive sexual activity under the piers at night. This forced the acknowledgement that this *did* occur but was not commonplace.

It is perhaps the case that the focus group context restricted what participants felt able to contribute about their own attitudes and experiences. Indeed, after a focus group with members of a Mother's Union group – who, judging by their responses, had expected a less risqué discussion – one older woman approached Angela and explained how difficult she found it to speak up about some of the issues because: *'You see, I'm divorced myself'*. Thus discussions with older focus group participants often evoked an initial response to questions about 'illicit' sexual activity 'then' and 'now' which suggested that things were different in their day. However, a more tentative exploration of the issues stimulated reports of a range of activities which were deemed socially 'taboo'. However, with the exception of one 38-year-old participant in a very small, mixed-age women's group, participants did not generally report their own *direct* experience of these, nor that of family or friends. Rather, such accounts were reserved for the privacy of the individual interviews, as data throughout this book demonstrate. Nonetheless, some participants sustained their insistence that moral standards 'then' were very different to 'now'. This, they speculated, was in part attributable to contemporary children's increased awareness of sexual and reproductive matters from a young age.

Interviewees who grew up during the interwar period were therefore markedly consistent in noting considerable differences between the experiences of their own age cohort and contemporary practice. With regard to their own awareness of sexual aspects of growing up heterosexual, they stated repeatedly that:

It wasn't a subject that was talked about in those days, was it, certainly not in our family anyway (Valerie Mills, 67).

I was as green as grass when I got married, I didn't know all the . . . (Anita Smith, 70).

they didn't talk about anything like that in those days (Evelyn Taylor, 81).

Oh! Absolutely wasn't talked of in my young day . . . *I mean you didn't talk about anybody being pregnant or anybody [.] anything sexy [LAUGHS] at all in those days* (Felicity Archer, 90).

When recalling what they knew about their own bodies as they approached marriage, these women found their ignorance laughable, particularly when viewed from a present-day social world where *'they know it when they're ever so young, don't they?'* Seventy year-old Anita Smith, for example, said: *'Well, I always thought the slightest touch of a man and a woman, that was it . . . '* When Angela asked, *'What, like any type of touch?'* Anita responded: *'No, with his . . . '* She thus betrays her difficulty in articulating the name of a sexual part of the body, one which mirrors her ignorance when growing up and, as noted below, suggests an ongoing concern with 'respectability' that demanded the avoidance of explicitly sexual references or behaviours. Eighty-one year-old Evelyn Taylor echoed this point: *'I mean, they never mentioned about how you got babies or anything. That was an experience you found out when you got married.'* When asked if she understood her body in a sexual or reproductive sense as she grew up, 67-year-old Jenny Hodge said:

Vaguely, very vaguely [.] very vaguely [.] yes, er, to be honest, I'd no idea how babies were born [.] when I had my first child [. . .] no, honestly, my sister, er, was a nurse . . . and, er, it was she, she who told me [.] how they were born and what to expect.

What is striking within these women's accounts is the critical perspective from which they now reflect upon their early experiences. Their testimonies are shot through with qualifying phrases such as: *'it sounds, sounds absolutely mad now doesn't it really?'*; *'it just shows how naïve you were'*; *'I mean, it's all pretty daft really'*; *'It might sound silly, but I was very naïve'*; *'now they say, "Oh, you're thick", but, I didn't know nothing'*; *'I was daft, seriously'*; *'Stupid really, wan't it'*; *'I was as daft as a brush, thought the moon was made of green cheese when you're 17'*.

In Chapter 8 we ask how the familial context can shape the passing of sexual knowledge, but here we focus on the way interviewees from this age cohort are expressing criticism of the cultural environment within which they grew up. Thus they look back into their pasts from a twenty-first-century perspective which is informed by vast changes in sexual mores, in women's place within the public world and indeed in the ideological and material circumstances of women's lives which result from feminist thought and action. In 1964, 63 300 children were born outside marriage, compared with 269 724 thousand in 2004 (ONS, 2006a). Similarly, 22 per cent of all families were headed by a lone parent in 1995, compared with 7 per cent in 1972 (Bernardes, 1997), a proportion which had risen to 24 per cent by 2004 (ONS, 2006b). From a contemporary perspective, then, these older women's reflections on their pasts are at best *self*-mocking, at worst *self*-reproachful about their lack of knowledge.

Although Humphries (1988) offers persuasive evidence that young women clearly *were* sexually active during this period, the testimonies cited above suggest that, for *these* women, it was primarily *after* marriage that any kind of sexual knowledge or practice developed. Ninety year-old Felicity Archer, for example, said:

> *you weren't expected to, sort of, sleep with anyone or anything else 'til you were married you know, it was all so very [.] naïve and [.] prim . . . I mean, it wasn't done [LAUGHS] to do anything improper so you just didn't, you know what I mean, this was unheard of in our days, I mean, my parents, well I had two maiden aunts, they were sort of brought up in the Edwardian age and you know, all that sort of rubs off on you, so I suppose we were sort of brought up in the same [.] way in a way.*

Discussions with working-class interviewees confirm both Humphries' findings and the existence of a powerful taboo concerning sex outside marriage. Seventy year-old Irene Nash describes how: *'a girl down the terrace, she had a baby, and my mother came and, you know, the way she went on about it, as though it was the worst thing in the world that could happen'.*

The Second World War, however, had a significant impact in disrupting marriage, family and sexual mores. H. E. Norman, formerly Secretary of the National Association of Probation Officers, in his (1949) book *Sex in Social Life*, lamented that during the war, 'there has been an exhibition of sexual incontinence and shameless conduct in our streets and lanes which must have shocked many more than just the old-fashioned Christians' (cited in Jeffreys, 1993: 7). And David Mace's (1948) *Marriage Crisis* – written in 'the tone of a friendly vicar giving a fireside chat to rather disillusioned parishioners about the necessity of keeping up the wartime spirit' (Jeffreys, 1993: 8) – observed the 'havoc of family life' wrought by the war:

> It was a pretty painful business – the evacuation of children, the life in the shelters, the black-out, the frantic embarkation leave marriages, the have-a-good-time-tonight-because-you-might-get-bumped-off-tomorrow atmosphere. (Mace, cited in Jeffreys, 1993: 7)

Examples of such disruption are evidenced in some of our participants' accounts. For example, Anita Smith's (71) early life had been affected by both evacuation during the Second World War and her mother's affair with one of the family's lodgers. Becoming pregnant by the lodger, she felt obliged to leave Anita's father and the children she had by him.

Even when the new relationship proved difficult, her mother felt she could not come back. Anita said: *'If she'd have thought on, she could have done, by what I've heard, you know, bits what my gran said, they'd have welcomed her back with Jean* [the baby]. *But you see then, it was scandalous, scandal, you see, wasn't it.'* A more 'light-hearted' example was offered by older women in one of our focus groups who recalled:

> *Maggie: I mean, I know what I was, but there was a lot of girls, say between the war breaking out, 1939, they knew what everything was about because [.] they'd been around a bit.*
> *Audrey: Been around a bit.*
> *All: [LAUGHTER]*
> *Maggie: I know because I worked in a factory and you listen to 'em talking,*
> *(?): God they had some good times.*
> *Elaine: Yeah [LAUGHS]*
> *Audrey: There were kids who lived down our street and their dads were in the army, but by eck, they had a lot of uncles.*
> *All: [LAUGHTER]*
> *Elaine: American [LAUGHS]*
> *Maggie: [QUIETLY] There were a woman (lived next door to me) when we was young he was coming home as a sailor was running out.*
> *All: [LAUGHTER]*

When asked about local responses to her position as a single parent, Bernice Parr (78) explained that women who found themselves in her situation during the war were *'all classed the same'*, whether they were 'promiscuous' or otherwise.

Bernice's comments about how women who violated the taboo were viewed at that time parallels Lees' (1993) account of the ways in which much later twentieth-century heterosexist verbal aggression and abuse drew on forms of categorisation which collapsed differences between different women's sexual experience, subsuming it to heteronormative stigmatisation: the 'tight bitches' and the 'slags' among the adolescent girls she worked with. It is also echoed in 70-year-old Joan Davis' account of training to be a nurse during the 1950s, when 10 o'clock curfews and prohibitions on male visitors at nurses' homes were still the norm. She described responses to an unmarried colleague's pregnancy in the following terms: *'she wasn't shunned, but . . . her apron got tighter and tighter and . . . it just didn't happen then, did it?'* Joan is testifying to the value attached to female pre-marital ignorance and celibacy at that time, a perspective held in place by the stigma and secrecy which surrounded young women's actual sexual practices. And indeed many interviewees from this age cohort were evasive or claimed to have forgotten the details of early sexual experiences.

Weeks (1989) notes that among working-class men during the 1930s, there was evidence that '[r]esponsiveness in their wives was hardly expected, and there was some suggestion that where the wife was more sensually disposed than her husband, her "hot nature" was disapproved, and even feared' (1989: 209). This is echoed by interviewees who described sex simply as a 'chore'. Whether sexual practice was subjectively less pleasurable, or whether instead it figured differently for people within heterosexual social identification is not self-evident. For example, if sex was largely invisible within public discourses of heterosexuality, does this make it more difficult to recall and to describe in the present?

In terms of the gendered identities of heterosexual partners between the wars, the concept of mutual sexual pleasure within companionate marriage referred to above was grounded in nineteenth-century medicalised notions of male sexual drives and female reproductive energy (Jordanova, 1989). The importance of female virginity and male experience when a couple married was therefore still in evidence, a cornerstone of van de Velde's *Ideal Marriage* (cited in Weeks, 1989: 206–7). This echoed Havelock Ellis' (see Weeks, 2000a) and Marie Stopes' concern with sex as a learned practice and was widely read between 1926 and 1932. This perspective on gendered sexual identities was evident in 70-year-old Joan Davis' assertion that boys did 'the running'. Of her first kiss Joan said: *'Yes, I think he was probably keen, but I wasn't, so, he kissed me, rather than we kissed.'* She spoke evasively of first sex saved for her wedding night and agreed that it was something of an anti-climax:

AM: *What did you expect?*
Joan: *[. .] Don't know, burst of sunlight or heavens open, or, no I don't suppose it was that, but both of us pretty, fumbling, or, um [. .].*

And she went on to affirm that: *'I think you do always expect men to take the lead, to be the, to be the authority on things, (. . .) I think [. . . .] I can't remember, um [. .] no, I really can't remember.'*

Eighty-three year-old Maggie Finch's account of first sex between the wars clearly indicates how our memories of the past are shaped by the tools we have to articulate them in the present: *'I suppose you would call it date rape these days'*, she said. *Then*, there was no term to describe what we now recognise as 'date rape' and Maggie explains that this was a perception she had only recently shared with anyone other than her husband. She says:

> *I didn't enjoy it [.] at all ... he, sort of ... kept me ... had me hands together, you know ... you don't think that men are so much stronger than women, but they are.*

This experience impacted profoundly on Maggie and, despite the hetero-normativity of marriage, she avoided men for ten years, until she met her husband aged 26. Sex became enjoyable only after her children were born. She said: *'I think that that first [.] contact with the other man [...] made a deeper impression than I thought.'* Though Maggie recalls that *'there was nothing nice about it at all'* and she *'finished with him'* immediately, her difficulty in categorising the experience as 'rape' reflected her belief that men are more easily sexually aroused than women.

These data suggest that interviewees' agency within heterosexual rela-tionships was limited to saying 'no'. However, Weeks (1989) notes that *forms* of control over women's sexuality were relaxing, for example, with the decline of chaperonage during the First World War, the growth of employment opportunities for women, and the establishment of mixed leisure venues such as cinemas and dancehalls. Both Maggie's and Joan's accounts of growing up showed them becoming independent early in life. Maggie left her family's remote farm for a career in nursing, as did Joan in later years. And Joan recalled hitching to the South of France with a friend at 18, despite it being, in her view, *'unheard of in those days'.*

'Modern times are wherever you are'

> Sexual intercourse began
> In nineteen sixty-three
> (Which was rather late for me) –
> Between the end of the *Chatterley* ban
> And the Beatles' first LP.

(from *Annus Mirabilis*, Philip Larkin, 1974)

In Chapter 9, we return to some of the broader social changes which shaped and influenced our participants' lives, notably the emergence of companionate marriage. Core to *this* chapter are matters of sex and sexuality since, from a comparative historical perspective, this was what preoccupied our participants' perceptions, as discussed above. Interestingly, when older focus group participants were asked when they believed 'modern times' to have begun, the responses varied, depending upon their age and gender. Below, we observe contradictions between what Audrey (in her mid-70s) says about the 1960s – the period when, in her view, *'everything went downhill'*, and Elaine (in her mid-50s) who has fond memories of her courtship during that time.

Audrey: *[Oh, that was] all free love and liberation. Everything went downhill then.*
Elaine: *That was the 70s, wasn't it, the flower power? The 60s, well I was courting from 64, I was married in 67. So from then onwards,*
Audrey: *It was sex, drugs and rock 'n' roll.*
Elaine: *It was good though, we had a good time.*
Kathy: *(Me dad says) 'But that was down South that, it never happened in Hull'*
All: *[LAUGHTER]*
AM: *Well what was it like then, courting in the 60s?*
Elaine: *It was good, it was good. We had more freedom.*

For the men attending a day centre whose data are presented below, 'modern times' were not the 'golden age' of 1940s tea dances remembered by older female counterparts, but:

Bert: *In the 60s, 50s and 60s.*
AM: *What makes you say that Bert?*
Bert: *Because, I remember up to the 40s and 50s, (they) were 'orrible. But the late 50s and 60s were great.*
AM: *Why was that previous time horrible? What was horrible about it and what was great about the late 50s and 60s?*
Bert: *Well, there wasn't things to do.*
AM: *Mm,*
Bert: *You know, you used to go in the Tower and have a dance, [.] come home, [. .] but now you can get all dressed up and dance the night away all night.*
AM: *So are you thinking, like, rock and roll*
Bert: *Yeah,*
AM: *And Elvis and Bill Haley and everything?*
(Ernie): *[Laughs] ( ) rock and roll and ( ) [Laughs].*

Turning to a group of retired professionals, their discussion explored the subjective nature of historical time, highlighting the importance of individual biography. Asked when 'modern times' began, they responded:

> *Joyce: The 60s.*
> *W?: Modern times are wherever you are.*
> *W?: Flapper girls could have been called modern in their day.*
>   *?: [Beatles. 60s].*
> *AM: You're being very unruly! So, people have got different ideas about when these modern times began.*
> *W?: The 1850s were modern times then.*
> *AM: So it's all relative to how old you are?*
> *W?: Whenever you're young.*
> *AM: The people that said the 60s, what made you say that?*
>   *?: [It was all free love and the drugs and travelling to India].*
> *W?: The pill.*
> *AM: The pill? Would anyone agree with that?*
> *W/Lots: Yes*
> *W?: Women's liberation.*
> *AM: Do you think that modern times have been a good thing for relationships?*
> *Lots: No.*

This resounding *'no'* echoes Weeks' argument that the term 'permissive society', as applied to the 1960s onwards, was not embraced by women and men seeking greater personal freedoms, but rather acted as a label which mobilised moral panic and subsequently helped generate 'mass support for authoritarian solutions' (1989: 249) to social problems during the 1980s. As stated above, it can be difficult to establish how the institution of heterosexuality was actually practised in the past – for example, within the marriages and families of the 1950s and 1960s. The sociology of the time reflected a spirit of optimism that the welfare state had seen off the oppressively restricted family lives of the 1920s and 1930s. Home-centred 'cosiness' and increased prosperity were felt to augur well for the long-term stability of marriage. Even public concern about 'juvenile delinquency' and divorce did little to dent the optimism of 1950s and 1960s sociology. It was indeed the case that post-1960s state support for greater sexual freedom became the context within which family life unfolded (Hawkes, 1996: 107), as discussed in greater depth in Chapter 9. Key events were the 1970s women's movement and the implications of HIV/AIDS for sexual mores in the 1980s. Plummer (1995: 38) argues that these have contributed to the feminisation of sex, the demo-cratisation of intimacy and a shedding of taboos around sexuality.

In this age of greater affluence, *many* areas of social life underwent change: 'from class relations to moral attitudes and family life, leading to the emergence of new social opportunities, new sub-classes, changed political allegiances, significant modifications in the relations between the sexes, an explosion of youth cultures, the fragmentation of the moral consensus – and in the end, acute social tensions' (Weeks, 1989: 250).

Interviewees who grew up during this period described leaving home whilst still single, just as young women in the previous generation had done. However, for them, establishing their independence facilitated sexual practice, albeit in ways which remained in tension with their heterosexual aspirations, as we go on to discuss in Chapter 7. As Finch and Summerfield (1999) argue, the ideal type model of 'companion-ship' which was believed to ground relationships between women and men after the Second World War was founded on a welfarist concern to stabilise the family. Marriage, then, retained many of its traditional features as a site at which hegemonic heterosexuality was being repro-duced and, as Chapter 1 described, it remained immensely popular, despite the growth in lone parent headed families.

Thus 43-year-old Sarah Davis and 50-year-old Jayne Finch both left home as teenagers. Sarah described herself confounding stereotypes of femininity by becoming a tomboy until the age of 16. Compared with the older generation of women, she was willing to describe her (hetero)sexual practices: kissing her first 'serious boyfriend' at a disco during the 1970s, wooed by his air-guitar emulation of Status Quo. She said: *'I think my knees felt weak . . . it was a very strange sensation, but certainly, yes my knees felt weak I'm sure.'* Their 18-month relationship included planned first sex at a friend's house, in her parents' absence, and she recalled her friend having first *'turn'* with her own boyfriend, upstairs in the bedroom:

I know we were in the living room listening to music and drinking coffee . . . we could hear the bed creaking upstairs and we tried very hard not to make any comments and, you know, concentrate very hard on the music . . . we were very much aware . . . I suppose then that it would be my turn next.

Though Sarah felt empowered to make choices such as this, the language she used still reflects the notion that boys do 'the running': she says that while *'we'* listened to the couple upstairs, *'we'* were aware that it would be *'my'* turn next. By implication, it was her, rather than her boyfriend, who was about to have 'first sex'. So alongside the claiming of these kinds of freedoms, traditional heterosexual practice persisted: marriage was more popular than ever, the 1911 figures of 552 women in every 1000 aged between 21 and 39 being married, comparing with 96 per cent of women under the age of 45 having been married by the mid-1960s (Weeks, 1989: 256–7). 'Marriage more than ever was "an inevitable step in the transition to adult life" ' argues Weeks (1989: 257). And indeed while Sarah travelled the world with the merchant navy, she went on to marry, albeit with sufficient sexual experience to exercise agency within the couple's sexual relationship.

Jayne Finch describes the sexual opportunities she discovered on leaving home to take up seasonal hotel work in 1970s Cornwall. She said:

> *I loved it. I looked round and there were boys, there were chefs, there were waiters, there were these dolly girls, they were all young, I was eighteen, and . . . I thought 'This is it!' . . . I'd landed in my own group.*

Surrounded by people doing drugs and *'sleeping around'*, Jayne felt free to have first sex at 18. However, her choice of an older man – a 34-year-old chef from the Middle East – again reflects the assumption that men, rather than women, are expected to be sexually experienced agents, even though women's ignorance and celibacy were less central to a desirable heterosexual identity. Like Sarah, Jayne could describe his first kiss: *'I nearly collapsed, it was just fabulous (. . .) it was heaven.'* First sex, too, was recalled in detail, even though it failed to provide erotic pleasure:

> *I remember being extremely disappointed that [. . .] it was so quick . . . Well, it just wasn't enough because [.] yes, it was painful the first time and [.] I [.] bled like a stuck pig, I didn't have time to take it any further or, you know, do [.] whatever I'd dreamt about or seen in the pictures or what people had talked about.*

Thus while both historical and biographical material attests to changes in the framing of heterosexual sex, continuities are also in evidence. As Holland et al. (1996) observe, among young women and men growing up in the late 1980s/early 1990s, 'conceptions of first intercourse as about women's pleasure, performance or achievement of adult status are strikingly absent' (1996: 153). Although Weeks describes the growth of a 'legal acceptance of moral pluralism' (1989: 273) during this period, Hawkes (1996) suggests that heterosexual practice remained resilient to change, persisting even within liberalising discourses under the guise of new lifestyle 'choices' for women. Our data nonetheless evidence what Weeks refers to as 'a growing interest in less orthodox sexualities' during the 1970s, including 'the social exploration of lesbianism' (1989: 263). Jayne, for example, cohabited with a woman for two years, the relationship ending only because her friend would not 'come out' as a lesbian, for fear of parental distress. Jayne's adult identity as heterosexual was not therefore an inevitability, but partly the outcome of choice, although not entirely her own.

Forever young

From the 1960s onwards, boundaries between childhood and adulthood became increasingly ragged. Physiologically girls were experiencing menarche on average at 13–14, compared with 16–17 a century earlier; and boys were reaching full growth and sexual potential on average at 17, compared with 23 at the beginning of the century (Weeks, 1989: 252). Yet economic and legislative changes began to delay previous possibilities for independence: for example, the raising of the school leaving age and the growth of unemployment from the 1970s onwards. Brannen and Nilsen (2002: 515) have argued that by the turn of the twentieth century, adolescence had become extended, with markers of adulthood, such as leaving home, marriage and transitions to parenthood being deferred. Countering modernist notions of a deterministically chronologised life course (Hockey and James, 2003), Brannen suggests that ambiguous transitions of the kind she is describing evidence the view that '[a] child may be constituted as a young adolescent in one context and with respect to a particular generational order and quite differently in another' (1999: 144).

What all this meant for the youngest cohort we interviewed was that extended 'childlike' dependency upon parents went hand in hand with potentially greater sexual licence. This paradoxical combination of circumstances appeared to disrupt the relationship between heterosexual identification and adulthood. For example, while interviewees from the youngest age-cohort used far more sexually explicit language than individuals from older cohorts, they saw discrepancies of all kinds between the sexual practices they permitted themselves and their notions of adult heterosexuality-as-imagined. Abigail Davis (17) spoke of being *'fingered'*; Liz Kirk (15) said a boy of her age had asked if he could *'knob'* her. And Andrew Jones (21) referred to *'anal'*, *'tit-wanks'* and wanting to *'come over'* his partner's face. Yet while referring to (hetero)sexual *practice*, the use of these terms did not signify the accomplishment of adulthood. Indeed stark references to the body and its parts could discredit the romantic language/discourse through which both young men and young women framed desired heterosexuality. This issue is discussed in greater depth in Chapter 6.

Our discussions with participants from the youngest cohort revealed an interesting paradox: on the one hand they access far more information about the 'facts of life' and enjoy greater freedom to practise, yet on the other, they express ignorance, confusion and dissatisfaction about aspects of heterosexuality which extend beyond the purely sexual. A narrow focus on the sexual aspects of heterosexuality appears problematic for young people struggling to reconcile the implications of a permissive discourse for their practice (Hollway, 1984; Wight, 1996), with a desire for an ill-defined something more – or different. For example, Andrew Jones (21), who lived in Hull and worked as a nightclub barman, described the mismatch between his permissive sexual practice and adult heterosexuality. This concern was expressed in terms of his emotional confusion around 'one night stands'. He said:

> *Unfortunately, and I hate to say it, but . . . I didn't really like going out with girls, I liked having sex with them, but that was . . . I didn't like . . . going out with a girl for a few months, fucking her and then fucking off.*

As his interview shows, Andrew felt that his emotional responses to this situation failed to conform to prevailing assumptions about heterosexual sex and relatedness: '. . . *every time I had had sex, afterwards, . . . I don't know, I started distancing myself from them, and I don't know why.*' Peer group pressure made Andrew more than aware of what an appropriate response might have been. He said:

> *I had quite a few angry people about that, which I can fully understand . . . ex-girlfriends, and a lot of their friends, when I was out they'd lay into me or whatever, have a bit of a go at you, which is fine, yeah, I understand why they do it, but [. .] I didn't appreciate it at the time, and I don't think they understand, understood how I felt, but then again, neither did I, so . . .*

Joanne Smith (21) also lived in Hull and was employed in seasonal hotel work. Though she now has a boyfriend, she described earlier teenage years when, like Andrew, she found herself unable to engage with heterosexual coupledom, yet felt her response required some kind of explanation. Rather than his straightforward, albeit 'inexplicable' unwillingness to enter into a 'couple' relationship, Joanne felt neither 'casual sex' *nor* a relationship were what she wanted. She began by saying:

> *Yeah, just that sort of thing, see each other at the end of the night, snog each other, see each other when you was in like, whatever clubs you was in, and that, been like now and again, but not anything really serious, which is what I wanted at the time.*

However Angela reminded her that she had previously said *'that you'd turned round to him and said, "Oh, this is doing my head in". Was it the fact that you were just having sex casually that was doing your head in, without any meaning?'* Joanne struggled to reply to this question and then said:

> *I don't really know how to describe it, it was um, just sleeping with him and not anything, not any relationship with it and what-have-you, which I was thinking, well, I don't really want a relationship, but then I don't really want this either. I wanted something in between, but it didn't work out like that... I don't know what I had in mind, but I wasn't happy how it was, so, but then I wasn't happy how it ended up either, so, something, like I say, in between, but (I) found that with him, it was either all or nothing, I think, with him.*

These data reveal a sense of dissatisfaction being experienced by young people as they engage in an emotional struggle to reconcile their sexual practices and behaviour with what they feel they *ought* to be doing. In the absence of a metanarrative around heterosexuality, they appear not to know what to expect, or how they and 'it' should be. That said, they retain the sense of 'accountability' as gendered, heterosexual individuals which was discussed in Chapter 1. And this, it would seem, exercises them. While participants from the older generations struggled with issues around accessing sexual knowledge and the freedom to practise their sexuality, such freedoms could present problems for young people. Paradoxically, whilst the achievement of adult heterosexuality might seem to be a matter of gaining sexual knowledge and practice, they still did not feel 'grown up'. What appears lacking is a persuasive discourse which relates this particular aspect of adult heterosexuality to heterosexual emotionality, or indeed heterosexual practices more broadly; for example, creating and sustaining family relationships and domestic life. Young people's accounts therefore suggest that heterosexuality is experienced as both taken-for-granted, yet elusive; as 'doing sex', yet potentially something more than that. Thus, while heterosexuality is reduced only to the sexual in the popular imagination, for young people there remains a sense of something not adding up, a 'critical lack of fit' (Hockey and James, 2003) between their expectations and the contours of hegemonic heterosexuality. Data such as these inform the debates raised in Chapter 2 where we ask whether the 'riskiness' which Giddens (1992) associates with the post-traditional loss of consistent metanarratives brings the benefits of personal choice and empowerment, or the dangers of risk and uncertainty.

Conclusion

The comparative material presented here suggests a radical shift in the practices through which heterosexuality has been lived out during the last 80 years, the most pronounced changes emerging in the late 1960s and 1970s. While data from the interwar period describe boys pursuing passive and sexually ignorant girls, the 1970s bore witness to greater agency among women, along with more scope for exercising it as a result of increased freedom and mobility, both in work and leisure activities. However, achieving heterosexual adulthood requires more than simply participation in (hetero)sex and access to sexual knowledge, and greater scope for practice did not necessarily erase ignorance and confusion about how to grow up heterosexual. The chapters which follow explore some of the complexities involved in negotiating heterosexuality when it is apparently so powerfully framed and entangled within sexual *practice* in people's lives.

Having explored the theoretical and methodological challenges of working with a pervasive yet 'invisible' category of mundane experience; introduced the body of feminist work which underpins the project, and to which it contributes; and laid out some of the profound changes which have taken place within the ways in which heterosexuality has been lived out during the last 80 years, Chapter 5 reviews the analytic resources through which our data can be made sense of. First we ask how the emergence of particular kinds of heterosexual subjectivity can be understood and how these might relate to changes within the institution, suggesting that what is left out, sequestered or silenced within heterosexual practice and experience is, arguably, as key to its viability *and* mutability as what is seen, heard and enacted. In examining potential theoretical resources, then, Chapter 5 asks how distinctions might be made between practices and experiences which can and cannot be included within hegemonic heterosexuality, highlighting the heuristic value of a focus on the discourses, narratives, representations and language which together constitute the 'heterosexual imaginary' (Ingraham, 1996, 1999, 2005).

Chapter 6 develops the issue of how aspects of institutionalised hetero-sexuality may be represented, imagined and spoken about, through a detailed examination of what was said – or not said – by parti-cipants. Chapters 7 and 8 then explore heterosexuality as *lived out*, within everyday life, and at key or extreme heterosexual moments – and, subsequently, within the home. The relationship between conceptions of institutionalised or hegemonic heterosexuality and the practices of everyday life, or mundane heterosexualities, is the subject of Chapter 9's historical comparison between concerns about the body and the emotions and, as such, brings together a focus on discourse and narrative with that grounded in the materialities of cross-generational family life.

5
Getting the Story Straight

Chapter 3 explored the case study of one older woman whose lifetime had coincided with major social changes such as a broader social acceptance of birth outside marriage and a growing association between major health risks and unprotected sex. These data were located within a reflexive account of the position from which we are investigating heterosexuality. It included our political and intellectual standpoints as feminists – and their methodological implications. Working in this area inevitably raises issues of power, and related sociological questions of structure and agency – and Chapter 3 came rapidly to the question of how we might interpret material derived from conversation with someone who had set out on heterosexual married life before even the very oldest of the book's three authors had started school. As our discussion of Jean Brown's life history shows, it was data which revealed the taken-for-granted yet powerfully gendered patterning of the everyday. And Jean's passage through schoolgirl bike-shed kissing, dating, marriage and motherhood exemplify the living out of an unremarkable, 'ordinary' heterosexual life. Yet Jean also resisted the silences and sanctions of such a life when they failed to conform to her own beliefs or to satisfy her needs. She reflected, critically, and resisted when, in her view, it was appropriate. Her agency is well evidenced – yet she exercised it in order to generate the heterosexual life which she has chosen.

This discussion takes us to the heart of a feminist engagement with women's and men's lives. It asks how diversity, conformity and resistance should be made sense of, both intellectually but also politically. In order to address such questions, however, we need to understand how particular lives come to be lived, and how heterosexuality is reproduced and amended, or indeed resisted. It is this task which the present chapter begins to address. As noted in Chapter 1, as a silent category, heterosexuality is a challenging focus for empirical research and one of the avenues we have therefore explored is the notion of heterosexuality as a *residual* category. That is to say, we can begin to make sense of what it is all about by examining what it is not. This therefore raises the concept of failed heterosexual lives, of transgressions, of omissions, of contradictions, important points which the present chapter and the one to follow will develop. Clearly heterosexuality also *demands* certain behaviours, attitudes and values, yet, as we argue, these can be more difficult to articulate since this process of interpellation is enmeshed in the institution's status as 'natural'. Using the notion of the residual category – and that which fails to be accommodated within it – therefore follows the flow of our interviewees' subjectivities more closely.

This approach is exemplified in Essig's work on the Mermaid Parade in Coney Island, USA, an event she describes as 'a space on the edge of the heterosexual imagination' (2005: 162). What she argues is that while once mermaids posed a Christian riddle as to whether or not they had souls, in a post-Christian era their questionable possession of a soul has been replaced by uncertainty as to whether or not they have a vagina. The mermaid's vagina, in her view, 'stands in for our larger cultural obsession with women's bodies and their accessibility to men' (2005: 151–2). If she is in possession of a vagina, the mermaid represents an idealised heterosexual fantasy figure; if she does not then her seductiveness is monstrous, a vehicle for enticing men to their deaths by drowning without ever providing them with penetrative heterosexual intercourse. As a result the mermaid 'swims at the edge of the heterosexual imagination as a potential lover and a potential monster' (2005: 152). Out there on the margins, the mermaid may strike the reader as an unlikely source of insight into the institution of heterosexuality. Yet Essig's (2005) account of the individuals who take part in Coney Island's Mermaid Parade shows that while they

> push the limits of the heterosexual imagination, they also remain firmly within it. These mermaids on the edge of respectable heterosexuality are able to explore a suspect topic like sex with a different species precisely because they are so clearly heterosexual. Their desires are firmly located within the only truly legitimate sexual practices of our culture, the desire for heterosexual intercourse, for the insertion of the penis into a vagina, even if that vagina belongs to a fish.
> (2005: 161)

Attention to the limits of heterosexuality as a way of understanding what might lie at its core is therefore a way of approaching something not readily articulated by individuals leading heterosexual lives. However, this approach does not necessarily deal directly with the question of power, the issue of structure and the possibility of agency. Chapters 2 and 3 provide an introduction to how we might understand these concepts and indeed trace them within the lived experiences of people we have spoken with. Yet when it comes to lived experience, can we produce an adequate explanation of how it all comes to happen? Already within this book we are placing particular emphasis on women's and men's agency, in part as a reflection of a feminist emancipatory agenda which would see research practice as oriented towards overcoming oppression (Harding, 1987). And to this end we have made reference to women's and men's creative capacities which transcend structural conditions (Wray, 2003: 514). With regard to the concept of structure – and the extensive feminist work on the ways in which structures such as patriarchy and capitalism sustain women's subordination – we are *resisting* a view of society as something existing independently of its members, as something to which they must strive to adjust (Cohen, 1994: 21). So as we seek to make sense of our data, we are avoiding a view of the individual as someone under pressure to conform to an abstract institution which exists outwith their everyday lives, a point we develop further in Chapter 7. Rather, we are interested in our interviewees' subjectivities as embodied, socio-emotional, heterosexual individuals who make choices, albeit within constrained parameters or circumstances.

How then would we respond to authors such as Hall (1996) or Ingraham (1996), both of whom talk in terms of 'discourses' or 'cultural imaginaries' as the sources of individuals' identities and aspirations? For both these authors, Althusserian concepts of interpellation, of the masking of the historical and material conditions of life, are important. Hall, for example, refers to discourses and practices which can 'hail us into place as the social subjects of particular discourses' (1996: 5). How do these positions mesh with a theoretical wariness of the idea that there is something 'out there' to which we feel a compulsion to conform? As Jenkins (2002: 78) says, if we are reliant on the presence of something 'out there' as a way of explaining human behaviour, then we have to be able to demonstrate that it exists – and we can't. Nor can we explain how it might connect with the everyday choices and actions of human beings. And if the something 'out there', broadly recognised by sociologists as 'structure', is but an analytic device for making sense of what people choose to do, then it cannot, in itself, effect anything at all – apart from our understanding of the social world.

What Jenkins (2002: 81–3) then points towards, however, is the possibility of something which *does* lie beyond the sum of society's individual members, albeit remaining part of the knowable world of everyday life. In other words it does not disappear into the abstractions of 'structure'. What he is referring to are the capacities of human beings to imaginatively transcend the here and now of the material moment; to identify with other people within groups; to draw on shared symbolic systems such as language; to participate in the dynamics of group interactions; and to agree upon a stable time-space called 'the present' (Jenkins, 2002). When we turn towards our interviewees and their life histories, it is this sense of the indivisibility of the individual and society which informs our analytic project. So on the one hand we are wary of what Geertz describes as those 'grand realities' (1975: 21) which signal their abstract status via the use of capital letters – in our case, Patriarchy and Capitalism. Yet on the other, we understand our interviewees as people whose agency is not simply an individualised 'inner' propensity exercised vis-à-vis an externalised abstraction such as 'structure', or indeed 'hegemonic heterosexuality'. Rather, their agency is something we see as integral to their nature as *social* beings, as members of the kinds of imaginative and socially interactive collectivities which Jenkins is describing. Indeed our focus on the cross-generational family, rather than the individual, as our site of investigation reflects Jenkins' notion of 'the immanent "more-ness" of collectivity revealed in the practices of everyday life' (2002: 81).

Such perspectives take us some way towards a position from which we can engage with our interviewees' accounts of their experiences, but they still leave aside issues of power and subjectivity. We remain with the question of how heterosexual subjectivities come to be constituted and while the family which surrounds us may evidence the nature of heterosexual life, we still need to understand how any one individual's subjectivity comes into being. However, since we are concerned with heterosexuality as a social institution, we draw on the perspectives of the social sciences, rather than psychology or psychoanalysis, seeking to transcend more individualistic approaches. This is not say that we eschew the 'inner' person since, as Chapter 2 highlights, there is a persuasive case to suggest that the very division between an 'inner' and an 'outer' world is particular to western conceptions of the self. Instead, therefore, subjectivity can more effectively be re-cast as *intersubjectivity*, individuals conceiving of and experiencing themselves not simply as insular, bounded entities.

Jackson raises this question of how subjectivities emerge when she asks a more focused question about the constitution of heterosexual *desire*, that is, how can we avoid 'conflating heterosexuality as an institution with heterosexual practice, experience and identity' (1996: 21)? While her starting point may be the return of agency to heterosexual women, her agenda also forces the question of how institutions and subjectivities should be understood and whether they can be seen as entities which stand in some kind of relationship with one another. Her review of political and theoretical perspectives on heterosexual subjectivities leads her to state somewhat despondently that: 'Psychoanalysis has established a virtual monopoly on theorising the construction of sexuality at the level of subjectivity' (1996: 27). And this, she suggests, can be explained by the fact that 'psychoanalysis retains its tenacious hold in part because of the lack of viable alternatives. It is not that there are no other theories, but that they are either inadequate or underdeveloped' (1996: 27).

Throughout this entire discussion, Jackson's theoretical agenda parallels the question we raised above – 'how does it all come to happen?', or as she puts it: 'How did I get this way?'(1996: 28). Her responses to this question include disciplinary practices such as the threat of male violence and harassment which potentially leads all women to manage their bodies with care in public spaces; discourses and representations of sexuality which privilege phallocentric sex; the heterosexualisation of feminine identities such as wife, girlfriend, daughter or mother; the framing of housework as loving service; the centrality of sexual attractiveness to femininity – and perhaps most profoundly, as a precondition for the resonance of all these micro practices, the primacy of gender as an aspect of social identity. This discussion then moves us into the domain of everyday experience, of the assumptions which inform our mundane tasks. When Jackson asks, for example, about how sexual practice relates to sexual experience, or, as she puts it, how 'what is felt both sensually and emotionally' relates to 'what is thought' (1996: 32), her answer then states that discourses, narratives and scripts resource the interpretative processes through which we connect our practices with our experiences of them. All of this therefore admits the participative nature of 'how things come to happen' or 'how I got this way'. Indeed Jackson (1999) stresses that we *work ourselves into* the 'immanent "more-ness" ' which Jenkins (2002: 81) refers to – and which in our view corresponds to the discourses and narratives which Jackson refers to. And to draw on her explanation of this process, we can argue that this 'work' involves

'participating in sets of meanings constructed, interpreted, dissemin-
ated and deployed throughout our culture, through learning scripts,
positioning ourselves within discourses, constructing narratives of self'
(Jackson, 1999: 106).

Agency is therefore writ somewhat larger in Jackson's (1996) and
Jenkins' (2002) accounts, along with a diminishing of the often abstract
nature of 'structure'. To believe in something beyond everyday materialities, to identify with family or indeed nation, to use a shared language,
to engage in the dynamics of social interaction, and to share in an
agreed 'present' are all forms of engagement with something which transcends the individual and indeed the fleeting moment. Moreover, these
are all *active* processes, observable at the level of the individual, even
if they are not limited to the immediacies of their own private 'here-
and-now'. There remains, however, that aspect of agency which pertains
to change, to renegotiation, to resistance and refusal. All that we have
argued so far could be taken simply as an explanation of how everyday
heterosexuality reproduces itself, how we all jump onto more or less the
same bandwagon. Yet, as data presented in Chapter 6 will demonstrate,
the experience of heterosexuality involves a whole series of divergences
from any kind of collective notion of what that institution might be
about.

While Jenkins (2002) identifies the decisions and actions of individuals as indeed a source of change, what he points out is that our
notion of a stable social world which then undergoes change – and then
regains stability – is misleading. In his view, movement is ongoing. The
social world is dynamic. Change, however, refers to those aspects of that
overall pattern of movement which are *recognised*, acquire meaning and
on some level become institutionalised. Where does agency fit into all
this? As we have identified, Jean Brown's life history evidences agency at
many points – yet there is nothing to suggest that she sought to redefine
the parameters of heterosexuality. Equally there is nothing to suggest
that her choices were *not* part of an overall pattern of change within that
institution. So, if we treat the social world as continuously in flux, with
'change' defined as those shifts which acquire significance, this implies
that the socio-historical changes we might document in this book –
such as the rise of lone parent households or the growth in women's
paid employment – are not necessarily the consequences of *intentional*
human behaviour. They are, however, inevitably the outcome of something which someone somewhere actually did or said – or perhaps
chose *not* to do or say; that is, unless we begin to invoke supernatural
sources of change. We are talking, therefore, about the agency of *effect*

rather than intention (Latour, 1993). When it comes to those aspects of subjectivity which seem to be associated with agency, such as motivation or resistance, we are engaging with the distinction which Jackson (1999) makes between practice and experience, between what we do and how we understand it. In other words, they are likely to concern aspects of a dynamic everyday environment which the individual – or someone associated with them – has given weight to and indeed has reflected upon. They merit scrutiny as somehow potentially intrinsic to *change*. And all of this returns us to the pervasive power of the institution of heterosexuality which, in being naturalised and misleadingly sexualised, persistently slides out of reflective focus. If we wish to understand change, then, we need to consider those discourses which are constitutive of heterosexuality for it is these which enable particular moments or movements within a dynamic social world to be *recognised* as different, as better or indeed as worse. Our understanding of agency cannot therefore be limited to notions of intentions put into practice, for the outcomes of these are highly unpredictable. And by contrast we can be powerful agents of change without any projection of where or what our actions will lead to. It is all, we might argue, a matter of *recognition*, whether in relation to ourselves and our own choices – or those of others.

Reflections on heterosexual lives

This chapter has taken up some of the long-standing themes and debates within the social sciences and considered how theoretical concepts such as 'structure', 'agency', 'change' and 'subjectivity' might be made to do their work as the tools through which we can better understand and amend, if not transform, the gendered social world we inhabit. Core to this discussion has been the relationship between structure and agency and how we might understand the 'heterosexual individual' in terms of their beliefs and practices. Jackson's (2005) account of the distinction between the cultural and the social provides another take on the contribution of the concept of structure to our understanding of life. Arguing that 'the social world includes the cultural, it includes the realms of discourse and symbolic representation, but the cultural is not all there is to the social' (2005: 18), she flags the structural or material conditions of women's and men's lives along with the situated practices which make up embodied, everyday life. These more grounded dimensions of the social need to be included in our analytic work for, she argues, '[i]n concentrating on one aspect of the social, others disappear' (Jackson, 2006: 108).

What are the implications of this argument for the present inquiry? Do we agree with this position? As Chapter 1 noted, what we set out to explore were the ways in which individuals came to understand what being heterosexual meant – and meant *for them*. Sparked by our personal experiences of individuals engaging with this question – albeit via discussion of particular relationships – we recognised scope for an empirical investigation of issues which for too long had been addressed at a primarily theoretical level. What we gathered, as Chapters 1 and 3 describe, are the narratives of 72 individuals. These accounts lay out our interviewees' perceptions of heterosexual lives which vary in length between 17 and 90 years. Like most life histories they combine description with reflection.

These narratives form the starting point for undertaking this distinctive project and, as we go on to argue, lead us to make the cultural or discursive aspects of the social our starting point. Moreover, in our focus on everyday life, our attention has been directed to the 'ordinary'. This orientation means that, as Mackay states, 'we are less concerned with the powerful and that which is recorded and codified, and more concerned with the unpredictable, the improvised and with the routine activities and control of ordinary people as they go about their day-to-day lives' (1997: 7). This is not to say that we disagree with Jackson that 'who we are is a consequence of our location within gendered, class, racial and other divisions . . . ' (2005: 18), that social structural and material factors need to taken account of. While these are aspects of an environment and a set of institutions which transcend the immediacies of the individual's everyday life, we view their mutability or stability as the outcome of choices and actions undertaken by *individuals*. Nonetheless, in that our data concern the reflections of particular individuals, that these are our starting point, it is the cultural or discursive dimension of the social which we prioritise here, rather than the wider structural or material environment within which heterosexuality is lived out. As Jackson says of the different aspects of the social – whether structural, discursive, interactive or subjective – 'although these dimensions of the social are interrelated, they cut across each other, as well as interlocking, producing disjunctions between and within them. Moreover, it is difficult, if not impossible, to focus on all at once' (2006: 108).

In making our interviewees' narratives our starting point, then, we are foregrounding their sense-making practices, so privileging both the discursive and subjective dimensions of the social. And in so doing we draw on Jackson's earlier distinction between 'discourse' and 'narratives' (1998), the notion that 'discourse circumscribes what we can know and speak about, and how we can know and speak about it; it enables us to say and think some things rather than others, thus shaping our sense of social reality' (1998: 47). While narratives are simply stories, these interact with discourses, each one articulating with the other, for as Jackson observes, 'we draw on discourses culturally available to us in order to construct narrative accounts, enabling us to tell particular stories at particular times' (1998: 47). Moreover, according to Gilfoyle et al., discourse involves more than simply language; it also organises meaning and action (1993: 182).

In this chapter, then, we are laying out our theoretical understandings of 'how things come to happen' or 'how I got this way'. In treating 'the social' as an umbrella term which encompasses the cultural and in exploring the analytic role of concepts such as discourse and narrative our empirical project has involved critical engagement with Jackson's body of theoretical work. We now move on to explore other theoretical contributions to feminist scholarship, asking what light the work of Dworkin, Jeffreys, Skeggs, McRobbie, Plummer and Ingraham can shed on our empirical data.

From discourse to language

In order to develop understanding of the connections between discourse, narrative and language and the ways in which they resource particular kinds of social relationships – and inequalities – we begin with the example of Andrea Dworkin's discussion (1987) of what she describes as the 'dirty words' associated with sexual intercourse. These contribute to a discourse which she and other radical feminists see as facilitating both the objectification of women and the occupation of women's 'inferior' and 'contaminating' bodies by men in the role of exploiters, conquerors and occupiers. Such perceptions, Dworkin argues, have been enhanced and proliferated through language and the representation of women in pornography. Indeed, in the early 1990s, Jeffreys (1993) described sex as contested political ground shared by both feminists and libertarians, one in which language, or its absence, is complicit in women's oppression. She argues: 'Part of the repertoire of techniques for political control is the control of language. It is hard to "think" about things for which there is no word available. Women are not supposed to think in a way which is positive about sex' (Jeffreys, 1993: 304). Women are therefore left to draw upon dominant cultural narratives relating to sex which are located within discourses to which men and women do not enjoy equal access, and through which men usually dominate as subjects, rather than objects.

Crawford et al. (1994) develop this view in their study of intersubjectivity and women and men's sex talk, noting that male discourses are hegemonic and that media and cultural representations ensure that women see themselves to some extent through men's eyes. So, while women know – or think they know – how men may feel during a sexual encounter, the same cannot be said of men in relation to women. Thus, they argue: 'the occasioned meanings which emerge within such encounters are produced with reference to dominant discourses, and are shaped and transformed in reference to them' (1994: 574). Skeggs (1997) introduces the issue of social class into these debates, arguing that our capacity to occupy and relate to dominant discourses is affected by more than just gender. Social class, as we go on to argue, also shapes our capacity to occupy subject positions in relation to sexuality. Within this project, therefore, we develop Jackson's (1998) and Gilfoyle et al.'s (1993) notion that discourse and language frame experience, asking how these may vary at different points in time and according to factors such as gender and social class. In the process we consider whether arguments such as those expressed about sex by radical feminists continue to have resonance in the twenty-first century, or, indeed, whether they were ever relevant to the lives of older participants in our sample.

Representing heterosexuality

While our primary empirical data are verbal, making sense of them requires us to take account of other ways in which the discourses surrounding heterosexuality might find expression. As Chapter 2 argues, the heterosexual narratives through which women and men make sense of themselves as they grow up include forms of cultural representation such as film (see Ingraham (1999) on wedding movies and television shows and Cokely (2005) on Disney), and romantic fiction (see Lewallen (1988) on blockbuster novels). Such representations, we argued, can be seen as facets of what Ingraham describes as illusory heterosexuality, one which is romanticised through a 'heterosexual imaginary' (2002: 79). This Ingraham defines as 'that image or representation of reality which masks the historical and material conditions of life' (2002: 79), imaginary being a Lacanian term which Althusser borrowed for his theory of ideology.

Whilst we might be wary of the notion of some kind of free-floating structure of ideas which potentially acts upon us, the notion that we work ourselves into sets of imagery and ideals which transcend the privacy of our own here-and-now, offers a less dualistic model of the social nature of everyday private life. Thus, for example, following Ingraham, heterosexuality – as recognised and practised within American society – can be seen to reside in 'rules on everything from who pays for the date or the rehearsal dinner to who leads while dancing, drives the car, cooks the dinner, or initiates sex' (Ingraham, 1999: 4). In Ingraham's (1999) work on white weddings and their associated representations – wedding movies and television shows – she shows how heterosexual partnering and all that it entails is both romanticised and also made accessible.

This perspective is echoed in Lewallen's (1988) earlier work on romance fiction. Here she refers to the view that it is 'a form of sexual foreplay that can function simultaneously as an expression and a containment of female desire, the fulfilment of which we imagine takes place in the nuptials promised at the close of the story . . . [t]he heroine wants sex, but only within the marriage bed, and thus these romances illustrate women's lack of social and psychological freedom to express their sexuality' (1988: 86–7). Hawkes (1996) exemplifies this perspective in her discussion of women's monthly magazines. Here she suggests that the explicit sexual detail of articles on erotic practice prioritises men's pleasure, even as it offers women advice on sexualising all aspects of their everyday lives, from work-time phone calls, through to undressing, taking a bath, and mundane domestic proximity to a male partner. Such magazines' promotion of the 'every-dayness' of sex through, for example, readers' letters which describe a different sexual practice for every day of the week is coupled with the additional requirement that 'sex must not be "dull" at any costs, even if we must now not lie back and think of England but go and tog up in rubber' (Hawkes, 1996: 119). In Hawkes' view, then, '[a] sense of autonomy of self, particularly for women, is negated in the exhortations to stoke the fires of desire. One can never let up sexually' (1996: 119). Lewallen (1988), however, took a different view of representations of women as sexual agents. What she argued was that a 1980s blockbuster novel, such as Shirley Conran's *Lace*, although framed within a discourse of bourgeois liberalism, did acknowledge women's potential for sexual agency within spheres which transcend marriage and economic dependency.

Lewallen's (1988) argument – that the shifting forms of romantic representation can reflect resistance to traditional heterosexual mores – is echoed in McRobbie's (1991) examination of magazines for girls and young women between the 1960s and 1980s. Her work documents the changes which have taken place in falsely unified consumerist perceptions of a common experience of girl/womanhood, one in which constructions of femininity hinge upon knowing how to 'catch a boy' (McRobbie, 1991: 84), and then keep him. Indeed, as Skeggs notes, not to be in a relationship with someone can be experienced as cultural exclusion (1997: 115), a lesson apparently learnt early by the readership of these magazines. Indeed, as data presented in Chapter 7 indicate, to have a boyfriend is to have social and cultural capital for many women. In her analysis of romance presented in the picture stories published in *Jackie* magazine in the 1960s, McRobbie evidences the manifestation of a 'to have/hold' or romantic discourse. Often drawing upon scenes from everyday life and depicting the trials and tribulations of typically older girls/women, these stories present a construction of heterosexuality to which every young girl was presumed to aspire. For teenage girls at that particular moment in time, boys were therefore constructed as objects of romantic love, rather than sex (McRobbie, 1991: 101).

However, by the 1980s, the emphasis on romance had given way to an increasing acknowledgement of girls, and young women in particular, as social *and* sexual agents with the emergence of magazines such as *Just Seventeen* and *Mizz*. No longer presented as the 'victims' of romance, these magazines had begun to portray girls as more equal protagonists within relationships than they had done previously (McRobbie, 1991: 148), a cultural representation of sexuality which parallels the block-buster novels of the same period. And among those magazines currently targeted towards an older teenage audience – for example *More!* and *19* – readers were characterised as more knowing sexual agents. *More!*, in particular, as Jackson (1999) notes, is (in)famous for its 'position of the fortnight' feature and contains articles on orgasm and female sexual pleasure. Interestingly, while Jackson notes the absence of information about relationships within materials read by teenage boys, anecdotal evidence suggests that the 'position of the fortnight' is a feature read by older *men*.

Given such evidence of a more active female sexuality emerging in recent decades, we therefore have to question the continuing reson-ance of Dworkin's claims about the imposition of a passive and objecti-fied female sexuality. Indeed, while Jackson does not share McRobbie's optimism that such magazines represent the potential for less uniform or monolithic modes of femininity (1999: 142), she nonetheless acknowledges that they begin to provide girls with a language which they can use in negotiating sex with boys, and in asserting their own sexual desires. This, she says, is precisely because they 'speak to them in terms which make sense in the light of their everyday experiences – even as they simultaneously help to construct that experience' (1999: 148).

Speaking of sex

The arguments explored above debate the issue of whether women lack access to a nuanced sexual language – something which concerned us when planning the topic guide for the interviews. Alongside more contemporary studies, we can place Skeggs' (1997) account of the historical silencing of women on matters of sexuality: for example, the requirement that sixteenth-century English court ladies use euphemisms, constructed from male fantasies, to speak about sex (1997: 120). Empirical work undertaken by Meadows (1997), does demonstrate a continuing paucity of language in use among the women she interviewed about sexual issues. She found her mid-life interviewees' choice of language ranged from medicalised or derogatory terms to innuendo. Holland et al. argue that while male interviewees involved in the Men's Risk and AIDS Project in the 1990s might have been empowered by accessing traditionally 'feminine' emotional discourses, in their parallel study of women it was less obviously empowering for men's female counterparts to engage in a male instrumental language of sexuality (1998: 104). Moreover, as our review of work on girls' and young women's magazines confirms, masculinised, derogatory expressions such as 'shagging' and 'fingering' are now freely 'owned' by young women. However, as Chapter 6 illustrates, the reliance by our younger respondents on these kinds of words signalled an absence of language to *reflect* on their sexual experiences. Instead they used body-focused, 'dirty' terms, such as *'knobbing'* and *'fingering'*, which proved inadequate when young women were asked about the emotional context of these experiences. What we go on to consider in Chapter 6, then, are the heterosexual discourses being drawn upon in narratives articulated through language of this kind – and what their implications for individual subjectivities might be.

This point is taken up in Wight's (1996) study of young Glaswegian men, one which develops Hollway's (1984) typology of the discourses available for speaking of sexual relationships. Wight (1996) brings out the complexity of making sense of how people understand, reflect upon and articulate their experiences. Although his analysis relates to young men, the discourses described are evident within our own study. Importantly, he reminds us that the discourses through which people represent themselves at the time of reflection may not be those they drew upon at the time of the experience. Indeed, they may slip between these different discourses during their interview. So, while it would be easy to assume that ownership of 'crude' language drawn from a 'permissive discourse' (Hollway, 1984; Wight, 1996) is specific to young people, a product of post-1960s liberalisation, among the older women we interviewed this kind of language was also evident, as was the case for some of Meadows' (1997) mid-life interviewees. In this example, two working-class women are discussing the 'scoring' system used in their youth to describe and categorise their sexual activities. The terms used may not necessarily have been felt as appropriate at *that* time, even if they experienced no discomfort drawing upon them in mid-life:

25'd mebbe be a snog, 50'd be touchin' your boobs, 75'd be fingerin' an' 100 was 'avin' full blown sex' (Anita Leigh, 50)

Well 5 was holding hands, 10 was putting his arm round you, 25 was snogging, 50 they used to say was touching the tits, and 75 was a fingering job, 150 was a shag, and then we used to say, been down to back of fields for a 75, we always used to say that [LAUGH] (Sandy Kirk, 39)

These women had, of course, grown up post-1960s. If we look towards the previous age cohort, we might assume that they not only lacked language which could carry bodily as well as emotional information, but would also have difficulty using crude or 'dirty' language to describe sexual practice. As Chapter 4 highlights, some of the women we interviewed even struggled to name the particular body parts that they wanted to refer to. Across the socio-economic spectrum, members of this age-cohort also insisted that: ' *you didn't talk about . . . anything sexy [LAUGHS] at all in those days'*, indicating their perception of the predominance of a 'to have/hold or romantic discourse' (Wight, 1996: 159) during their youth.

By contrast, however, Humphries' (1988) data, derived from the period 1900–50, indicate that although certain euphemisms may have been in use, for example 'having connections' (1988: 108), much more explicit sex talk *did* take place. One man who grew up in the 1920s described sexual explorations undertaken in hay lofts, fields, parks and other places beyond adult control in his childhood. He recalls how a

12-year-old farmer's daughter had invited him to 'bull' her (1988: 37). Regardless of regional variations in slang, this language could not carry the bodily and *emotional* aspects of sexual experience, but instead reflected the concept of male conquest and violation of forbidden female territory. Indeed the metaphor of cross-species sexual practice reinforces hierarchically opposed definitions of masculinity and femininity. The continued use of this kind of language more than 80 years later might indicate that little has changed, leaving us with an ongoing concep-tualisation of sexual practice from the perspective of dominant male sexuality (see Holland and Ramazanoglu, 1994). Moreover, the contem-porary acceptance and 'normalisation' of such language by women and the media raises questions about the complicity of women in their sexual subordination, at least at the level of language.

That said, Dworkin's notion that 'dirty words' are drawn from a discourse within which heterosexual sexual intercourse involves the objectification of women's bodies by men has also been challenged. Hawkes (1996), for example, argues that Dworkin's views allow us to see sexuality as a political act, but that speaking of women's physic-ality in this way downplays the pleasures heterosexuality may afford to women and so occludes any possibilities of heterosexuality being seen as fulfilling. Indeed, such arguments deny women's embodied agency (see also Smart, 1996).

Conclusion

This chapter has raised questions about how heterosexual subjectiv-ities come into being, exploring issues of agency, structure and social change and the question of how the cultural might figure within the social. This has led us to give particular attention to discursive and subjective dimensions of the social – and to explore the ways in which the discourses which surround heterosexuality are drawn upon in the narratives through which it is both represented and reflected upon. As argued, it is the task of working with empirical data which take the form of personal and familial accounts of heterosexual lives that guides us in our choice of focus here.

As Chapter 4 notes, Plummer has suggested that the 'modern western world has become cluttered with sexual stories' (1995: 4), the result, he argues, of an erosion of the boundary between private and public with the media providing 'a veritable erotopian landscape to millions of lives' (1995: 4). While he views storytelling as core to human conscious-ness, a primary route to meaning-making, contemporary western society is now recognising its centrality to human experience. Jackson too observes that: 'We constantly tell stories to ourselves and others and we continually construct and reconstruct our own biographies in narrative form' (1993: 46).

Nonetheless, as this chapter has shown, storytelling, or the creation of narratives, is a process which both draws upon and contributes to existing discourses. And these in turn are manifested in particular forms of language which may or may not be accessed by individuals on the basis of their age, gender and social class. In addition, as already discussed, there is not only the question of who may say what, but also the issue of whether *any* language is available for the expression of particular forms of experience: for example, a nuanced language of female desire. As Chapter 6 reveals, moreover, what concerns us here is not just discursive and subjective dimensions of the social, but also the situated interactions which make up everyday life. What can be said is not enabled or restricted simply in terms of one's age, gender or social class. Instead, as language manifests itself in speech, so the intersubjective nature of what may be said by whom and to whom is crucial. In that our data concern the family lives of individuals who stand in parental, marital and filial relationships to one another, and where generational identities exist in parallel with membership of age-based cohorts, storytelling and silences come to life in ways which reveal much about heterosexuality's role as an organising principle which pervades the experience of both the life course and family life.

In that Plummer (1995) is concerned with the late twentieth-century politicisation of the sexual and the oppressions which individuals then began to speak about, his argument resonates with data which testify to the silencing of stigmatised sexual identities and sexual suffering and – in some cases – the articulation of those silences, whether in later life reflection, for example, or the revelations of other family members. Preparedness to speak out can signal a reframing of the moral and indeed economic dimensions of heterosexuality. Yet we should not assume that heterosexual lives have become transparent as a result. Silences and obfuscations remain evident, even during interviews with the youngest cohort. So, for example, when young women engaged in sexual encounters with men who were not potential heterosexual partners, there still tended to be secrecy and embarrassment surrounding these experiences.

Chapter 6, then, demonstrates our concern both with what was *not* said during interviews – and what interviewees *said* was unsayable. So we not only listened out for silences but also attended to discussion of these silences. Thus, some interviewees talked at length about what it was that could not or had not been articulated within their families, marriages or partnerships, so remaining anything but silent themselves. Interviewing within extended families proved particularly beneficial here in that it allowed the gaps in one interview to become apparent when additional material was discovered in another. From whatever perspective silence was discovered, however, what it reveals is that which cannot readily be accommodated within the category of hegemonic heterosexuality.

In addition, we can identity two very different categories of silence, both of them enabling the living out of heterosexuality. On the one hand, there are those surrounding failed or transgressive heterosexualities or heterosexual relationships and families. These are of analytic value in then revealing heterosexuality as it *ought* to be, a way of uncovering an often implicit set of beliefs which many people have difficulty in articulating. By contrast, there are the silences referred to by 78-year-old Bernice Parr, for example, cited in Chapter 4. She says of growing up heterosexual: *'in those days, it wasn't as much talked about as what it is now'*. Statements such as hers point towards questions as to whether an appropriate language was unavailable; whether age, gender or social class militated against talking about 'it'; or whether it was within particular familial or age-based relationships that 'it' was silenced. These latter forms of silence, or indirect communication (see Hendry and Watson, 2001), can therefore be seen as powerful in that they help *shape* heterosexualities, for example, by creating both closeness as well as distances within families along gendered and generational lines.

What was left unsaid, either during the interview or within the relationships which constituted 'marriage', 'coupledom' or 'family, therefore constitutes one kind of narrative of heterosexuality. As Wilden argues, silence is itself a form of communication: 'every act, every pause, every movement in living and social systems is also a message; silence is communication; short of death it is impossible for an organism or a person not to communicate' (1987: 124).

6
Getting it Together? Carnal and Romantic Discourses

This chapter draws on earlier discussions of the theoretical and methodological challenges of working empirically with an unmarked, yet pervasive social category. As Chapter 5 notes, our starting point was the question of how people made sense of their everyday heterosexual lives and what reflections might contribute to its stability and its openness to change. Interview and focus group data were therefore the material we chose to work with. What this chapter shows is how interviewees' voices provide a route into understanding the living out of heterosexuality (see Meah et al., 2004). Chapter 5 discussed the discursive dimensions of the social, the way discourses resource the narratives, the representations and the language through which human beings reproduce, reflect upon and resist aspects of their everyday lives. Here we take up those narratives in order to demonstrate their scope for shedding light on these lives. We begin by focusing on what *was* said and how this might be interpreted. In so doing we pay attention to the limits of the sayable and in the second half of the chapter we discuss what could *not* be said – and its implications for developing our understanding of heterosexuality. What we argue is that heterosexual narratives can give clues as to the discourses which resource everyday heterosexual life *and* to the exclusionary narrative strategies which sustain heterosexuality as a residual category, one sustained through the silencing of that which it is not.

Telling heterosexual tales

If once, and not so long ago, our sexualities were shrouded in silence, for some they have now crescendoed into a cacophonous din. We have become the sexual story tellers of a sexual story telling society. (Plummer, 1995: 4–5)

If the Victorian era was marked by anxiety and taboo regarding sexual matters and characterised by resounding silences in these matters, Plummer argues that in contemporary society, 'Outside the world of formal story telling, we are all being enjoined to do it daily to each other. Somehow, the truth of our lives lies in better communication: in telling all' (1995: 4). Sexual stories can therefore be seen as a product of their time, and are both produced and consumed under specific social conditions. Moreover, as Plummer notes, 'different moments have highlighted different stories' (1995: 4).

If narratives are to be a means of getting at the discourses through which particular social arrangements are kept in place or resisted, then we need to consider how best they might be examined. Plummer (1995) suggests that they evolve at four levels: the personal, the situational, the organisational and the cultural/historical. While the personal level relates to the motives which lead individuals to share their stories, the situational refers to the processes through which people come to find their stories *and* how they find themselves in their stories. The organisational level, however, is the frame of the interview, or other social situations in which stories are elicited and offered; for example, via the relationship between interviewee/interviewer. Finally, stories' cultural and historical dimensions enable us to explore how they enter public discourse at particular historical moments in time, and not at others. As Plummer observes, many stories exist in silence, 'dormant, awaiting their historical moment' (1995: 35).

While Chapter 3 prioritised methodological discussion, here we engage with the organisational and cultural/historical dimensions of heterosexual storytelling and the question of how such stories reflect the discourses which resource them, how the language(s) drawn upon derive from and contribute to particular moments in time. In addition, a story's *presentation* at a specific moment in time in relation to specific individuals is also important. As Chapter 3 describes, data were generated within interviews and focus groups facilitated by Angela, a mixed-race, working-class woman, aged 29 at that time – a heterosexual, androgynous feminist who grew up as a tomboy with older brothers in the armed services. These data are the outcome of a negotiated relationship between a historical past reconstructed in a contemporary interaction between two people who, whilst different from one another, may share similarities, perhaps in age, gender or social class (Fawcett and Hearn,

2004). Such issues can represent elements, stages or layers within an interactive process of establishing mutual understanding of some kind and as such require careful examination.

Given the heterogeneity of our interviewees, engendering sufficient trust to elicit frank responses, without harming or, indeed, leading the participant in specific directions was a challenge. Indeed participants' perceptions of our inquiry clearly varied, with some anticipating simply a discussion of their family life. While older participants often drew on 'props' – sepia photographs of sweethearts, weddings, family events, now curled at the edges, or lovingly preserved in family albums; a wedding trousseau; drawings of heart-throbs of the day; a family tree – most inter-viewees were reliant upon language to share material derived from inter-nalised memory processes. And, as we discovered, the sensitive nature of much of what concerned both them and us raised a crucial ques-tion: does the cue as to the appropriate use of language to communicate intimate reflections come from the researcher or the interviewee? As Chapter 3 indicated, if the interviewer, seeking to establish trust, adapts her language to the participant, how might she differentiate between sensitivity and ageism, for example? Similarly, how might her gendered assumptions impact upon the interviewee – and indeed, theirs upon her? At risk is the possibility that her language might *direct* rather than enable the speaker. Marsden (2004) argues the case for a more challen-ging, but intrusive methodology and it is the implications of such an 'intrusive' methodology which concern us here.

What we find within interviews is a mutual testing and monitoring of each party's assumptions about the other, both of them contributing to the organisational processes through which these stories emerge. Moreover, many of the stories may have been adapted and embel-lished in successive retellings, each one potentially introducing distance between the teller and the events which took place. Indeed, Plummer observes: 'When talking about their lives, people lie sometimes, forget a lot, exaggerate, become confused, and get things wrong. Yet they are revealing truths. These truths do not reveal the past "as it actually was", aspiring to a standard of objectivity. They give us instead the truth of our experiences' (1995: 167).

That said, it is the organisational context of this talk which concerns us here if we are to explore its relationship with experience. As Holland and Ramazanoglu (1994) note in their study of young people and sexu-ality in the context of AIDS, interviewees may require the interviewer's 'permission' before using their customary colloquialisms. As we suggest, this seeking and granting of permission needs to be understood as an often implicit dimension of the process of testing assumptions. Yet, as Chapter 3 notes, one young male interviewee had been warned by his mother to *'keep it clean'*, perhaps highlighting a continuing legacy of the association of sex with 'dirt'. What she would regard as *un*clean remains obscure, since she herself (Anita Leigh) used the expression *'fingering'* when interviewed. Twenty year-old Stuart, her son, in describing where *'groping'* might lead him, said:

> *Stuart: The usual place, breasts, (buttocks), you know.*
> *AM: Nothing down your trollies or anything like that?*
> *Stuart: Oh, no, no sticky fingers, if that's what you call it, but . . .*

Stuart's implicit question mark about his language (*'if that's what you call it?'*) is noted by Angela, who says:

> *AM: Feel free to use whatever language that you'd normally use, so if you would have said 'tits', that's fine.*
> *Stuart: I've got a ( ) my mum said, 'Oh, keep it (clean)'.*
> *AM: . . . just use, talk in whatever way you would talk.*
> *Stuart: Cause I feel daft saying stuff like that, and I wouldn't say 'breast' in front of a (mate) I'd say 'tit' or 'bap' or ('molders') or whatever . . . (I was worried) how I would have come across to you, you know.*

Clearly, then, Stuart has censored his language, reflecting his assumptions about Angela – yet also testing the possibility of using his more customary terms. Sometimes, however, she *took* the cue from an interviewee, as with Jean Brown who initiated explicit discussion of her sexual experience. In sum, articulating intimate, often sexual aspects of everyday heterosexual life was hedged about with risk. What language to use and what content to reveal or elicit were questions which preoccupied both participants and researcher. As such, these methodological challenges not only speak to the wider context of the interaction taking place, the subtleties of body language, tone of voice and facial expression not captured in a transcript, they also point towards the ways in which heterosexuality is shaped and experienced through socially mediated discourses.

From narrative to discourse

In the example of Dworkin's (1987) account of 'dirty words' (Chapter 5) we noted her argument that these contributed to a discourse which facilitated both the objectification of women and the occupation of their 'inferior'/'contaminating' bodies by men – as exploiters, conquerors and occupiers. Working from our interviewees' accounts we now attempt to unravel the discourses which resource and constrain their language and narratives. As Holland et al. (1998) argued, language, in their view, has the capacity to produce young people's sexuality as 'male' and 'female' and their data show a consistent distinction between 'doing sex', that is, fulfilling an active, masculine role, and 'having sex done to you', an aspect of a passive, feminine role.

Among our participants, 15-year-old Liz Kirk was propositioned with the words: ' "*Can I knob you?*" ', and made what she believed was her sexual debut at a house party. Her description fails to resonate with any discourse of emotion or romance, instead representing her as a passive young woman encountering the archetypal 'predatory male' (Wight, 1996), for whom penetrative sex is the goal. In the excerpt below we can ask how this persona might have informed Angela's tentative exploration of whether or not penetration took place:

AM: *Did you enjoy it?*

Liz: *[..] Um*

AM: *Or did you think you enjoyed, I mean, did it hurt?*

Liz: *My first time didn't, but my second time did.*

AM: *Your first time didn't, that's interesting. Did you bleed?*

Liz: *Yeah, a bit.*

AM: *Do you think, I mean, how to say this, bit graphic and horrible, were he a big lad Richie?*

Liz: *Yeah.*

AM: *And it didn't hurt? When I say big, I mean, in the trouser department.*

Liz: *Yeah, it was real weird, 'cause we'd kind of do it on the side of the bath, so, I don't know, everybody was like knocking on the door, and Katie, was like, 'Come on, let's go', so maybe it was that.*

AM: *The excitement of it, do you think, or?*

Liz: *Well, you see, he was trying to go for it and I was, everybody was knocking on the door and I was trying to move away from him, some of it was that.*

AM: *That he didn't actually fully penetrate you?*

Liz: *Yeah.*

AM: *But he did penetrate you?*

Liz: *(I don't)*

AM: *I mean, was he actually inside you?*

> *Liz: D'you know, I don't really know, to be honest, but that's what he, he*
> *said he did, but,*
> *AM: I think you'd have known about it, if he had.*
> *Liz: Yeah.*

Many younger interviewees did become awkward when encouraged to recall their early sexual activities. Some were dismissive of the emotional implications of what were presented as casual activities, but does their silence in this area reflect a lack of access to language within which to frame these recollections, a failure to reflect critically on sexual experience, or a fear of being judged promiscuous or unassertive by the interviewer (see Gilfoyle et al., 1993)? Holland and Ramazanoglu (1994) argue that young female interviewees' difficulties in talking about sex transcend the interview situation and instead reflect the contradictory nature of femininity: for instance, a pressure to accommodate to a conception of heterosexuality as inherent to *masculinity* and male sexuality, whilst simultaneously making sense of themselves and their 'otherness'. As Weeks (2004) notes, sexuality is constituted in a highly gendered world. That male sexuality is the benchmark against which all other forms are measured is an unremarked given, or, as Dyer puts it, like air: 'you breathe it in all the time, but you aren't much aware of it' (1985: 28). Twenty-one year-old Joanne Smith's account of a period during which she had sex with someone, whilst not wanting to be in a relationship, flags the contradiction which Holland and Ramazanoglu (1994) refer to. Joanne says: *'I was thinking, "I don't really want a relationship, but then I don't really want this either", I wanted something in between.'* Although it is Joanne who does not want a 'relationship', she remains uneasy with the casual nature of this particular relationship. Whilst articulating her own agency, it remains unclear as to whether Joanne's unease reflects her search for a more permissive discourse within which to frame her sexuality, and perhaps a sense of failing to live up to an acceptable form of femininity.

While Wight (1996) observes that within the permissive discourse women *theoretically* initiate sexual encounters for their own gratification, in reality, permissiveness does not extend equally to women, particularly given the enduring importance of sexual reputation in working-class culture (1996: 169) (see also Holland et al. 1998). As Chapter 8 shows, young women appeared uneasy describing encounters which failed to live up to an imagined heterosexuality, a vision of intimacy involving a 'couple-type' relationship which reflects a 'to have/hold', or romantic discourse. In contrast with the passivity intrinsic to such discourses, however, Hollway (1984) suggests that women *can* be positioned as subjects, actively attracting and keeping their men.

Mother and daughter, Elaine and Michelle Ogden, for example, offer their shared narrative of *desirable heterosexuality*. In recalling meeting the men they later married, both describe an instant recognition which evokes popular constructions of 'love at first sight'. When Elaine first met her husband, Andrew, at work when she was 16, she recalls thinking: ' *"I'm going to marry him. I'm definitely going to marry him".'* Her daughter, Michelle, met her second husband at work and says: *'I knew that I was going to get married to him and have a relationship. I knew that he was the one for me for the rest of my life.'* Indeed, Michelle's entire narrative evokes Brunt's (1988) assertion that falling in love is like 'getting to star in your own movie' (1988: 19), showing how the discourse or cultural script of love which Elaine draws upon is transmitted across the generations to Michelle (Jackson, 1996). Elaine, for example, says: *'I think you have to love somebody, I think you have to love them . . . with Andrew, it was just love, he could have done whatever . . . and I just loved him and felt he did me.'* And Michelle, in turn, affirms: *'The main thing is obviously, has got to be that you really love each other . . . not just love, but love each other, you know, very deeply . . . then you'll be alright.'* For both these women their children are also viewed through the lens of a discourse of romantic love. Of her son, Elaine says: *'I can remember thinking, he's only here because I love Andrew* [husband] *so much . . . you know, that's the reason he is here, because I love him so much.'* And Michelle then says of her daughter: *'we've got Jessica because we love each other'.* If learning what 'love' is involves articulating narratives resourced by romantic discourses, then for Michelle, they reside not only within popular culture, but also her parents' relationship.

Debates as to how particular discourses might inhibit or engender women's agency resonate with discussion in Chapter 3 as to how contemporary feminists might make sense of Jean Brown's heterosexual life. Fay Roberts (50), for example, described the sexual pleasure she derived from early schoolgirl fumblings, outwith any romantic entailment, yet her comments on the lack of intimacy in her present marriage evoke Dworkin's (1987) reference to Tennessee Williams' words: ' "I have been haunted by the obsession that to desire a thing or to love a thing intensely is to place yourself in a vulnerable position, to be the possible, if not probable, loser of what you most want" ' (1987: 54). As Fay reflects:

Fay: Yeah, yeah, yeah, it was, he was very attentive and very aware of how I felt, you know, what I was getting out of it, which was nice. The only thing was [. .] that it wasn't often. I think I'm more highly-sexed

than he is, I think probably be more highly-sexed, apart from Graham,
probably more highly-sexed than any of them [LAUGH] but [..] in
a loving relationship, because Graham once said, that if I hadn't have
had the upbringing I had, I could have been a prostitute. And I
said, 'It's not my upbringing, it's that I don't', sex is part of a loving
relationship to me.
AM: *It's how you express that?*
Fay: *Yeah,*
AM: *Physically?*
Fay: *Yeah.*

Fay's capacity to secure sexual intimacy as an expression of love is
thus limited by her husband's power to deny her. His own reflections upon their apparent sexual estrangement, however, show that, for
Graham (46), his wife's association of sex with love disturbs him (see
also Chapter 9): *'I started equating it with love and closeness, instead of*
just sex, and I stopped wanting it . . . It was the first time that it came to me
that it was an act of closeness and love between me and her, and it scared
me . . . ' Whilst Fay's agency would therefore seem to be limited, Graham
himself is vulnerable to the agency of his own emotion and we return
to the question of constraints on men's power later in this chapter.

Carnal masculinity and romantic femininity?

As noted, Holland et al. (1998) view language as not only capable of
producing young people's sexuality as 'male' and 'female', but also
locating sexual agency at the site of masculinity. This view reflects
a long-standing discourse of sexual difference which, as Chapter 4
describes, has its roots in Victorian attempts to stabilise the new bourgeois model of the family. If middle-class women were romanticised as
virtuous 'angels in the house' then middle-class men were vulnerable to
the carnal enticements of 'fallen women' who gave sexual favours freely
(Jamieson, 1998).

Dichotomies between masculinity and femininity which seem to map
onto sexualised and romanticised conceptions of heterosexuality were
evident in the discourses drawn upon by our interviewees. A number of
women reported feeling 'used' for sex; among young men some apparently conformed to stereotypes of the 'objectifying' predatory male.
For example, Ryan Finch (25) said he liked *'real big tits'* and detailed
his first *'blow job'*, along with videoing sex and bondage; 21-year-old
Andrew Jones described wanting *'anal sex'*, *'coming on their faces'* and
'getting a tit-wank', albeit feeling hampered by a view of his girlfriend

as a *'nice girl'*. While young women did use instrumental language such as 'shag' to describe sex (Holland et al., 1998: 89), they still differentiated between carnal and romantic heterosexual sex. For example, Di Elliot (34) describes being *'upset'* by sexual positions which *'made me feel like [.] he didn't love me [.] so [.] I used to have a real problem with not being able to have eye contact'*. Leanne Cook (22) was at best ambivalent about her sexual debut with a Scandanavian professional athlete, a one-off event, which brought kudos among her peer group, followed by pregnancy and termination. Here Leanne reproaches herself for inadvertently taking emotional risks through not seeking a romantic attachment:

> *I was cross in the fact, like [. . .] I mean I was a little bit more [.] I was naïve about that sort of thing then [.] and I was cross that I didn't [. . .] I didn't [. . .] I don't know if I would have not done it had I thought about it but [. . .] I was cross that, cross with myself that, you know, I'd done that [.] an' he obviously just didn't want me for anything more [. . .] but I suppose I did just see 'im as a [.] 'trolley dolly' really, so [LAUGHS].*

Shortly afterwards, aged 19, she *did* invest emotionally in a man ten years her senior. Forming what she understood as a *'proper couple'*, she nonetheless scrutinised this 'coupledom' against a romantic notion of heterosexuality. Thus, although *'he was just so different because, obviously, you know, we were, sort of, seein' each other properly and he cared about me'*, she also observed that:

> Leanne: . . . *after a few months, you know, you need a bit more than that, you don't [.] you don't just want to have the excitement you want somebody [.] I genuinely felt that he [.] at the time I felt that he wasn't givin' me what, more than [.] he was holding back with something.*
>
> AM: *Emotionally?*
>
> Leanne: *Yeah, but I genuinely feel, at that time, he didn't know how to give it [.] maybe, he hadn't ever given it [.] away [.] and there was just something, I couldn't put my finger on it but, like, when I told 'im it was over and everything, I expected, because I felt that he was detached in some way,*

Despite Leanne's disappointments, however, she remains committed to pursuing heterosexual experience which transcends 'just sex':

I don't even go after anybody just for sex or anything, it doesn't appeal to me at all so [.] you know, I just [. . .] I don't know, 'cos I would like to have a relationship but not just with anybody [. . .] it's like, my friend always says 'the right person will come along for you and you will just say "I'm getting married" and that's it', whereas, you know, she's always is like 'oh, I'm getting married next week' and it'll be to a person that she's known [.] two weeks, I'm not like that at all but, you know, it's just, I don't know.

So can we therefore argue for the persistence of parallel dichotomies between masculinity and feminity *and* carnal and romantic hetero-sexuality? Among male participants of varying social-class backgrounds, some reflected carefully about both the sexual *and* emotional aspects of their relationships, confounding feminist claims about male emotional inarticulacy (see Williams, 2001). Stuart Leigh (20), for example, described being challenged by a young woman for refusing sex:

Stuart: *There was one time, that I was seeing a bird, and I think only after a couple of weeks, she asked me to sleep with her, but I respected her, I didn't love her, but I respected her, and she wanted me to sleep with her, and I said, 'No, I think it's too soon', and she said, 'Are you gay or what?' All I was doing was trying to put her feelings first, you know, I didn't think it was just a quick shag and that's all I wanted from her.*

AM: *Did you try explaining that to her?*

Stuart: *No, I've never talked like this to anybody before, not anyone . . .*

AM: *Why do you think that is, is it just that –*

Stuart: *I don't know.*

AM: *It's personal, it's private and you wouldn't know how to express it?*

Stuart: *I suppose it's not a normal thing to do is it, to express your feelings to somebody like that, I suppose.*

AM: *Do you think it made you a bit vulnerable as well?*

Stuart: *Well, you're putting your heart on your sleeve aren't you? You're offering, you explain everything what you feel about somebody, and if they don't like what you're telling them or they'll probably think I'm a pansy or whatever. Again, I think it's down to what they think of you, if they think the less of you, I suppose.*

In addition, as in Wight's (1996) study, some men believed that sex should take place when two people loved each other. While Stuart had difficulty articulating his feelings, Paul Archer (29) explained how *he* struggled to come to terms with his girlfriend's failure to engage with him emotionally and its impact upon their sexual intimacy. He reflects:

> Paul: *I didn't sort of [. . .] looking back, I didn't sort of do my part to [.] help arouse her, arouse her in different ways [.] I wasn't, sort of, intimate with the use of fingers or anything like that . . . I mean, this was during the period of time when she would be kind of putting up the emotional kind of walls, and having the, the problems there as well, which probably, looking back, will've kind of affected our, sort of, intimacy as well, but yes it was, kind of, yeah, the end of kind of physical frustration, and it was relief and [.] yeah, I mean, I know, it was a good feeling, it was a moment to share, I don't think it was [.] particularly fulfilling sexually for her, but it was, yeah, a moment that we both appreciated and shared and you know.*
>
> AM: *Did the earth move, or was it an emotional thing?*
>
> Paul: *Yeah, it was more of a little tremble I suppose, but more of an emotional thing and, you know, we were kind of [.] we were physically close and clingy and everything afterwards and the next day, I mean, I remember walking to university together the next day and, kind of, sort of felt like you're kind of walking a couple of inches off the ground, that sort of stuff . . . I felt a bit [.] inadequate in a way 'cos I didn't know how to kind of [.] um, help her achieve an orgasm.*

So young men as well as women slipped between a 'language of love' and a 'carnal language' when differentiating between relationships. David Gold (28), for example, describes first performing oral sex on a woman:

> Yeah, I was probably akin to a dog licking milk out of a bowl, huge tongue [LAUGH]. At that age you don't really know what your tongue's for . . . So, yeah, that was like the next sexual experience, wasn't till about six months later, before I first made love to a girl.

Angela asked how his use of carnal or romantic language related to his experience:

> AM: *. . . It's interesting that you use the term 'made love' as opposed to 'a shag', or 'getting your end away', or 'losing your virginity' or whatever, so you did see it as making love, or is that retrospective?*
>
> David: *Yeah, it was, I was, I really liked the girl . . . er, we sort of, kissing and caressing each other and I asked her, I was prepared for*

> *it, so I mean, I had some condoms, and I asked her, 'Do you want to make love?', and we'd talked about it before, and she did, so we decided that was the time that we both felt happy with doing it, and we did it . . . We made love as best we could, and then cuddled up and afterwards and talked about it, and she was like, obviously embarrassed about bleeding, and I sort of said, 'Well . . . are you alright?', you know, sort of thing, and that was it.*

What we have explored here, therefore, are the ways in which the language used and the narratives deployed in accounts of heterosexual coupling might be resourced by traditional discourses of masculinity and femininity. In that both women and men drew on romantic as well as carnal discourses, however, we argue that the living out of particular gendered *strategies* potentially contributes to the ascendancy or otherwise of varied and innovative framings of everyday heterosexual life. Here, therefore, what was *said* has been our focus. In the section to follow we move on to consider that which was left unsaid, what was hidden, a contrast which nonetheless belies the similar roles of language *and* silence in contributing to and contesting the heterosexual imaginary.

A residual category

In discussing the work of both Rich (1980) and Butler (1990), Hanson (1997) describes how heterosexuality emerges through the repression or denial of the 'other'. This notion of heterosexuality as that which is *not* underpins our argument that one way of exploring heterosexuality empirically is to view it as a residual category which remains intact whilst energy and anxiety are directed towards its margins, so defining its boundaries. Hanson's focus is the homosexual 'other' and she discusses Rich's view of heterosexuality as a compulsory, something 'enforced for women, superimposed, as it were, on an "original" homosexuality' (1997: 56). Rich's concept of a lesbian continuum traces women's physical and emotional intimacy with one another from 'the infant suckling at her mother's breast', to 'the grown woman experiencing orgasmic sensations while suckling her own child', and 'the woman dying at ninety, touched and handled by women' (Rich, 1980, cited in Hanson, 1997: 56). In Butler's work, however, Hanson identifies a Foucauldian approach which provides a less essentialist account of how homosexuality relates to heterosexuality, arguing that 'the taboo on homosexuality produces a homosexuality which is disavowed within the heterosexual frame' (1997: 56). If homosexuality is produced from within 'the regime of power-knowledge-pleasure that sustains the discourse on human sexuality' (Foucault, cited in Hanson, 1997: 56), then, in Hanson's view, a *generative* process is at work: for example, 'one of the mechanisms whereby heterosexuality is inculcated for women might be via the internalisation . . . of the tabooed female Other' (1997: 57).

Building on this view, we argue that homosexuality may be but one among a whole range of 'taboo' desires and practices which serve to generate heterosexuality. What lies at the boundaries of this institution, whether it be a partner from a different social class or ethnic background, a sexual liaison not oriented towards coupledom, or a celibate marriage, is precisely that which shores up heterosexuality as everyday life's 'known', yet implicit organising principle. Cline (1993), for example, exposes the incompatibility of celibacy and marriage, showing that even when men have privately agreed to their partners' decision to be celibate, if the partner then 'outs' their relationship as celibate, they feel stigmatised by being seen to break an 'unwritten code' (1993: 75–6). Thus, while Jackson (2006) argues that heteronormativity regulates those within the boundaries of heterosexuality as well as those outside it, the intensity surrounding transgressive heterosexuality among our participants suggests that we can usefully consider it as a category situated at the boundaries of hegemonic heterosexuality alongside homosexuality – that as a marginalised experience it too has generative potential. As argued throughout this book, normative or hegemonic heterosexuality itself is something which many of our participants found hard to define.

Telling it straight

In response to the offer of confidentiality, many interviewees explored with us those aspects of their heterosexual lives which troubled them. Yet despite this openness, for some their troubles were felt to be so stigmatising that these were precisely the areas omitted from their accounts. Working with these data, then, we attended carefully to its confessional, contradictory and evasive qualities. So while some participants attributed chastity, monogamy and sexual restraint with high moral status, they acknowledged the vagaries of sexual practice between individuals they knew personally, including themselves.

As Chapter 1 notes, many potential interviewees failed to co-opt other family members into our project. And data bear out the fears which may have inhibited participation. Family members gave contradictory accounts of shared events; generations revealed one another's secrets, as in the case of the Underhill family. Sixty-four year-old Audrey had a rural working-class background and was now a pillar of her market-town community. While she dwelt on her public life when interviewed, Jennifer, her 44-year-old daughter, brought out other aspects of her mother's heterosexual life. These disclosures were prompted by Jennifer's account of becoming pregnant before marriage, so infuriating Audrey and her husband. Confiding her mother's anger to her grandmother and uncle, she was told by her grandmother: ' "*Well, I don't know why she's* [Audrey/her mother] *like that, because all the people she's had, all the men she's had up Wold Road".*' Jennifer went on: '*a few hints were dropped, and . . . grandma told him* [her uncle] *to* "*Shut up, it's not any of your business", it was never brought up really . . .* ' The secret surfaced again during a row between Jennifer and her father and at this point she also learned that her father was not biologically related to her. This silence had been sustained until Jennifer was in her mid-twenties, although Jennifer had never felt close to her parents and, aged 12, told her best friend that ' "*I'm sure there's something not right here, I'm sure I'm adopted or something".*' On reflection she now concludes that '*I suppose every time she* [her mother] *sees you* [me], *she thinks, "Hmm, there's my mistake".*' So Jennifer not only described the silencing of her parents' failure to conform to hegemonic heterosexuality, but also drew attention to the silences within her mother's interview.

Sarah Davis (43), from a well-off rural background, also described the secrecy surrounding transgressive heterosexuality within her family. Not only was talk of reproductive and sexual matters silenced – evidence of a tension between respectability and sexuality – but also her father's extra-marital relationships. Thus, Sarah describes how, as a child: '*at the tea table, all of us sat round the tea table, I remember coming out with this story* [about Tampax] *and my father went very, very purple in the face and walked out of the room and my mother said "Oh we don't talk about that at the tea table, Sarah".*' Yet Sarah went on to say that '*I don't think he was as Victorian as he made out . . . I think I realised later [.] that perhaps he'd [.] don't know if strayed is the right word, but there'd been something going on with other people in the past, sort of reading between the lines.*' She said '*I could tell something was wrong and you shut your mind to it 'cause you don't want to think about it.*' She then described her father's extra-marital affairs and his eventual, permanent move out of the family to join a new female partner.

Silence therefore not only obscures transgressions; it also represents an absence which resonates with other family members, calling their attention to heterosexuality as imagined and alerting them to its instability. Sarah said that her father's repeated absences for 'business' led her, at about 13 or 14, to suspect *'there was something going on, I just had that feeling.'* Yet, until she was 20, it was only by *'reading between the lines'* that she could *'tell something was wrong'*.

The potency of these secrets and silences led some interviewees to 'groom' each other prior to interviews: a woman in her late 70s said: '[my daughter] *hasn't told you about her first marriage, she said she didn't want to talk about it. Well I suppose I shouldn't either.'* Thus secrets may have a currency, and indeed agency, all of their own. In the Davis family, sisters Abigail (17) and Helen (18) buffered one another from their parents, concealing each other's drunkenness and meetings with boys in the city. Yet rather than confidantes, the sisters spied on one another, each a potential conduit of information between the generations. If one exposed a secret to their parents, retaliation would occur.

Practices of concealment therefore emerged as an aspect of the living out of heterosexuality. Jayne Finch (50), for example, had misperceived her parents' relationship:

> *you've been [.] taught what's right, what's wrong and maybe you should wait 'til you get married 'cos that's comes from [.] your mum and dad, um, well, you assume that's what you did... I know me mum had sex before she was married but I didn't know that when I was growing up as a child... that's come through since [...] I was older and probably married.*

Families' conceptions of authentic heterosexuality are thus revealed in their grasp of what might put it at risk, risk-factors varying between age-cohorts. While pre-marital sex between partners who subsequently married carried potential stigma among older individuals, an unplanned pregnancy which made their children's 'private' practices *public* troubled the parents of our youngest age-cohort.

As Chapter 7 argues, heterosexuality is an organising principle which transcends the simply sexual. So a heterosexual couple's failure to manifest marital harmony could also be silenced. Audrey Underhill recalled how the mental health problems which undermined her parents' marriage were sequestered:

> *No, no, we were never beaten up, no, my mother would, but he [her father] was nasty with my mother, very nasty with my mother, and, so, um, she had that to contend with, but she knew it wasn't the man, when he came back from war... because he was in the trenches and he saw all his mates*

crawling with rats and what-have-you and it disturbed his mind . . . 'cause in those days you didn't get counselled . . . and I think . . . my mother had a very rough time on it, but she didn't take it out of us, because she knew he was an ill man.

Audrey said she remembered her father's cruelty: '*Yes, very deeply, but I don't talk about it, because, um, er, because, well, yes, he was cruel to her, but he wasn't cruel to us.*'

The failure of parents to conform to hegemonic heterosexuality can therefore derive from different sources. Yet where this pertains, it can be masked through silence, so leaving the residual category of heterosexuality largely intact.

Respectability, heterosexuality and social class

If gender can militate against access to particular forms of language, so too can class. As Skeggs argues, the class-based notion of 'respectability' is one to which women aspire, yet are denied equal access (Skeggs, 1997). Lawler, for example, notes that the media vilification of working-class women who participated in the Paulsgrove 'anti-paedophile' riots in 2000 was grounded in their inability to demonstrate the right 'kind of femininity'. From a middle-class perspective, then, working-class women are 'marked as the "Other", pathologised as bad mothers, laden with sexuality and dirt or displaying the wrong type of femininity' (Lawler, 2002: 107). Indeed, Skeggs (1997) highlights representations of working-class women as sexually 'deviant'. As a discourse of normativity, then, Skeggs argues that respectability is:

> one way in which sexual practice is evaluated, distinctions drawn, legitimated and maintained between groups. This means that heterosexuality is not occupied equally precisely because it is mediated by respectability and some women are, by class and race location, already categorised as non-respectable. (1997: 118)

As a result, for working-class women, 'sexual practice and respectability seem to be at odds with each other' (Skeggs, 1997: 124). Moreover, heterosexuality, respectability and femininity are enmeshed and, in Skeggs' view, the successful attainment of femininity is, for *most* women, impossible since 'it would be *to be* without agency, to be a sign of powerlessness' (original emphasis, 1997: 102). In addition, Skeggs' argument that 'structural positioning and access to discourses and meanings is already circumscribed by social location' (1997: 120) calls attention to other differences between women and raises the question of how age might intersect with class around notions of 'respectability'. Among our older working-class participants, some spoke openly about their sexual experiences. Jean Brown (74) felt she *'enjoyed it too much to feel guilty'* and Mo Innes (66) said of her sexual debut: *'could've just laid there an left it in all night [. . .] which I 'ave done [. . .] coulda done then an' all'*. Yet 83-year-old Maggie Finch chose to describe her date rape in part because she only now had the language to conceptualise it. Seventy years previously it had been virtually silenced. When she broached it with her daughter, Jayne, and grand-daughter, Claire, over a meal in a pub, however, they in turn had no ready language to frame a response within this context. Claire's explanation for their silence was: *'. . . you know, [eating] prawn cocktail and, she's never mentioned it since, and I wouldn't ask her'*. Other working-class women described marital rape, and – despite middle-class participants' claims that sex *'wasn't talked of in my young day'* – there were accounts of and from women who had conceived outside marriage during wartime.

Links between respectability, shame and sex are nonetheless power-fully evident in 85-year-old Marion Ogden's account of her elder sister's pregnancy which breached the taboos of both pre-marital and extra-marital sex because her child's father was married. At the time of the study, Marion was widowed after 35 years of marriage, Elaine her daughter after 25 years of marriage, while grand-daughter, Michelle's first marriage ended in divorce. Marion grew up in the 1920s/1930s within a community where sex out of appropriate time and place was shameful, silenced and made invisible. Thus her elder sister's pregnancy was hidden from her mother until the baby was born, a decision which anticipated the consequences of the birth: her sister was sent away and Marion forbidden contact with her. Moreover, Marion's contact with boys was then scrutinised exhaustively, her relationships termin-ated or questioned by her mother for reasons such as: the young men were fishermen and, therefore, beneath her; they were in the armed services and had made another girl pregnant. Marion did side-step this scrutiny, however, again through secrecy: *'I used to go out with, well, never used to tell her who I was going with, used to go with different people, and she never, you know, never used to ask me.'* When Marion eventually found a boyfriend acceptable to her mother because he attended the same chapel, the relationship was still curtailed when *his* parents discovered her sister's pregnancy. By way of resistance Marion could only refuse to go to chapel. Her family's 'reputation' within their community had thus undermined Marion's heterosexual prospects. Indeed, as Skeggs (1997) and Lawler (2002) argue, working-class women are by definition sexualised, a position which differentiates them from middle-class women and precludes authentic femininity. Respectability, as Strathern (cited in Skeggs, 1997: 3) suggests, makes morality public, an object of knowledge. For Marion's family respectability was an achieved but fragile status, one they sought to rescue through silencing and exclusion.

If Marion's data exemplify aspects of the social environment within which the oldest cohort grew up, they also give insight into the transmission of a heterosexual imaginary between generations. Elaine, her 54-year-old daughter, grew up in the 1950s. Like her mother she learned to be wary of boys, for example, by being made to return the sixpence a boy gave her and refused permission to play with boys when menstruating, albeit without explanation. For Elaine these boys were simply 'friends', yet these prohibitions resonate with theoretical work on heterosexuality which highlights the centrality of *difference* to this institution (Richardson, 1996, 2000) (see Chapter 2). Through parenting practices such as these, boys are 'othered', made unapproachable or dangerous.

Like her mother, Elaine described the sequestration of experience which failed to conform to hegemonic heterosexuality, such as the secret of her pre-marital sexual experience. Her silence, however, alerted Marion to the possibility that her daughter married rapidly whilst pregnant, even though she never admitted this. During her interview she said she became pregnant early in the marriage and miscarried. Although Elaine looked *back* to taboos on pre-marital sex among young people in the early 1960s, describing the refusal of hotel rooms to unmarried couples, she sustains a sense of youthful shame by concealing her pre-marital pregnancy, despite the contemporary relaxation of stigma in this area. Moreover she continues to conceal risky aspects of her current experience, such as the emotional unhappiness within her present partnership which potentially delegitimates it. Rarely speaking of her relationship with friends or family, Elaine has become a focus for Marion's concerns in that her daughter conceals her failure to conform to hegemonic heterosexuality.

By contrast, Michelle, Elaine's daughter, did describe her experience of sex outside marriage. By the 1980s, sex had been uncoupled from marriage and reproduction (Hawkes, 1996: 105), and Michelle took sexual activity for granted. Dating someone sexually experienced, she says: *'I remember thinking "I'm going to be expected to have sex now".'* She told her mother: ' *"I need to go on the pill." I felt it was better to have permis-*

sion in a way. I wanted her to know about it. I felt as if I wanted her to know that I was being sensible and thinking about it.' At this point hegemonic heterosexuality required not abstinence or secrecy, but 'being sensible'. Yet Michelle never told her parents that she shared her boyfriend's bedroom at his parents' house, in *their* knowledge: *'I used to say that I slept downstairs or something like that.'* Though contradictory, given her openness about contraception, the *social* dimensions of secrecy are evident here. What could be made explicit between mother and daughter in the 1980s, had to remain hidden within the community. Were Elaine to realise that the boyfriend's parents knew of her daughter's sexual activities, she would no longer feel in control of her daughter's sexual reputation; and open sexual practice prior to marriage still jeopardised that reputation.

These data show a marked if changing consensus around the boundaries of hegemonic heterosexuality. How transgressions would be dealt with if they did come to light is, however, less predictable as individuals exercise agency in relation to heteronormativity. Thus other ways of being heterosexual could be accommodated, however costly they might prove. Agency therefore needs to be seen as integral to the gradual changes we have identified within the institution. For example, not only 44-year-old Jennifer Underhill, but also her 65-year-old mother, Audrey, had become pregnant outside marriage. Although *'hurt'* by Audrey's untimely pregnancy, *her* mother was supportive and the couple escaped the whisperings of their market-town community by removing themselves to Audrey's husband's parents in another village. When Jennifer became pregnant 18 years later, Audrey was less sympathetic. She recalls:

> But Jennifer, like me, she got caught with a baby, with Karen, and that devastated me, absolutely, that, that devastated me and Neil [husband], I thought Neil and I were going to part at that time . . . I've never known him blow up, and he just blew up, went berserk. 'She's got to be adopted, she's got to be adopted', these were all voices coming from these people, telling me what to do . . . I think this is when, I let Jennifer down, I let Jennifer down. They said, 'There's a home in Yorkshire, she can go to, and she can have the baby in Gildervale Hospital, and the baby, she can keep her for four days or five days, and then she will go up for adoption'.

However, Audrey's response changed with the arrival of the baby. She says:

I knew I let her down, I've known I'm letting her down, and I must apologise to her before I've gone to a better land, and, um, so, anyway she went and she had the baby, and Neil and I went to see her, went to see Jennifer, and she said, 'Have you seen Karen?' I said, 'No, I don't want to see her', I said, 'I can't'. She said, 'Please go and have a look at her'. So, I went and had a look at her, and somehow she just opened her little eye at me, and I thought, 'Oh god, you're not going anywhere'.

These data concern the heterosexual lives of participants with a working-class background, one, we note from Skeggs (1997), where respectability is both sought after yet elusive. This raises the question of how the greater unwillingness of middle-class interviewees to describe their sexual lives relates to class-based notions of respectability. What may be the case is that for them respectability, in representing a given, was recognised as a key resource which they avoided putting at risk. As noted, secrecy prevailed among the well-to-do Davis family, and indeed masked transgressive heterosexuality among members of all three generations. Although 43-year-old Sarah Davis had developed a pattern of resourcefulness during her childhood which resulted in her joining the merchant navy as a teenager, she grew up with strict codes around sexual behaviour. Nonetheless, during adolescence she grasped the opportunity to experiment with sex and vividly recalled her sexual debut at a friend's house, while the parents were away (see Chapter 4). Yet while courting her future husband, her younger sister spitefully *'spragged'* on her for sleeping with him. She recalls:

Yes, she said 'You don't mind about Sarah do you?!', and of course mum thought 'What about Sarah?', and we'd actually been out for a drive, Richard was teaching me to drive, and we came back in absolutely full of it 'I did a three point turn!', and she was absolutely wooden faced and she cut me dead and she said: 'Are you sleeping with [.] Richard?' or something, and I said [.] 'Yes', she said 'Well, that's a turn up for the books isn't it?!' And she was very angry . . . [. . .] but she took it very, very badly, in fact she didn't talk to me for several months. [. . .] I went back to college and I used to phone up, you know, to talk to them and, um, she wouldn't talk to me. There'd always be some excuse, dad would come to the phone and talk to me and say 'Oh you know, mother's busy'.

Sarah particularly resented her mother's tolerance of her younger sister sleeping with *her* boyfriend, a punitive double standard which reveals the situatedness of conformity to hegemonic heterosexuality. Eventually her mother acknowledged that her distress resulted from discovering that the *'goody-goody'* of the family had fallen from her *'pedestal'*. When Sarah's mother, Joan, described her divorce from Sarah's father following her discovery of his affair, her interview provided insight into the particularity of her anger towards Sarah. Once again secrecy had undermined her assumptions about her family's conformity to a heterosexual imaginary.

While there had been some relaxation of sexual constraints between each generation of this family, Sarah's daughter, Abigail, freely describing being *'fingered'* while drunk at a Young Farmer's party, her 18-year-old sister, Helen, had less sexual experience to reflect upon. Nonetheless, Helen talked openly about the emotional aspects of her experiences thus far, and made critical observations about her parents' relationship and how it had shaped her aspirations for her own heterosexual future. Refusing social pressure to acquire a boyfriend, she asserts: *'I actually like being single at the moment, because if all the men around, because all the blokes I seem to bump into are only interested in one thing, but I'm quite happy as I am.'*

Conclusion

Grounding itself in participants' narratives, this chapter has set out to explore the discourses which resource them, tracing the contours of a heterosexual imaginary which works to shore up particular notions of masculinity and femininity. Beginning with that which was *said* by our participants, we examined the language through which they not only articulated but also reflected upon their experiences. In engaging critically with the institution of heterosexuality, then, attention was paid to its diversity and potential mutability, to the intersection of age, gender and social class within the contingent, discursive possibilities accessed by different individuals. In addition, weight was given to the intersubjectivity of knowledge produced within an interview involving two socially located individuals, taking account of how the assumptions of both participants about the other inform the language used to discuss a heterosexual life.

During the second half of the chapter, we also examined the contradictions, evasions and silences which act to marginalise those 'heterosexual' desires and practices that are felt to be transgressive. In making sense of the sequestration of such experiences, Butler's argument that homosexuality acts to generate heterosexuality via the inculcation of a refusal of the homosexual cathexis is suggestive (see Hanson, 1997:

56). What we argue, however, is that rather than simply foregrounding a sexuality conceived of as oppositional to heterosexuality, we should instead give far greater scope to a whole range of everyday beliefs, desires and practices which somehow fail to be incorporated within hegemonic heterosexuality – and in so doing contribute to our interviewees' sense of what it is heterosexuality somehow demands of them.

Given the centrality of silence to this theoretical perspective, discussion *of* those silences contributes significantly to this chapter's exploration of the heterosexual imaginary. As a source of promise and fulfilment, this imaginary is represented in institutions as elevated as the white wedding and routines as mundane as who drives the car (Ingraham, 2002). In the romantic mystification of the gendered hierarchies which intersect with heterosexual institutions such as marriage and the family, we have a wealth of images, representations and narratives, all of which potentially act as markers against which individuals may evaluate not only their own experience but also that of their heterosexual partners, their parents and their children and grandchildren. Where a 'critical lack of fit' (Hockey and James, 2003) is strongly in evidence what we tend to find are silences which, as noted above, in Wilden's view 'cannot be overlooked' (1987: 69), in that they constitute messages which on some level draw attention to the otherwise unmarked category of mundane heterosexuality. As such, these communications remind individuals not only of its instability as an institution, but also of the social, emotional and economic implications of transgressing its contours and boundaries.

7
What's Sex Got to Do With It? Heterosexuality as an Organising Principle

In Chapters 5 and 6 we examined the discourses that people draw upon in constructing their narratives of heterosexuality – but the question we address now, in this and the following chapter, is what happens in practice as people live out their diverse heterosexual lives? Does the prioritising of the sexual in their accounts tell us the whole story about heterosexuality? Here, we examine its wider sphere of influence as an organising principle and ask how this is expressed in family practices (Morgan, 1996) – where, our data show, it is clearly a matter of something more than sex.

Scott (2004) argues that sociology, as a discipline, still brackets off sex and sexuality as a special area of human life at the very edges of the social and the cultural. To address this, she argues for a need to focus the theoretical gaze on the institution of heterosexuality and on sexuality as everyday practice, two factors which are fundamental to the underlying aims of our research in both its original conception and analysis of data. Thus, while the concept of 'being heterosexual' is commonly seen to be primarily an issue of ('normal') sexual preference, this chapter will show that although, as Scott argues, heterosexuality needs to be examined as a key site of sex and sexuality, such practices or preferences by no means exhaust the scope and meaning of this category.

We have used VanEvery's (1996) conception of heterosexuality as a (social) institution which provides the organising principle within areas of life that extend far beyond what we might think of as simply 'sexual'. She also argues that in seeing heterosexuality as an institution, and not merely as a sexual preference, we begin to understand heterosexual relations as an important context within which traditional forms of femininity and masculinity are reproduced. These points relate to the following questions which have underpinned the previous chapters' discussions:

- To what extent are patterns of heterosexuality produced and repro-duced within families and across generations?
- To what extent do generations differ from one another, perhaps as resistance to, or rejection of the relationships of the previous gener-ations?
- What kinds of relationships are people actually making – and can we speak of a diversity of heterosexualities?

What this chapter offers is a development of these discussions through the suggestion that heterosexuality remains relatively unproblematised – adhering to the status of an unmarked category – by virtue of its role as an organising principle within everyday life. In other words, although individuals may think critically about 'the opposite sex' or 'getting hitched', heterosexual pairing itself, and the centrality of gendered difference, remains difficult to reflect on objectively as simply one of many possible ways of organising social life. In other words, as Ingraham (2005) notes, we learn to both act 'straight' and think 'straight'. Through data from participants belonging to all three age-cohorts, we show how bodily information about growing up, peer group relations and social status in adolescence, the structuring of both public and domestic space and the attainment of desirable age-based identities were all organised according to the principle of heterosexuality – though none of these are directly associated with sexual desire or practice. Yet, as Ingraham (2005) points out, we create a set of identity categories and corres-ponding belief systems to produce an illusion that sexuality is fixed and unchanging. Further, she argues, these categories are then used to posi-tion us hierarchically within a value system, and we then claim both social status and legitimacy from our place within this framework. From this, '[c]onstructed notions of sexual behavior and sexual identity have become primary organizing categories for many key aspects of social life including but not limited to marriage, family, politics, religion, work, and education' (Ingraham, 2005: 2).

Our data show how, empirically, heterosexuality may have been understood in terms of 'sex', rather than its other aspects, and we have explored how this view can be expressed via multiple layers of language. This chapter's focus on embodied life moves on to demonstrate how heterosexuality infuses the times and spaces of everyday life, therefore reproducing itself through experience which, whilst embodied, may not necessarily be sexual. Instead, we argue, heterosexuality is constituted in those 'key heterosexual moments' such as the acquisition of gender and age-based social status in adolescence, introduced in Chapter 4. In working with this material we offer a framework which allows us to conceptualise the relationship between the mundane and the extremes of heterosexual experience. Arguably, it is the power of the mundane which not only keeps heterosexuality 'in place', but also, at times, reveals disruptions to it. We are interested too in how extreme events such as a recollection of 'date rape' or empirical evidence of domestic violence are sutured into more mundane experiences of heterosexuality. Robinson (2004) has argued, in relation to sporting masculinities, that an explora-tion of mundane and extreme experiences in 'extreme sports' reveals the *everyday* nature of the practices which constitute rock climbing or wind-surfing. She suggests, therefore, that the 'exceptional' is very quickly routinised and comes to consist of largely standardised activities. With regard to our project here, however, we will argue *conversely*, that the pervasively mundane quality of heterosexual life can shape the way people make sense of extreme events. This means, for example, that memories of an extreme event are likely to be remembered and recalled in some detail by virtue of the fact that they disrupted mundane activ-ities such as eating. What we find within our data, then, are examples of participants' reflections on 'extreme mundanities'.

Chapter 1 contextualised this aspect of our work in terms of Schutz's ([1932] 1972) argument that social reality is constantly reconstructed through the everyday actions of individuals. Also important is recogni-tion of the everyday in more recent work on consumption (see Mackay, 1997), which concerns itself with the unpredictable, improvised and routine activities of people's everyday lives. The unmarked mundanity of heterosexuality to which, nevertheless, we feel expected to conform, is our focus here. Our data, we argue, complicate Mies' (1983) notion that people cannot reflect consciously on oppressive relationships as long as their 'normality' goes unchallenged. Our interviewees did, at times, reflect and sometimes act upon their circumstances, despite the absence of disruption or extreme occurrences. However, our 'scrutiny' of the everyday also draws on the feminist tradition of seeing the mundane aspects of everyday life, such as the minutiae of past and present rela-tionships, as, on one level at least, re-enforcing patriarchal notions. The feminist gaze on the world, according to Smith (1987), attempts to problematise this everyday 'normality'. Like Felski, however, we also see women's connections to the everyday world as something to be made evident, even celebrated, especially where women are involved with the messy, chaotic, embodied realities of life (1999–2000: 352).

Also like Felski, we have argued that men too are 'embodied, embedded subjects, who live, for the most part, repetitive, familiar and ordinary lives' (1999–2000: 353). Nonetheless, as this volume argues, we know little about masculinity in relation to how heterosexuality is practised in the everyday world – and our study draws on empirical data to address that theoretical void. To this end we have drawn out differences between women and men in how they think about, and practise, heterosexual relationships. How heterosexuality is 'done' is, as we have emphasised, something which happens differently, across generation, class and gender. Finally, it is in the everyday, especially through the concept of 'mundane extremities', that, following Gardiner (2000), we can see the everyday as open to redemption and trans-formation, yet still acknowledge its ambivalence and contradictions. In other words, heterosexuality still needs to be critiqued, as it has been in the past, by feminists who have emphasised its oppressive aspects. Nonetheless it can also be seen in terms of its contradictory, yet enduring appeal for many people seeking to create and sustain an everyday life and set of close relationships. If, as Silva and Bennett argue, '(t)he attention to research on everyday life identifies a range of small changes, and implies that these can have significant cumulative effects' (2004: 16), our discussion of how change might be theorised (see Chapter 5) is here developed through the notion of mundanities, extreme or otherwise. This, we argue, allows us to explore these 'cumu-lative effects', starting with the idea that heterosexuality is not simply about 'sex'.

What's heterosexuality got to do with sex?

As our data implicitly demonstrate, heterosexuality is not simply a matter of attraction to members of the opposite sex. Chapter 1 has already questioned its status as the outcome of some kind of natural instinct and argued the case for another explanation for its pervasive-ness. Instead, it was suggested, heterosexuality operates as the implicit organising principle of much of everyday life, and so needs recog-nising as a social rather than sexual identity. As Richardson (1996), argues, heterosexuality encodes and structures everyday life. While we anticipated difficulties in encouraging respondents to reflect on their experiences of heterosexuality as a social category, we were unpre-pared for colleagues' difficulties with the notion that heterosexuality was an organising principle, rather than a *sexual* category. For them, data describing the onset of menstruation or first sexual experiences, for example, should be coded under 'sexuality'.

As the example below indicates, however, 'non-sexual' practices can be crucial to the pervasiveness of heterosexuality. Thus, Audrey Underhill, aged 65, from a rural background, talks about the first boyfriend she had when she was 16:

> Audrey: Oh, we just liked each other, we liked, you know, we used to dance together at the Marwell and all that, and he used to come to Nottingley to see me, and I can remember, he was the only one, the only Easter egg I'd ever have had bought and it was bought by Philip.
>
> AM: Easter egg?
>
> Audrey: Yeah, and he bought me this Easter egg, and I can always remember it was in like a gold wrapping with a bow on, not a box, and he just said, there you are, and it was the first Easter egg I've ever had in my life.
>
> AM: Quite special then?
>
> Audrey: Yes.
>
> AM: First and last?
>
> Audrey: Yes, I've never had one bought me since.

She then uses this memory to reflect on her current relationship with her husband in which he is found wanting:

> AM: So, if you got together then, after he came back, after his National Service, how did he woo you? How did he make you feel bothered about?
>
> Audrey: Oh, Neil isn't that type of person, he never has been and he never will be.
>
> AM: I can tell, if he's never bought you an Easter egg. [LAUGH]
>
> Audrey: No, he's not the type of man who can, no, he isn't.

Much of our data similarly shows the centrality of 'non-sexual' memories to recollections of key heterosexual moments and relationships and so point towards the 'something more' which constitutes hegemonic heterosexuality. As such, they problematise the notion that ('normal') sexual desire lies at the *heart* of the institution of heterosexuality, with other emotions and practices, loving or caring, for example, providing something akin to the gold wrapping on Audrey Underhill's one and only Easter egg. We have inherited an Anglican service for the solemnization of matrimony which, among other reasons, states that marriage is ordained by God 'as a remedy against sin, and to avoid fornication', in other words, a proper place for the unwieldy human tendency to feel and act upon sexual desire. Yet our project is one of decentring heterosexuality, of asking where – if anywhere – sex might be located within it. And, as this book demonstrates, that question is one which can only be addressed empirically, regardless of the ordinances of the Anglican Church. As argued, it is within the everyday that heterosexuality is embedded, and where, therefore, it occupies the status of a 'natural' practice.

Practising heterosexuality

VanEvery (1996) asserts that when we investigate the family or marriage/coupledom, we are looking at one of the hegemonic forms of heterosexuality – that is, a form of heterosexuality which is implicitly assumed to be the most appropriate or the most natural – and this assumption is powerful precisely because it is taken-for-granted rather than thought through. This means that we can see heterosexuality as the principle which underpins 'family practices', the term that Morgan (1999) uses to describe the processes through which individuals live out the concept of 'family'. 'Family' therefore emerges out of people's interaction with one another, rather than being 'a thing-like object of detached social investigation' (Morgan, 1999: 16), which lies beyond its members' control or making. As such, family practices can also be seen as gendered practices or age-based practices, for example, making this a multifaceted concept which allows us to explore the diverse aspects of heterosexualities.

In Morgan's work, then, the concept of practices conveys the following: a sense of the active; an interplay between the perspectives of the social actor, the individual whose actions are described and the observer's perspective; a focus on the everyday; a stress on regularities; a sense of fluidity and an interplay between history and biography. If, as Silva and Smart (1999) note, Morgan's framework makes it possible to think of individuals 'doing' family (or heterosexuality or masculinity), and not passively residing within a pre-given structure which determines social behaviour, then his idea of practices stresses their routine nature and, importantly, does not imply an opposition between structure and agency. Nonetheless, tensions can of course arise from different and conflicting practices, which may be age- or class-related, for instance, and it is this perception of a dynamic, fluid and mutable relation between structure and agency which our work on heterosexuality draws upon.

In Chapters 5 and 6, we argued that practices were intimately related to, and constructed within discourses. Within the data that follow the family practices through which people learn to achieve 'heterosexuality' are exemplified. What is striking is the lack of explicit reference to sexual attraction or sexual practice. Whilst people learn about the changes in young women's bodies and about attracting the attention of the opposite sex, these are communicated through the mundane experiences of being told to wash more scrupulously, for example, or of *not* being told about something which one's peers and elders clearly find engrossing. In this way, young people grow up and into what we can regard as the more 'extreme' aspects or peak moments of heterosexuality: the marriage ceremony; the first penile penetration; the divorce. And indeed, as our data reveal, it remains the mundane through which these more 'extreme' experiences are then recalled and recounted during interviews.

So when it comes to bodily change, what participants were told – and not told – carry heterosexual implications. Yet sex itself is never mentioned. Instead, young people are learning to grow up as an appropriately heterosexual woman or man. Amongst female participants, some, for example, described how they were warned against sitting on *'cold slabs'*, taking baths and *'touching meat'* – which menstruation would then putrefy. While these body-focused warnings are not explicitly concerned with sex, they are, we suggest, implicitly about appropriate heterosexual embodiment. It is important to note that this form of ambiguous communication is not some old-fashioned residue but has more recent parallels in the obscuring of the materialities of the body. For example, one female member of our middle generation described how:

> *even things like, um, your underwear, your bras an' your pants [.] you always 'ad a clothes 'orse round the fire, but if dad was comin' in, everything 'ad to be took off and moved away . . . I don't think 'e would've been cross, I think 'e would've been embarrassed* (Anita Leigh, 50).

Andrea Queens (41) also describes how she was told that she couldn't swim while menstruating, but no explanation was given for this. She goes on to describe hiding menstruation from her brothers and purchasing packets of sanitary towels in paper bags for her mother as a child and being told that they were *'firelighters'*.

When it comes to getting the interest of a member of the opposite sex, apparently a self-evident requirement if sexual coupling is to take place, we can ask about the extent to which it *was* simply motivated by bodily 'urges'. What our data indicate is that for both young women and young men a boyfriend or girlfriend gave them considerable social status among peers. While the recollection embarrassed her, Anita Leigh (50) described physically fighting for her first boyfriend when she was 14. So intense was her desire for 'victory' over another contender that the very fact that *'I was prepared to fight for 'im [.]. . . made 'er back down'*.

Even sexual practice itself is described less as a source of private pleasure or personal fulfilment, and more as a way of measuring yourself against peers. In other words, it represented a quantifiable currency which might buy social kudos. Here, middle-class participants spoke of a *'points scale'*, previously referred to by working-class interviewees in Chapter 6, one which allowed private practice to be evaluated publicly:

> *Well, there was a check-list that used to go around, that you were meant to sign, and everything was a stage, of the sort of meeting boys, courtship, right down to the ultimate, and you were meant to, score certain points [LAUGH] you know, and I of course, you know, I was sort of, nought, nothing . . . I forget what age we were, but that was sort of current at one time, trying to sort of out-do each other in how daring you've managed to be* (Lynne Archer, 55).

David Gold (28) gives his version:

> *I don't know, it's like a ladder, you start off with a peck, well, holding hands, then the peck on the cheek, then there was the snog, and the snog and the grope, and it was like, that ladder, took everything in steps.*

A high score was one way of gaining social status through sexual 'conquest'. But our data show other ways of evaluating a conquest. Fay Roberts (50), for example, was thrilled because her first boyfriend looked like Mike Nesmith from The Monkees pop group; women were attracted to men with motorbikes (particularly in the 1970s); Joanna Hodge (46) went to agricultural college so that she could meet someone who would 'count' within her local community, another farmer; and Leanne Cook (22) describes how her reputation was enhanced by kissing a particular boy: *'I was big and hard because I'd kissed him'*. She later inflated it further by making her sexual debut with a Scandinavian professional athlete:

Oh god I was [.] really, really happy [LAUGHS] oh god [.] 'e was, like, 'e was such a conquest, and that's all 'e was really, I can't say that 'e was [.] that 'is brain made me want 'im [.] even more, but 'e was just such a conquest.

This was no less of an issue for some male members of our sample. For example, Graham Nash (46) reflects on his first girlfriend:

it was just, um, bravado, wasn't it, it was, 'Oh, I've got a girlfriend, or I'm going out with Diane Campbell', I mean, she was a good-looker.

So what these data indicate is that 'sex' is somehow not central, either to information about bodily changes or to the experience of attracting the opposite sex. As an institution, heterosexuality is more all-embracing. Implicit within the everyday lives and practices of young people growing up, encoding and structuring their bodily experience and their peer group relationships, heterosexuality far exceeds the more limited category of 'sex'.

Growing up and becoming sexual? Becoming sexual and growing up?

As these data suggest, heterosexuality informs ideas about how the body should be managed as well as representing a source of status among peers. For those who grow up within this social framework, its hegemony as an institution is effectively affirmed. Thus, we can begin to understand its pervasiveness without simply resorting to essentialist notions of a 'natural sex drive' (see Weeks, 1989: 142–3) – and once we adopt this position we can reflect on and amend the institution.

We now move on to consider the centrality of heterosexuality – rather than simply sex – to acquiring an adult status. As the social study of childhood affirms, this period of the life-course is characterised by dependency and diminished access to social power (see James et al., 1998). As a result, 'growing up' is a highly valued project among children and young people – and here again, heterosexuality represents an important indicator of social status (see Ingraham, 2005).

Thus, our data suggest that reaching puberty and actually being 'sexual' constitutes a marker of achieving adulthood: this, rather than chronological age, prompting the start of sexual practice. For example, describing the moment she told her mother that she had started her periods, Anna Leigh (28) recalls her sister's resentment that she had over-taken her in the race towards adulthood, despite being chronologically younger:

> *she started crying, 'Oh my baby, [LAUGH], oh my baby!'. 'Cause my sister's older than me, she's eleven months older, but she still hadn't started her periods, so I started before she did, yeah, and she didn't speak to me for about three months [LAUGH].*

For women of more than one age cohort, starting their period was seen as a 'rite of passage' into adulthood. Both Di Elliot (34) and Claire Finch (23) talked about their impatience to start theirs, without explaining why, exactly, while Claire's mother, Jayne (50) says she *'knicker-gazed for months, years'*. And when it happened to Fay Roberts (50), her aunt *'flung her arms round me and she said, "Oh, Fay, you're a woman"'*. While not necessarily linked with any discussion of sex itself, the beginning of a reproductive life which is conventionally linked with heterosexuality is desired and celebrated. It carries social value.

The progression towards heterosexual adulthood was further accel-erated by early brushes with the opposite sex. Both male and female members of our sample said that having a girl/boyfriend (even as young as age 12) made them feel more 'grown up'. Indeed, one woman describes both her own and her mother's response to her first 'date':

> *Well you felt quite [. . .] you know, me first boyfriend [LAUGHS] (also) you felt 'Ooh, first boyfriend [.] Going on a date'. I remember me mum, d'you know, I remember that, I remember me mum saying [WHISPERS] 'Oh, your first date'* (Dorothy Cook, 54).

And when Sadie Innes (54) described her first kiss as an *'awakening'*, there is a sense in which that awakening is as much about a transition to a higher status age-category as an initial experience of physical desire.

Becoming a wo/man

In seeking to understand how implicit claims to a heterosexual iden-tity mesh with the process of becoming adult, we also need to consider the importance of *gendered* identities. Growing up heterosexual occurs within a western social context where both heterosexuality and adult-hood represent not only dominant social categories which are implic-ated in the marginalisation of other sexualities (Richardson, 1996), and indeed, other life-course categories, such as 'childhood' and 'old age' (Hockey and James, 1993, 2003). Thus, as our data indicate, what interviewees were told or found out, what they did and their reflections on what they did, were integral to self-identification as both heterosexual *and* adult.

Our data therefore reveal the personal agendas through which individuals seek to realise or animate the social identity 'heterosexual adult'; the relationship between the desires, decisions and strategies of young people growing up, and the hegemonic models of heterosexuality available to them. The institution of heterosexuality thus emerges as an ideal type model in relation to which individuals manage everyday, embodied heterosexual lives. For example, 23-year-old Claire Finch, like other of our interviewees, had only recently considered leaving home, despite two years in a stable heterosexual relationship. This suggests, as Brannen and Nilsen (2002: 515) argue, that adolescence has become extended, with markers of adulthood, such as leaving home, marriage and transitions to parenthood being deferred. Among this cohort, therefore, potentially greater sexual licence (see Chapter 4) is coupled with childhood dependency upon parents. This combination of circumstances appeared to disrupt the relationship between heterosexual identification and adulthood. For example, while interviewees from the youngest cohort used far more sexually explicit language than the oldest one, they were less likely to view their experiences as compatible with or indicative of adult heterosexuality.

Claire Finch, for example, saw herself as sexually unattractive, a perception which led her to develop a crush on *'the first bloke that ever showed any interest in me, so I was besotted straightaway'*. Grateful for heterosexual attention, she undertook sexual liaisons with other men, yet found these inadequate when it came to the claiming of a heterosexual identity for, as VanEvery argues, heterosexuality is an institution which 'encompasses much more than sexual desire or sexual acts' (1996: 41). One young man made her keep their activities secret because he was seeing other girls, so for her first sex was not part of an openly *'couple-type'* relationship. Whilst Sarah Davies and Jayne Finch, from the 1960s age cohort, at least had first sex within a relationship, albeit without the pleasure they had imagined, for Claire sex meant being used, rather than heterosexual coupledom. It was, nonetheless, an approximation she felt obliged to accept, and, indeed, encouraged by her mother, Jayne, eventually found a boy with whom she could become a public 'couple'.

Unlike Claire, 17-year-old Abigail Davis was preparing to leave home for university. However, at the time of interview she was tied to rural family life, dependent on family members for transport. Abigail did engage in sexual activities, secretly, but like Claire, she differentiated (hetero)sex from a desirable heterosexual identity. For her, a *'serious'* boyfriend involved more than *'holding hands and messing about'*, yet the experience of bodily desire did not add up to anything like the full assemblage of beliefs and relationships 'through which people become socially heterosexual and practice heterosexuality' (Holland et al., 1996: 144). When asked if she had experienced the 'sexual chemistry' of (hetero)sexual kissing, she said:

> *Yeah, he was [.]... a young farmer guy, and we were like, we went to a party and I'd be with him, and he'd be with me, but nothing would happen in between... in the end I just decided that... if I wanted a boyfriend I'd get someone that would be there all the time not just when I was drunk at a party* [emphasis added].

These data show young respondents coming to understand the contours of hegemonic heterosexuality via sexual experiences which were at odds with a prevailing heterosexual imaginary (Ingraham, 1996). Abigail, for example, described an experience where: *'I was stupidly drunk and there was just [.] a guy there that I think is absolutely minging... and I started kissing him, and my mum was there and that's like, how embarrassing [LAUGHS].'*

Clear about what they do not want, therefore, Claire and Abigail saw sex as but one facet of the institution of heterosexuality. Claire, for example, recognised heterosexual coupledom as something which fulfilled her desire for *intimacy*. Of her current boyfriend, she said:

> *... he wants to be with me as much as I want to be with him... he's the first (person), he respects me, and he listens to me, and he's not after anything, you know, like (the others) were just after one thing, they just wanted somebody to get their end away.*

Achieving heterosexual adulthood therefore requires more than simply participation in (hetero)sex, as evidenced in the way young women judged relationships or practices as inadequate bases for heterosexual identification. While the institution may encompass, and indeed, fulfil, private bodily or emotional needs, the strategic choices made by young people at different historical moments demonstrate its social nature as experience, practice and identity, a status which must be both negotiated and sustained.

Extreme mundanities

Through the data presented above we have explored 'common experiences' (Lefebvre, 1991) of living out heterosexual relationships, yet we are also concerned with finding out and problematising precisely what a 'common experience' of the everyday is for different people. We want to sift through theoretical claims and assumptions such as those detailed below, to explore, for example, the future of intimacy as a form of democracy within heterosexual coupledom; and to interrogate the emotional experiences of men in the practices that constitute (new and old) forms of masculinity. As Chapter 2 argued, the historical and cross-cultural variability of gender differences is made invisible within the naturalising processes of living out heterosexuality. A conception of the mundane and the extreme, we go on to argue, enables exploration of these new emotional and intimate territories and makes visible the potentially shifting nature of gender differences.

Recognising the importance of the mundane, or everyday, has a long history in the context of sociology (and anthropology). It can be defined as a 'largely taken for granted world that remains clandestine, yet constitutes what Lefebvre calls the "common ground" or "connective tissue" of all conceivable human thoughts and activities' (cited in Gardiner, 2000: 2) (see also Smith, 1987; Nettleton and Watson, 1998; Bennett and Watson, 2002; Chaney, 2002; Highmore, 2002; and Silva and Bennett, 2004). For Gardiner, however, the purpose of studying the everyday is not only to describe it, but also to change lived experience. Chaney (2002) suggests that the everyday acts as a space for whatever 'other ways of being' can be envisaged; and, in tracing the significance of changes, everyday life and what is orderly or disorderly about it needs to be closely investigated. He sees the 'common experience of normality' as giving people's lives order and stability and is what makes experiences meaningful.

Analyses of data already presented demonstrate that the agency of social actors is central to the study of the everyday, for people are self-reflexive about their experiences, and neither 'cultural dopes' nor unwilling victims. But it is important to note, as Gardiner does, that: 'Increasingly, the "everyday" is evoked in a gestural sense as a bulwark of creativity and resistance, regardless of the question of asymmetries of power, class relations, or increasingly globalized market forces' (Gardiner, 2000: 8). So although a concentration on everyday events can, for Gardiner, sidestep sociological roles or structures, nonetheless, as Chapter 5 argues, structural constraints on mundane heterosexual relations still need to be recognised.

Some of the older women we interviewed took for granted the status of gendered roles and practices, such as the necessity of the male bread-winner and female homemaker, seeing them as necessary to the survival of a marriage. Not only did they see this as relevant for themselves, but also for people much younger than they were. Gendered roles and prac-tices were often conceived of in relation to the mundane and to private, domestic space; who does the ironing and washing, the decorating or the gardening and cooking. Older men and women reflected on court-ship and romance via recollections of dancing in the 1940s. For some of the men, this was also seen as mundane, because *'there wasn't things to do'*, beyond the routines of the local dancehall. People's materially grounded memories were also clearly orchestrated around their daily, weekly or annual routines. Thus, in discussing emotions with the inter-viewees, love was remembered by one male focus group participant in his sixties as when a man and a woman *'want to share everything. You want to know what she had for breakfast or what she had for tea, where she's gonna be tomorrow'*. His courtship days were recalled by detailing the routines of whose house they went to for tea, the anticipation of waiting for her to arrive, of wanting to be alone with her and not sharing her with anyone. Also, one of the older women in another focus group had been advised by her vicar about marriage. In similar terms, he said: *' "Can you bear to see that same face at the breakfast table for the next 50 years? If the answer is yes, go ahead, if the answer is no, don't do it".'* However, Highmore (2002) conceptualises the everyday as potentially having an extraordinary element to it, one which can be characterised as mysterious – or even bizarre – and so exceptional. This element, he suggests, can be found in our everyday lives, informing the contradictory and paradoxical nature of the everyday. Nevertheless, the differences, contradictions and continuities in people's perceptions of and experi-ences of heterosexuality can be seen in the everyday mundanities, rather than necessarily 'revealed' in extreme or peak moments. This is borne out in our discovery that when people are asked to be reflexive about their experiences, they do so in everyday terms.

Mundane memories

As argued above, our data show the mundane informing people's experi-ences on different levels, shaping how they make sense of extreme events in both public and private spheres. While the everyday is often thought of simply in terms of routines, it seems to us that the term 'mundane' is preferable as it incorporates both routines *and* other aspects of everyday experiences. For example, Sonia Elliot (55) associated psychological abuse by her violent partner around food and an evening meal:

> *I was due to go to hospital, and the night before we went out with some friends and 'e knew I was nervous about [.] goin' into hospital, anaesthetic an', as we was goin' 'ome in the car 'e said 'I 'ope the anaesthetic goes wrong and you end up bein' a vegetable' [.] an' 'e started sayin' all this stuff an' our friends were really surprised, an' 'e stopped the car to go and get a Chinese an' I got out the car an' ran off.*

Similarly, Sandy Kirk (39) also associates food preparation and mealtimes with her former husband's cruelty. She recalls:

> *I remember once cooking this spaghetti bolognese and he was decorating and he'd, because my sister's a cook, and he'd asked me to ring her, how to make . . . and I don't know whether I'd got it wrong or what, but it was absolutely horrendous, and he made me sit down and eat it all. So, to this day I won't eat bloody spaghetti bolognese [LAUGHS].*

Food is also used in Sonia's recollections to convey the contradictory feelings her husband had for her:

> *I remember 'is friends all comin' back one weekend, one Saturday night, and I used to bake quite a lot then and one of 'is friends went into the kitchen and 'e went 'Hey come an' 'ave a look at this lot what Sonia's done, hey, she actually bakes!' You know, 'cos their wives didn't, they just sort of went off boozin' and that was it [.] An' 'e was quite proud of the things I did, and he always [.] He was always complimentin' me on how I looked, used to say 'you always look so lovely' an' that, an' yet there was this other side to 'im [.] aggressive.*

The contradictory nature of his behaviour is captured here and made sense of by Sonia as she recalls her performance of some of the mundane aspects of a stereotypical division of domestic labour in the home. The normality of these gendered tasks (and compliments about her femininity) gives an order and stability within which the extreme aspects of her partnership are located, so helping to stabilise and sustain a set of oppressive relations of power. Craib (1999) has noted that dominant discourses should not be conflated with the volatile nature of people's emotions and this is relevant in making sense of Sonia's recollections of a situation in which there was struggle, flux and contradiction within an oppressive heterosexual relationship. As well as the everyday and mundane helping to stabilise this relationship, however, it also operated as a lens through which she eventually sees the relationship in a new light, and in exercising agency, leaves it.

The everyday or apparently trivial can therefore tell as much about the 'doing' of gender, heterosexuality and masculinity and so on, as much as more 'dramatic' events. What the above examples suggest is that the mundane interacts with the extreme in everyday living in a dynamic manner, with the mundane acting as an interpretative framework for the extreme. This allows Sonia and Sandy to be reflexive and aware of the unacceptability of their ex-husbands' past behaviour, while also treating it as everyday and unsurprising. It also enables Maggie Finch (83) to 'forget' an experience of date rape for many years, because it was embedded in ordinary and everyday activities: walking down country lanes near her home. In Sonia's recollections, the mundane and the extreme had become enmeshed and inseparable, so that distinguishing the ordinary from the extraordinary was problematic, and indeed, unsustainable.

The mundane, in acting as an interpretative framework for the extreme, can also stand in for deep seated feelings about sexuality based on gender stereotypes and notions of respectability, especially as played out in the public sphere (issues we have discussed in Chapter 6). Talking about her honeymoon in London, Audrey Underhill (65) says:

> *Audrey:* Yes, we went to London, we went to, yeah, went to London, I'd never been to London in my life before, so, we went to London.
> *AM:* It must have been quite an eye-opener?
> *Audrey:* Yes, it was, yes, I must admit, he gave me a good time, and I, um, I, he took me down, is it Soho, and, this'll make you laugh, white shoes, I never bought a pair of white shoes, since he told me what
> *AM:* What white shoes meant?
> *Audrey:* Yes, well, we were down where all the prostitutes were and I says, why are those ladies all wearing white shoes, Neil? Whether it was just a tale, he just says, well, you know what they are, and I looked at him and said, no, and he says, well, they're prostitutes, and I've never worn a pair of white shoes since. I will not buy any, no, and they had little chains round their, sorry about that.

By refusing to ever wear white shoes again, once they had been revealed to her as a symbol of 'loose' female sexuality, Audrey demonstrates her fear of the social stigma she would risk if she did so. Her data therefore indicate how the mundane act of putting on a pair of white shoes meshes with her conceptions of what is considered, both by her and other people, to be a disreputable sexual identity. Thus, the mundane here allows aspects of 'extreme' sexuality to be not only refused but also regulated, without the body ever being foregrounded in a sexual sense.

Thinking about the 'inevitable' experience of performing mundane domestic chores in her very traditional marriage allows another interviewee, Lynne Archer (55), to implicitly reflect on heterosexuality as an identity, one which involves a shift from being a person in her own right, to being married and being seen as someone's wife, something which she resented:

> *Exactly, because even, you see, I'd lived at home when I was teaching primary school, either walked or cycled to school, and (mum), on everything, spoiled me rotten, and, I mean, I was so lazy, I still am if I can get away with it. I blame myself, but I blame mum, because she didn't make me do things for myself, and it wasn't until I was married and I had to, you know, that I found how awful it was, and how terrible housework was, washing and, oh god!*

In the rest of Lynne's interview, her consciousness of a loss of identity was evident, yet she frames this issue in terms of being expected to submerge herself in mundane domestic activities, things she had never done before. Felski's argument (1999–2000), that the mundane brings ontological security and scope for agency may well be true for many people, and in many circumstances, but for Lynne, and in a different way for Sonia Elliot, it is the ontological *loss* of self as experienced in the mundane which eventually led to self-reflection and the eventual recovery of agency. Clothing was an aspect of how Sonia recalled her husband's sustained violence and callousness towards their daughter, but one such incident led to her realising that *'something had to be done'*, and ultimately to greater agency in changing the relationship:

> *like once 'e slapped 'er [.] They sat at the table eatin', she 'ad a, I mean, why on earth I don't know, but she had this underskirt on with a bit of lace showing above her dress, an' 'e slapped 'er across the face 'cos of this underskirt [. . .] so, you know, that's when I thought 'I've got to do something about this'.*

Gardiner (2000) highlights the reflexive potential of everyday experiences for people coping with ongoing challenges or crises, something which is illustrated by Sonia's realisation and its basis in her husband's mundane, but symbolically resonant, violent reaction to the *'bit of lace'*, showing above her daughter's dress. Concentrating on the apparently mundane also enables 'such static sociological abstractions as "roles" or "structures"' (Gardiner, 2000: 208) to be sidestepped, instead bringing the focus onto the minutiae of lived social relations which can lead to new identities and behaviours. However, the potentially oppressive nature and power dimensions of gendered relationships need to inform this emphasis on agency, for it was only when Sonia feared for her daughter (a reaction echoed in interviews by other women in this project), that she felt able to leave the relationship.

A different aspect of masculinity is revealed in Sarah Davis' (43) comments about her marriage. This does not concern the refraction of the extreme through the mundane, as with Sonia, but rather Sarah's response to her male partner's (non) performance of mundane domestic tasks:

> *I'd like him to think about things that need doing rather than it always being down to me [. . .] and, um, those sort of basic [.] I'm very practical and I do nearly all the maintenance but it would be nice if he suddenly sort of came home and he said 'Oh well, I'll clear the gutters out, they need doing', or [.] I'd like him to show some interest.*

Sarah's disappointment in the relationship is given overt acknowledgement in her account of her husband's lack of interest and implied incompetence or unwillingness to undertake domestic chores. His rejection of the importance of the domestic mundane for her constitutes an inadequate heterosexual relationship, and this impacts on her feelings for him, which she details in the rest of the interview. The everyday is important, not as a set of structures or 'roles', but as practices invested with meaning: while it is dealing with gutters, or not, that is important for Sarah, how she invests particular domestic routines with a (gendered) meaning reveals the way she makes sense of their relationship.

Conclusion

In the materially grounded recollections of bodies, food, clothing, and guttering we find exemplified a diversity of mundane experiences of being heterosexual. In that hegemonic heterosexuality involves the proximity of bodies – and, indeed, their production and reproduction; the spatial segregation of the couple and eventually their children; and the materialities of shared eating, sleeping and washing arrangements – we can begin to understand it as one of everyday life's key organising principles. More than this, though, our data show individuals generating 'heterosexuality', 'courtship', 'marriage' and 'coupledom' through sets of everyday *practices*, rather than consciously following any overt social script. Nonetheless, it must be recognised that practices which potentially destabilise one or both partners' implicit conceptions of the institution of heterosexuality and its associated beliefs and practices, demand attention, whether in the form of silencing, renegotiation, or abandonment of the relationship. Extreme experiences of heterosexuality, whether disruptive or confirming of individuals' heterosexual identities and arrangements, remain nonetheless accessible largely through their recollections of the mundane and it is the nuances of such recollections that this chapter has addressed. In contrast with the focus on discourse, language and sexuality in Chapters 5 and 6, we have also been concerned here with the embedding of heterosexuality within the everyday lives of our interviewees. In the next chapter, we continue to explore how heterosexuality operates as an organising principle, but particularly in relation to the spatial aspects of heterosexuality.

8
Nothing Natural? At Home with Heterosexuality

As our analysis of data in previous chapters demonstrates, we have both drawn on and informed feminist theories of how power and agency operate within heterosexuality (see for example, Maynard and Purvis, 1995; Jackson, 1996, 1999; Richardson, 1996, 2000; Smart, 1996). Key to our critical position has been the relatively underdeveloped empirical base of many theoretical positions, particularly those linked with the emotions: intimacy, faithfulness, commitment, personal privacy and independence. We therefore have approached heterosexuality as an embodied, spatially located emotional experience and this acknowledgement is central to the arguments made in this current chapter.

First, we discuss the key theoretical frameworks and concepts that underpin this chapter's findings, drawing on literature on spatialising heterosexuality, much of which is taken from recent theorising in the field of geography. Space (and time) have also been explored from sociological and cultural perspectives, allowing new understandings of everyday life and the different spaces of community, the street and home itself (see Bennett and Watson, 2002). However, heterosexuality as a construct is rarely, if ever, critically examined in these accounts of the 'everyday', neither in relation to the institution, nor the experiences, of heterosexuality. What we do find are acknowledgements of spatialised contradictions in some of these more sociological/cultural accounts of mundane environments, for example, in work which explores the historical developments of the modern concept of home and highlights cultures of domesticity and the position of women in the family. Furthermore, forces which bear on the organisation of home and the attendant activities have been theorised in terms of contradiction, where the home has been seen as a retreat from capitalism and bureaucracy, as well as being subjected to their rationalising influences (Bennett, 2002).

But we are interested in contradictions theorised at a different level. When one of our respondents confessed to *'What I used to do behind her back... on my mother's settee'* her statement, amongst others, prompted our thinking around the question of the difficulties experienced by individuals seeking to bring together their sexual and family lives and how both constraint and agency were implicated in managing the contradictions people experienced in doing this.

In analysing these findings we therefore draw on key contemporary debates around the spatialising of heterosexualities and their associated emotional geographies. For geographers in particular, heterosexuality has been explored in relation to 'immoral landscapes' and more recently 'moral landscapes' (Hubbard, 2000), particularly in the context of the home, shopping centres and churches. In our analysis of empirical data, then, we therefore draw on this body of work to identify the ways in which heterosexuality, as an institution, has provided an implicit organising principle through which materially grounded links between self, the emotions, the 'other', body, home and the public sphere have been produced and/or negotiated over the last 80 years.

Spatialised heterosexuality

Our aim here is to examine a *plurality* of heterosexual identities in an examination of 'home' as both a resource and a constraint within the negotiation of, and expression of, class, gender and age-based heterosexualities (see Robinson et al., 2004). Furthermore, we set out to explore how heterosexuality is learned, reproduced and resisted, both within and outside the family and particularly in relation to the acquisition of (sexual) knowledge, in particular spatial and temporal contexts.

In this chapter, therefore, we examine the ways in which heterosexual spaces have been sexualised or desexualised at different times by different family members, according to gender and age differences in particular. Indeed, we assert that whilst heterosexuality organises everyday (spatialised) life, its supposed roots in the sexual are paradoxically difficult to live out. If earlier we have argued that heterosexuality is a key organising principle of social relations, and, further, is about much more than 'sex', here we put forward the view that heterosexuality is key to how the family itself is organised, an environment where both sexual knowledge and practice are subject to constraint and sequestration. Thus our data show how hard it is for some family members to be able to talk about sex, let alone engage in sexual practice in the family home.

What we present are some of the dilemmas experienced within families when contradictory aspects of the institution of heterosexuality are encountered. These point towards people's diverse experiences of heterosexuality yet reveal the pervasive influence of a kind of 'hegemonic heterosexuality' (VanEvery, 1996). Thus, the dominant, 'common-sense' model of heterosexuality within which the conjugal family and 'legitimate sexuality' are entwined, powerfully informs the way individuals think about the emotional and bodily aspects of forming a relationship with someone of the opposite sex. Nonetheless, this elision of legitimate sexuality and the family stands in awkward contradiction to the unwillingness of family members to discuss sexual matters within the family itself. What our data reveal are the feelings and emotions engendered by mismatches with dominant models of heterosexuality. The dilemmas arise for individuals when they fail to live up to heterosexual norms or transgress them in some way. As a result, their *lived* experience of heterosexuality can either empower them or constrain their agency in both an emotional and spatial sense.

The contradiction that we focus on here concerns the respectability which family life accrues through maintaining a reserve, or even coyness with respect to sexual talk and practice (see Skeggs, 1997). This, we argue, can in practice be at odds with the relegation of legitimate sexuality to the heterosexual family. It can mean that sexual knowledge cannot be easily transmitted, sexual experiences cannot readily be discussed – sometimes even between heterosexual partners – and sexual practice can be engaged in only if all family members outside the couple remain unaware of its occurrence, or at least sustain the pretence of being so.

Building on Chapter 4's historical arguments, we note that from the late nineteenth century onwards, family, heterosexuality and home have, in many respects, become elided (Foucault, 1987). If we wish to provide an empirically based account of the institution of heterosexuality, as an emotionally embodied practice, then it is the family and its locations – the spaces it occupies and the spaces it abjects – which arguably need to be investigated. Bachelard ([1958] 1994), for example, explaining the association between emotion, intimacy and the culturally specific routines of everyday life, highlights the ways in which these are learned via embodied experience of the home: 'the house we were born in has engraved within us the hierarchy of the various functions of inhabiting'. He also points out, '[t]he word habit is too worn a word to express this passionate liaison of our bodies, which do not forget, with an unforgettable house' ([1958] 1994: 15). Crang and Thrift (2000) locate this argument historically when they refer to 'the historical development of spaces for the self through the evolution of privacy in the home' (2000: 242). Bourdieu (1977) provides a more theorised account of how self, home and everyday life interconnect via his concept of 'habitus'. Of this concept, Painter (2000) says, '[I]t is the mediating link between objective social structures and individual action and refers to the embodiment in individual actors of systems of social norms, understandings and patterns of behaviour' (2000: 242). We also acknowledge that, when we refer to the family, this term can encompass different spatial and emotional aspects for individual family members, for instance in relation to the separate but connected concepts of domestic space, the home and household (Madigan and Munro, 1999). In addition, while spatiality constitutes an important dimension of our approach, we do not treat it as a static category. As Crang and Thrift argue, space should be seen *'as process* and *in process* (that is space and time combined in becoming)' (2000: 3).

As the data to follow indicate, a focus on the family allows contradictory experiences of heterosexuality to be exposed. As we know from Foucault (1987), sexuality, in the west, became carefully confined to the home during the Victorian period. With this move, he argues, the *conjugal* family became the custodian of sexuality and 'the act' became intimately linked with reproduction. The prevalence of these beliefs exemplifies the ways in which heterosexuality, as an institution, has been seen as both sexualised and naturalised. Thus, the heterosexual couple became the model, the norm (Foucault, 1987: 3); indeed it is only via heterosexual, rather than gay or lesbian relationships, that 'real' families can be reproduced (Weeks et al., 1999). Moreover, the marital relationship is also set up as the 'ideal-type' model within which to reproduce the family structure. In addition to this model being the primary means through which morally sanctioned sexuality is deployed, it is also a site in which gendered identities are both reproduced and resisted through discourses which ground them in particular constructions of the body. For example, at the simplest level, Morgan (1996) argues that the act of penetration can be seen to affirm hegemonic masculinity, while a woman's true femininity is ultimately confirmed through motherhood.

While our data indicate that sexual practice is undertaken in the car, behind the bike sheds, in hotels, fields and alleyways, these are the favoured sites for more furtive sexual encounters; the *family* continues to emerge as the context within which 'respectable' and long-standing heterosexual relationships are meant to be accommodated. However, for the expression of illegitimate heterosexuality, whether in the casual relationship or by those family members for whom it is deemed inappropriate (usually on grounds of age, but also of gender), the family is less likely to provide a comfortable environment in which to explore sexual desires and curiosities. This finding resonates with Hubbard's (2000) conceptualisation of the coding of sexual spaces, with certain spaces being deemed or coded erotic, and others as perverted or immoral. Via the lens of age and gender the subtleties and fluidities of this conceptualisation are revealed.

Thus, age, generational location and gender, we argue, are linked with family-based sexual identity, constituting the bases for internal boundaries and divisions which can impede both the articulation of sexual knowledge and experience, as well as the emotional and bodily practices recognised as 'lovemaking' or 'sex'. We are consequently faced with the contradiction that despite the social insistence that the family be the legitimate site for the expression of one's sexuality, for some of its members, the family – both as an institution and a 'location' – can in practice represent a considerable barrier to sexual expression, communication or activity.

This chapter therefore explores the emotional demands which our interviewees testify to when they attempt to live out, or live up to, hegemonic heterosexuality. Our data reveal a fundamental tension between the imperative that sex be confined to its 'proper' place within the family on the one hand and, on the other, that within the closed social space of the family and the confined material environment of the home, sexual desire, practice, talk and knowledge, can often be shared only with difficulty, if at all.

We consider two aspects of this tension. The first explores the ways in which heterosexuality is learned, reproduced and resisted both within and outside the family. We argue that sources of sexual knowledge, paradoxically, lie outside the family and look at how individuals seek to incorporate this knowledge into family-based sexual relationships. Similarly, we ask if individuals are constrained by the expectations of their families to choose partners from within their own social groupings and from within similar families. And if so, what are the implications of connection with those who are socially *different* – and perhaps a sexually exotic representation of 'risk' and 'danger'? Do they capture something to be sought after, embraced and flaunted in front of the family? Conversely, do they offer something to be 'dabbled' in, before settling into a more conventional and 'safer' routine that is acceptable to other family members?

Our second aspect concerns the impact of the material space of the home as either a resource or constraint within the negotiation and expression of gendered, age and class-based heterosexual identities. Do age and generational-based expectations impinge on the legitimacy of (hetero) sexual practice and, indeed, the acknowledgement of the existence of embodied sexuality amongst both older and younger generations? Relatedly, how is the space of the home managed to facilitate the expression of gendered emotional identities, particularly when its scale and materiality can have a constraining impact? Gurney (2000), for example, highlights the problematic nature of 'privacy' as a distinctive feature of feeling 'at home'. Taking an embodied perspective on this, he points out that: 'For most people, the home is the place where solo or mutual sexual activity most frequently takes place. Being "at home" means having the freedom to represent or practice your sexuality without fear of embarrassment, sanction or ridicule and to maintain sexual secrets, in the form of pornography, erotic literature, sex toys, or evidence of infidelity, from partners' (2000: 40). However, his research into the public boundaries of the home in relation to coital noise suggests that the emotions linked with privacy – namely embarrassment – have a real impact on 'efforts to regulate corporeal noise' (2000: 43), of which, coital noise is a principal example. Experiences such as these are evident in the data we now explore. They derive from interviews with two families, the Archers and the Browns, chosen to reflect contrasting class-based social locations.

Learning, reproducing and resisting heterosexuality in the family

If we look first at how the oldest cohorts of women found their ways into heterosexual lives, one in the aftermath of the First World War, the other prior to and during the Second World War, both acknowledge that information about what is involved in 'becoming a woman' did not involve discussion of the relationship between menstruation, sex and pregnancy within their families (see also Chapter 4). Felicity, the older of the two women, was offered and accepted the *'gooseberry bush'* explanation of sex that supposedly explained how families reproduced themselves. The discussion by 74-year-old Jean Brown in Chapter 3 shows that she thought that the initial explanation of sex that she was given by a friend was *'a funny how-to-do'*. She felt she was fortunate enough to have had *'the facts of life'* explained to her by an adult neighbour, but despite the fact that her mother didn't have *'the words'* to do the job herself, *'she was most annoyed with Nancy'*, the neighbour, for doing it for her. It is perhaps the case that her mother's annoyance was directed more at herself than the neighbour precisely because she had failed to meet Jean's need for information about 'growing up'. Clearly there is a tension between preparing young people for adulthood and the pressure to maintain reserve and respectability that can be manifested through embarrassment among both parents and children. Nonetheless, knowledge *is* passed on within families, and this can take the form of 'indirect communication' (Hendry and Watson, 2001). Sexual knowledge is thus communicated, often with the hope of deterring illicit sexual practice, yet reticence is also demonstrated. As we note in Chapter 3, Jean, for example, acknowledges stumbling upon a copy of Marie Stopes' *Married Love* in her mother's drawer and, at the age of 16, having read it from cover to cover with her future husband and then sexual partner. Fulfilling her own need for sexual knowledge, while respecting the social pressure of respectability, Jean and her boyfriend read the book in secret.

However, she also describes more direct communication taking place when she was about to shift social category from 'single' to 'married woman'. This was marked by her mother presenting her with the book when her marriage approached some years later and she recalls, with some amusement, her efforts to feign surprise and gratitude, preserving her mother's belief in her innocence. Despite having developed a relatively liberal attitude towards sex and sexual knowledge in her youth and adult life, when it came to her own children, paradoxically, Jean was unable to recall a time when she sat her own children down and told them about the facts of life. She recalls: *'I never sat down and said, "This is it", but if they asked questions . . . They always asked questions when we were eating, always'*; an openness which would have been unheard of in her mother's home. For Jean, it was sufficient that the familial context was relaxed enough for her children to feel able to approach her with any questions or problems they might have. Although her daughter, Diane, cannot recall her mother having spoken to her about *'the actual mechanics of sex'*, she did say that she always felt that her mother was very open and available to talk to. Nonetheless, direct communication about sexual knowledge had not taken place. In this way, individuals negotiated the tension between communicating an appropriate 'code' of sexual practice whilst adhering to the norms of respectability by avoiding explicit sex talk.

Similarly, 90-year-old Felicity Archer was also unable to recall any discussions about the facts of life with her daughter, Lynne, and said she found that being surrounded by nature in the countryside a useful resource. Interestingly, Lynne explained that it was her own modesty and embarrassment that prevented her from having had more open discussions with her mother. She recalls her innocent imaginings, which clearly disassociate reproduction from the mode of conception:

> *I remember I had some weird ideas that somehow this convenient little trapdoor, that was never any use for anything else, would open and the baby would miraculously come from there. Where I quite imagined it was, I don't know . . . it was just sort of a little miracle opening, and also I seem to remember that, well, babies conceived in your sleep . . . Like, you woke up and you [LAUGHS] knew nothing about it.*

Her emotional response to this recollection of her own naïvety is indicative of how she, and other respondents, use humour to be able to recall a lack of knowledge which had potentially serious implications in relation to sexual practices. Paradoxically, although a source of embarrassment in her childhood and youth, Lynne spoke frankly and openly about her youthful explorations (including exploring her sexuality with a female friend as a teenager), her current sex life and her sexual needs as a woman in her fifties. Perhaps reflective of an emotional 'blocking out' of her role in giving her own children information about sex, Lynne cannot recall any occasion in which she told her children 'the facts of life'. However, her son, Paul (28), vividly recalls a conversation about this while driving to school one morning when he and his sister were approximately nine and six and a half years old: *'I remember a particular point on the journey just on this roundabout where she told us [.] the actual mechanics of it . . . it was a bit of a bolt out of the blue.'* In contrast to Jean Brown's family who felt comfortable having such discussions around the kitchen table, communication between Lynne and her children was achieved but in such a way as to avoid face-to-face contact or an extended discussion, notably outside the family home. Reserve was then maintained. In contrast to Lynne's own memories of these issues, Paul observes that:

> *she was quite keen for us to sort of know these things, there was no kind of [.] she didn't make us think [.] she didn't make us feel like it was [.] dirty thinking about it, or she didn't make us feel awkward or anything like that . . . I seem, I remembered at the time, you know, that this is quite a [.] decent way to find out really, felt like it was the right sort of time to, age, to find out . . .*

It is precisely these disclosures, avoidances and omissions which we seek to make sense of here. Family, it seems, both is and is *not* perceived and experienced as some kind of container for legitimate sexual expression. If explicit 'knowledge', directly communicated, was unforthcoming in these two families, what, then, can be said of the family members' relationships with potential sexual/marital partners in the external social environment?

While Felicity went to a single-sex boarding school where young girls would have *'crushes on the form mistress and . . . and teachers'* and older peers, Jean spent her school days at a mixed comprehensive where she has vivid memories of having been kissed behind the bike sheds. In the former case, it is noteworthy that in the absence of boys, the gendered hierarchy implicit within heterosexual desire is replaced by an age-based hierarchy, schoolgirls orienting themselves towards older peers and female teachers. Despite their different social experiences and levels of sexual knowledge, both women chose male life partners who were known to their families. Jean explained that although her friends were seeing servicemen from *'all over everywhere'*, her first *'proper boyfriend'* was a young man she had known *'all my life'*. Anticipating an objection to the fact that he was four years her senior, the argument she presented to her parents was: *' "well, at least you know him, you know his family", and I said, "Would you rather I went off to Bolton Palais?", well, there were no GIs then, but I mean, there were all sorts, and, so, they sort of accepted him right away really.'* Likewise, Felicity reported that knowing of her future husband's family was also important. Clearly, 'knowing' of their part-ners through shared social networks was significant in securing parental approval for both women, and the suggestion is that these shared social networks were seen as a safe extension of the family, which overrode any concerns about an inappropriate age difference in Jean's case. This appeared to be no less of an issue when it came to the evaluation of their daughters' partners. Thus, while *differences* of gender are seen as integral to hegemonic heterosexuality, *similarity* of class or social background underpins what is seen as the purely emotional experience of 'falling in love'. As Bourdieu says of love: 'The illusion of mutual election or predes-tination arises from ignorance of the *social conditions* for the harmony of aesthetic tastes or ethical leanings' (1977: 82, emphasis added). And the *social conditions* to which he refers are what he calls 'class homogamy' (1977: 82). Again, then, heterosexuality emerges as the organising prin-ciple through which social differences are sustained, whether based on class, occupation, or indeed, ethnicity. This perspective contrasts with the notion of marriage as simply a 'container' for 'natural' sexual desires and practices, discussed in Chapter 7.

While their respective daughters, Lynne and Diane, eventually settled down and had children with 'safe' men whose families were known to their own, both women had also dated men from outside their own social circles. For both women, these experiences represented difference, excitement and, as we shall see, emotional risk. In Diane's case, her first serious boyfriend was from a different religious denomination to her own and their eventual marriage in his church, rather than hers, was a source of tension within her family. The fact that the relationship was socially recognised *outside* a context that was familiar to and accepted by Diane's family was a source of considerable tension, which Jean struggled to keep from her daughter. Despite the initial attraction between the couple, the marriage did not last and ended with his adultery. Meanwhile, Lynne's middle-class status helped her to move away to study for a degree. During this period her social world was opened up and she became involved with young men during trips to Europe, in addition to a brief engagement that ended, unceremoniously, with her being *'dumped'* by letter. While she fondly recalls that a number of her former boyfriends were *'charmers'*, what Lynne eventually settled for was someone more ordinary, *'familiar'*, less risqué or dangerous, a young man more like her father, who she describes as *'more obviously husband material than boyfriend material'*. Having *'fallen in love'* or *'been infatuated'* with a number of boys, by the time she met the man who was to become her husband, Lynne says that: *'I made some conscious or unconscious decision, "OK, he may not be as glamorous as whatever, as outgoing, but this is more the marrying kind. This is more the kind I would, if I was being sensible, would marry".'* In its hegemonic, marital form then, heterosexuality transcends sexual 'infatuation' and instead embraces the characteristics which, whilst powerfully felt, are difficult to articulate. Yet Lynne, nonetheless, recognises 'husband material' when she encounters it.

Unsurprisingly, Lynne also spoke about her mother's approval of what she saw as constituting a good *'social match'*:

> *The families are friendly, and if mum could have hand-picked someone for me that she would approve of, it would have certainly been Simon* [husband] *[GIGGLE] . . . mum's a snob and she likes the idea of a big house, you know, and (we've) had a tennis court that, she remembers she used to play in tennis parties here, and, you know, the right social status and somebody like that.*

Again, Lynne's emotional response to the memory of her mother's approval which underpinned her own choice of a heterosexual partner at the time, is mediated through laughter, allowing her to recall this family pressure in an innocuous way.

Despite her apparent moral conservatism, Felicity's social concerns were no less evident with her grandson, Paul. Like his mother before him, Paul's move from his rural home to a large city facilitated his 'sexual awakening' while he was at university. Not only does the city provide greater anonymity for one's sexual explorations but, as Hubbard (2000) points out, the existence of different 'standards of personal and sexual morality' amongst the population of the inner-city contrasts with those of 'more stable and settled residents' (2000: 201) beyond, permitting increased sexual experimentation. Nonetheless, Paul explained his surprise when his *grandmother* had encouraged him to 'play the field' when he thought she would have a ' *"one person for life" kind of attitude'*. He went on to explain his understanding of the situation:

Yeah, it was strange that in a way, unless [.] she kind of thought the people I was seeing at university were a bit unsuitable, but she wanted [. . .] um, I think she was always tied into the fact that she was keen for me to, and still is, keen for me to take over the farm, think she wanted [.] ideally, for me to marry a local lass who'd be [.] know the farming world, know the area, the sort of person who'd want to [.] do the farm with me basically.

Although somewhat amused by his grandmother's attitude – as Paul said *'there was a respectable, religious, elderly woman who was almost advocating promiscuity'* – there is also a generational-based contradiction in that what she was suggesting was in conflict with how *he* believed a relationship should proceed:

she wasn't talking one night stands or anything like that I don't think, but [.] yeah, she was sort of saying 'Oh don't get too serious with the first girl you meet, don't get too involved' . . . I found that a bit discouraging in a way 'cos I was [.] hoping for the opposite of what she was hoping for really.

Clearly, Paul is disappointed by the absence of emotional support from his grandmother. Again, social status and financial and property considerations appear to override moral or emotional considerations for Felicity, a standpoint which again reveals the role of heterosexuality as an organising principle which can shore up other kinds of social hierarchies. The empirical evidence presented here reveals the diversity of strategies through which individuals negotiate the tension between the elision of legitimate heterosexuality, with home and family, and the demands of respectability which require reserve around sexual matters.

Spaces of heterosexuality

Following our exploration of the relationship between the containing space of the family and the acquisition of heterosexual knowledge and experience, we now consider the ways in which home, as the site of legitimate heterosexuality, is nonetheless riven by internal contradictions. That is to say, although sexual activity is a prescribed aspect of coupledom, it is also a practice which must remain hidden from other family members. These are often relatives whose age and generational location shape and are shaped by notions implicit within hegemonic heterosexuality. Yet, as we see in the data which follow, slippage can occur between the fixed relationships which connect generations ('I remain daughter to my parents, mother to my children and grandmother to their children') and the *process* of ageing. For Jean, for example, the location of Marie Stopes' *Married Love*, relatively hidden in her mother's drawer, then later placed in her hands, marked an age-based sexual transition which nonetheless left her still in the role of daughter vis-à-vis her mother.

Our data therefore illustrate that the permanence of generational identities can be in tension with shifting age-based sexual identities. For example, the question of whether or not to permit the partners of their grown-up children to stay overnight in the family home is one which continues to stump parents and children alike. So, what did our participants have to say on the matter? As the data which we explored in Chapter 3 indicate, despite evidence of cross-generational continuities, it remains an aspect of family-based heterosexuality that can confront individuals with contradictions. For example, while Jean's first sexual encounter occurred in a field in 1944, the absence of siblings meant that she and her future husband were in fact able to use their family homes as a resource when their parents were out. She told us that she felt comfortable about having sex outside of marriage, that she enjoyed having sex in the family home, and further, prioritised pleasure over any guilty feelings she might be expected to have felt. So, as Miller (2002) argues, phenomenological experience of geographical spaces is always emotional, and based on levels of intimacy or anonymity which we share with the others that surround us (or not, in the case of Jean's absent parents).

It was because of their own experiences that Jean and her husband were then open-minded in relation to their own children's emerging sexuality. Significantly, however, their decisions did not come easily. She recalls being asked by her teenage daughter if she and her boyfriend could spend a weekend in Wales: '... *Well Harry looked at me and I said, "How old were we when we went away?", and he said, "Aye, I know, that's what bothers me" [LAUGHS]'*. Her laughter here perhaps reveals her current appreciation of the tensions inherent in such decision-making at the time. Furthermore, whilst Jean and Harry are fully aware of what their daughter and her boyfriend would almost certainly get up to while they were away, Diane pointed out that: ' *"If we wanted to", she said, ... "you leave us in here, we're in ( ), we don't have to go to Wales, mum, do we?".'* Thus their daughter reminds them that the home is a sexual resource, in much the same way it had been to them in their youth.

Although Diane recalls her determination to explore her emerging sexual identity in the family home, she did experience ambivalent feelings: *'I just felt it were my room and I could do what I wanted in it really ... But didn't dare be upstairs in case she came back.'* Because of the fear of getting caught in her bedroom, Diane and her partner settled on her parents' sofa for her first sexual encounter. While not experiencing any guilt at the time, on reflection she says: *'my poor mother, you know, what I used to do behind her back ... on my mother's settee, which is really not very nice is it?'* As well as revealing a capacity for a changed emotional response in relation to past events, this also shows the *appearance* of conformity to hegemonic heterosexuality was therefore required if appropriate generationally located identities were to be adhered to. That sex out of place and time carried a potentially disruptive power is evident and this can be revealed in its subversive potential as a deliberate act of resistance. For example, while Diane had misgivings about her mother's settee as a site of sexual activity, these did not extend towards her first husband's oppressively Catholic mother. Indeed, she admits to having had sexual intercourse in this woman's house while she was out playing the organ at church, watched by images of the Virgin Mary and Sacred Heart and thinking: ' *"we'll show you" '*.

Apparently more open with her own children, Diane describes incidents involving her 23-year-old son (whom we were unable to interview):

Me and Jonathan used to laugh when [his girlfriend] had gone home 'cos I'd say 'Are you sure you're doing it right 'cos she screams an awful lot?' You know and you can be so open with him really. I mean once they discovered it, God they were in the shower all morning, I used to go out 'cos I were embarrassed in my own house, you know, they were so open.

Although open-minded in principle about the expression of her son's sexuality, in reality, the violation of her aural privacy through these non-silent performances (Gurney, 2000) precipitates her emotional response: embarrassment and discomfort. However, she accepts her son's behaviour, preferring him to feel comfortable enough to be open about his relationships in the family home.

The Archers have adhered to less liberal sexual attitudes. Felicity was a virgin when she and her husband married; for the situation to have been otherwise would have been *'wicked... from our parent's point of view'*. She drew upon these old-fashioned values, to an extent, in raising her own children, admitting that there was little she could do to alter their behaviour while away at college/university, but recalls reading *'the riot act'* when her son told her not to bother making up two beds when he brought a girlfriend home to stay: *' "under our roof, you do what we do" '*. In the meantime, Lynne admits to having engaged in some heavy petting in her parents' living room and in the caravan that was parked on their drive. As with Diane, when asked if she felt any sense of guilt, she expressed defiance: *'I don't know, no almost a little bit "Phworr!' Right under my parents' noses" if I did at all. There was a little bit of sort of, rebellion.'*

Despite these acts of resistance as a daughter, when Lynne became a mother, she and her very religious husband took a cautious approach in adjusting to their son's emerging sexuality. She describes how she initially made up separate rooms for Paul and his live-in partner: *'I knew they were living together, it was just... well, "This is my home", and, you know, but then gradually.'* Their acceptance of the situation was marked by an eventual move towards twin beds in the same room. In many ways, the move from separate to shared rooms indicates Lynne's acceptance of Paul's transition from son to fellow adult. This transition is, however, relational. That is, Paul and his partner themselves remained uncomfortable about flaunting the reality and so developed a strategy which they used to conceal their sleeping arrangements once permitted to share a room. While it appeared to be a rational strategy at the time, he now reflects on it with amusement: *'We used to [LAUGHS]... [.] pluck a few of Sally's hairs from my pillow and sprinkle them on the (camp bed) and ruffle*

the sheets up a little bit.' This relatively transparent family-based subter-
fuge is certainly very different to the clandestine meetings he described
with previous girlfriends down country lanes in the back of his mother's
car. Again, sex in the home precipitates the emotions of guilt and embarrassment, the fear of being caught and exposed whilst flouting the rules
of respectability, while locations beyond the home facilitate guilt-free
exploration. Home – and family – as sites of hegemonic heterosexuality
thus operate to frame and constrain sexual and emotional connections
between individuals, and shape their experiences of 'legitimate' and 'illegitimate' heterosexual relationships. It is also interesting to note that
in coming to terms with her children's developing sexuality, Lynne's
reasoning is specifically gendered. She acknowledges that the situation
might have been different had her daughter, Deborah, been the first one
to bring a partner home. She observes that: *'If Deborah had been the first
one, I certainly wouldn't have felt anywhere near comfortable as soon as I
had. The fact that Paul was a boy definitely made a difference there.'* In this
way then, heterosexuality provides the context within which not only
class, but gender hierarchies, are held in place.

The data presented so far provide an insight into some of the contradictions that interviewees encountered within the context of cross-
generational heterosexual family life, and the resulting accommodations
they achieved. In arguing that the institution of heterosexuality both
shapes and is shaped by the familial context, the question of how home
and family frame the living out of oppositional gendered identities needs
to be considered in more detail.

The material space of the home is frequently thought of as being
divided into gendered spaces (Madigan and Munro, 1999), with the
kitchen characterised as the woman's domain and the garden, garage
or workshop as the man's, environments into which each might
retreat, particularly in times of emotional tension. Within these spaces,
emotions themselves can be gendered and indeed emotional labour can
be divided between women and men (see for example, Seidler, 1989;
Delphy and Leonard, 1992; Rutherford, 1992; Duncombe and Marsden,
1993; Jackson, 1996, 1999; Petersen, 1998; Bernard, 2002; Whitehead,
2002). Many of these studies identify a more limited emotional articu-
lacy among men, when compared with women, and in exploring more
critical responses to this, we decided to ask our interviewees how they
and their partners managed difficult situations when they arose and
whether they used home space to sustain particular, gendered 'performances' of heterosexuality.

Both women of the oldest cohort stressed the importance of maintaining separate interests and identities within their relationships. Reflecting the notion of heterosexuality as an institution constituted through difference (Richardson, 1996), Felicity said that the key to maintaining a well-balanced relationship was the pursuit of separate, as well as shared, interests; as she put it: *'not being in each other's pockets all the time'*. However, for some women, gendered difference was understood more in terms of independence than complementarity. For example, Jean said that maintaining her own independence had proved crucial in her efforts to cope following her husband's death fifteen years ago: *'I had a life, apart from him, you know.'* The preservation of independent identities was also important for the youngest generation with Paul, Felicity's grandson, explaining how he and his partner insisted on spending time apart and having separate holidays which, he admitted, some of his friends found odd. Through the timing of movement between domestic and public space, independent *gendered* identities were sustained.

When it came to *sharing* domestic space, the older generations appeared to be participating in a far more structured process of setting up home together. Paul, however, appeared to view the period in which he and his partner first moved in together as a project of discovery, one which offered choice outside specific guidelines. For many young people, this is an exciting time which represents the forging of a shared identity as 'a couple' and has the novelty value of choosing furniture and décor, and the luxury of sexual togetherness without prying eyes, flapping ears and knowing looks, a clear indicator of the legitimacy of their heterosexual status.

Home is, of course, a space which is not exclusively occupied by couples. Indeed, although what is safe and familiar within the home and extended social networks can constitute a resource during difficult times, it can also be oppressive, particularly if still living with parents in a close-knit community. This is illustrated by Diane's feelings after her separation from her first husband after he had left her for another woman. She returned to her parents' home for some time but found this stifling. Consequently, she says: *'I escaped, I just went, I packed my job in'* and went to the South coast on a working holiday. There, she says, *'I could just be whoever I wanted to be, you know I didn't have to talk about Ian* [husband] *if I didn't want to or I don't know, I could just recover I think, lick my wounds really 'cos I knew I wasn't going to bump into either of them.'*

The physical space afforded by being away from home was also used by Lynne during her emotional recovery after the disappointment of her broken engagement. Instead of telling her parents about what had happened, she says that she *'brazened it out for ages'*. Being away enabled her to avoid answering *'awkward questions, I just kept up the pretence for a while, 'cos I was too ashamed to admit that I'd, I'd made a mistake. It was me that made the mistake.'* Her own experiences allowed her to realise the importance of physical and emotional distance for her own children while they were studying and/or living away from home. She observes that:

> *emotionally I was living my life, and just like when my own children were away at university, you were only told the things you want to be told, that they want to tell you and when they want to tell you it, and they're living their own lives when they're away from home.*

For Diane's daughter, Sam, things were sadly more complex. While at home, her 'room' was a place in which she isolated herself from the rest of her family. In addition it was a resource in which – unbeknown to her family – she repeatedly self-harmed. If the heterosexual life is to be lived out within the home and family, its boundedness emerges as key to its legitimacy. Within this sphere, family practices are lived out in ways which can preclude personal privacy – other than as a cover for illegitimate forms. Madigan and Munro, for example, cite an interviewee in their study of space, gender and privacy, who said: *'There isn't anything private in the house really, I mean we're pretty open with one another, we don't really have a private life as such, I don't think. I hope not'* (1999, 65–6).

Conclusion

The data examined in this chapter highlight the complexity of hetero-sexuality as an emotional, embodied and spatially located experience. On the one hand, heterosexuality is conventionally rooted within the moral landscape of family and home, wherein it becomes sanctioned and is thus given the guise of 'respectability'. On the other, both home-based cultural transmission of what and how heterosexuality is and 'ought' to be, along with its practical expression involves an awkward-ness felt by many people when it comes to sharing their knowledge of such matters with other family members, particularly from different generations. The living out of these contradictions highlighted by our data illustrate that heterosexual beliefs and practices differ markedly from what we reveal to family members outside the heterosexual couple, particularly those from different generations to our own. This strongly suggests that it is *via* contradictions such as these that the gendered institution of heterosexuality reproduces itself. As we can see, heterosexuality intersects powerfully with other social categorisations such as those based on class, and therefore respectability, and those based on gender, and the living out of feminine and masculine identities.

Thus, for example, we have Felicity, married for almost 50 years and born and raised in a context in which for women to have sex before marriage was *'wicked'*, who complains that *'there's no . . . morals'* these days, yet who encourages her grandson into the traditional male practice of 'playing the field'. By contrast, Jean acknowledges these contradictions and struggles to reconcile her own youthful sexual curiosity with her wish for what she sees as best for her own children. Indeed, through these case studies we are able to examine the tensions that exist between heterosexualised identities and those which are rooted in our roles as parents, grandparents, children or grandchildren. Within family-based heterosexuality, we are expected to occupy these various roles at different stages during the life-course. Because these roles are simultaneously complementary and conflicting, the successful management of the tensions that are created by their existence crucially impinges on our ability to perform each role successfully. Thus, for example, as far as Sam is concerned, she felt that her mother, Diane, failed to live out her maternal role and to notice her mental health problems because she was *'so occupied by being miserable and bad tempered'* as a result of the deteriorating relationship with her children's father.

Within the confined geography of 'home' and the potentially excluding social space of the family (and in the context of different emotional responses to these spaces, for example on a gendered basis), individual relationships can be profoundly influenced by a hegemonic model of heterosexuality. For some it represents an unachievable yardstick, for others an institution to resist or subvert. As our data indicate, as lived emotional and embodied experience, the institution of heterosexuality needs to be recognised as both constraining and as the outcome of individual agency and creativity, not only in the twenty-first century, but also during the earlier part of the twentieth century. In this way, the spatial articulation of how 'moral' heterosexualities are played out, and naturalised in different everyday settings (Hubbard, 2000), can be both recognised and explored.

9
Different Heterosexualities: Different Histories

Throughout this book we have explored the pervasiveness of heterosexuality as one of everyday life's taken-for-granted underpinning principles. This has involved examining what might account for its stability, for example, the family and its location as the legitimate site for the expression of sexuality, its centrality to the reproduction of hegemonic heterosexuality and the silences and omissions which characterise everyday – often mundane – lived experiences. We now shift our focus towards the *mutability* of heterosexuality and those social, structural and historical factors which have been argued to contribute to perceived changes in how heterosexuality has been negotiated, rejected, reproduced and lived out, particularly in the post-Second World War period. Indeed, if we concern ourselves with the 'making' of heterosexual relationships, as was the focus of our empirical study, what emerges from our data is an image of *heterosexualities* as neither imposed by one generation upon the next, nor as a form of top-down patriarchal control. Further, what we argue is that the institution of heterosexuality be seen as a residual discourse, a set of ideas and practices, which emerge by virtue of the silencing or exclusion of aspects of everyday experience which are either ambiguous or ill-fitting in terms of women's and men's implicit conceptions of themselves and their relationships as 'heterosexual', a naturalised *social*, rather than sexual identity.

Rather than advocating a monolithic view of heterosexuality, we have consistently engaged with a pluralistic notion of *heterosexualities*, since we see hegemonic heterosexuality as both historically and culturally located and, therefore, subject to change. Within this chapter, we take up and develop the historical perspectives introduced in Chapter 4, exploring in more detail the bodily and emotional nature of shifting heterosexualities across the last century and those factors believed to have contributed to their metamorphoses. Relatedly, we also address the question of what aspects of everyday heterosexual life might have been silenced or sequestered at different points in time in order for the ascendancy of the institution to be sustained.

This chapter therefore completes this book's project by examining heterosexuality's mutability as a category, so developing Chapter 6's argument that a powerful mechanism for revealing the nature of heterosexuality is an examination of that which is excluded from it. In suggesting that historical comparison can reveal the contingent nature of that which is excluded, it examines the body-focused nature of 'illegitimate' sexuality before the 1960s liberalisation of sexual mores, comparing it with the subsequent emphasis on the quality of emotional experience. In addition, it suggests that hegemonic heterosexuality was held in place more by external, community-based sources of power during the earlier period, internal self-monitoring becoming a more powerful source of control during the later period. We begin by revisiting our earlier discussion of changing historical eras (see Chapter 4). If we look back to the nineteenth century, we see particular social and historical moments which were to impinge crucially upon the living out of heterosexuality – as both a social *and* sexual construct – for cohorts to come. For example, writing about different forms of social organisation and associated forms of marriage, Engels identifies industrialisation and the intensification of production outside the home as representing the introduction of wage slavery, giving the man greater control over the instruments of labour, including the wife, thus unsettling the socioeconomic equilibrium that had marked pre-civilised society. 'Civilisation' and the emergent bourgeoisie therefore became associated with what he described as 'class-based monogamy, supplemented by adultery and prostitution' (Engels, 1986). But open sexual expression was potentially undermining of the newly emergent and insecure Victorian bourgeoisie and sex was relocated within the respectable confines of the (bourgeois) family. As Foucault observes: '(t)he conjugal family took custody of it and absorbed it into the serious function of reproduction' (1987: 3). Nonetheless, Weeks (1989) reminds us of the paradox of this age 'when sex was publicly, indeed ostentatiously denied, only to return, repressed, to flourish in the fertile undergrowth' (1989: 19). However, Foucault (1987) suggests that what we have commonly come to identify as the 'repression' of sex during the Victorian period was, in fact, a mechanism of social regulation, by which the bourgeoisie were able to exert disciplinary power over the working classes, ensuring that pleasurable pursuits did not interfere with the intensive work imperative (1987: 6). Indeed, Walkowitz (1980) documents how the relative fluidity of prostitution among urban poor women, who would move in and out of prostitution as financial circumstances dictated, was undermined by the Contagious Diseases Acts. These required the registration of prostitutes and an annual physical examination, forcing them to 'accept their status as public women by destroying their private identity' (Walkowitz, 1980: 73), often foreclosing the possibility of achieving 'respectable' status after their 'fall', an option which had previously been available.

The social and sexual contours of hegemonic heterosexuality underwent significant change in the 1960s with the uncoupling of sex from marriage and state-sanctioned relaxation of sexual mores (Hawkes, 1996: 106–12). While these changes marked the advent of a distinctively different way of constructing heterosexuality, Hawkes (1996) reminds us that there is the danger of oversimplification with the assumption that, in qualitative terms, 'different' equalled 'better'. Indeed, work undertaken in the 1960s by Betty Friedan, in the US, and Hannah Gavron, in the UK, detailed the lives of women who were 'captive wives and housebound mothers' (Gavron, 1966, cited in Hawkes, 1996: 110). According to Hawkes (1996), this 'captivity' manifested itself in the disproportionate numbers of women suffering from depression, tranquillizer addiction and alcohol dependency. Jeffreys suggests that rather than posing a threat to patriarchal marriage, the sexual revolution actually strengthened the institution and she observes that 'it was not intended to liberate [women] from anything other than their common sense and instinct for self-protection' (1993: 53). Clearly, particular embodied realities and emotional subjectivities have been emphasised as potentially problematic during different historical eras, and have, therefore, been sequestered and, to some degree, silenced as less positive by-products of what have otherwise been heralded as socio-historical 'golden ages'. As we continue to explore our empirical data, what we find is a corresponding shift in emphasis from the need to contain 'unruly bodies' and potentially disruptive sexuality in the first half of the last century, towards an increasing concern with the management of 'unruly emotions' from the 1960s onward, a transition which became apparent in data presented in Chapter 4.

Emotions, bodies, selves

A separation of bodily life from emotional subjectivity can be seen as a false dichotomy since the body and emotions are inextricably linked, and

Lupton (1998) observes that physical manifestations of an unbalanced emotional state are not a modern concern, but can be dated back to the early modern period. During this time, there was little social pressure for self-restraint and emotional imbalances were believed to lead to illness or certain personality traits, hence the use of leeches, for example, to balance 'humoral' fluids. Lupton notes that it was from the sixteenth century onwards that there came increasing pressure to regulate and civilise the body. She observes that: 'there emerged a conflation of bodily discipline with the disciplined self: without disciplining the body, the self would become unruly' (1998: 75). The Enlightenment heralded a period in which emotions were seen as irrational and the enemy of reason, while the nineteenth century witnessed the horror of the Victorian bourgeoisie when presented with the bodies of the working classes, the sick and the 'fallen' whose boundaries were not well contained (Walkowitz, 1980). Although 'Body McCarthyism' (Lupton, 1998: 86) continues to persist, particularly following the advent of HIV/AIDS and the consequent preoccupation with bodily fluids and potential damage to our immune systems, the situation regarding our emotional selves is rather more complex. To be 'in touch' with one's emotions is seen to be important, but perhaps even more crucial is the ability to *manage* our emotions effectively, preventing them from becoming troublesome in our everyday lives. Therapeutic models which adopt a 'confessional' approach to the disclosure and acknowledgement of emotions have become popularised, the focus being to ensure that once issues are addressed, they are appropriately managed, 'tied off' and made 'safe'. Women interviewed for our study who grew up during the 1960s and 1970s, were particularly predisposed towards a need to 'confess' stories of their youth, their courtships, their attempts – and failures – at marriage and parenthood, their expectations and their disappointments. A process of public self-reflexivity has therefore begun in earnest, one which had apparently been absent among members of older cohorts.

This volume has provided repeated examples of how people have reflected upon and negotiated the impact of social changes within their own lives at different points across the twentieth century. In so doing, it not only reveals a shift in emphasis as people of different age-cohorts construct their stories, but also a marked difference in the degree to which individuals engage reflexively during the interview. For our researcher, Angela, the challenge was both to raise a level of conscious reflection upon the organising principles of heterosexuality that extend beyond the bedroom, and to do so in a way which did not precipitate concerns about being assessed against a normative, hegemonic heterosexuality. While the older generation were the most reticent in engaging reflexively around such issues, those whose youth had taken place during the 1960s and 1970s were most vocal in their reflections upon their success, and failures, their expectations and disappointments.

The question we are left with as feminist researchers is whether it remains possible to speak of 'hegemonic heterosexuality' when confronted not only with modernity's close bonds within the nuclear family and the role which this played in the regulation of sexual behaviour and reinforcement of gendered roles, but also post-modern opportunities for increased equality, emotional fulfilment, intimacy and individualism. In the following section, we present our participants' reflections upon their experiences of learning about and adapting to differing models of heterosexuality which for them were important at different historical junctures, overlapping and transforming, embracing and sequestering some aspects and rejecting others. What we are ultimately left with is a vision of multiple, coexisting heterosexualities under the umbrella of an apparently monolithic 'institution'.

The data we now present have therefore been organised according to the perceived historical shifts which have taken place in relation to the family and its centrality as an organising principle in relation to heterosexuality. As Morgan (1991) observes, the twentieth century has seen an ideological shift in the story of family and marriage – from 'institution' to that of 'relationship'. What we therefore document is a shift away from 'institutional', familial or communal expectations vis-à-vis the management of heterosexual behaviour within/outside the family, to expectations about the management and expression of emotion and the prevalence of what Jamieson (1998) describes as 'disclosing intimacy', between partners since the 1960s.

Sequestering women's bodies, stigmatising 'unacceptable' sexuality

There was a consensus among interviewees who grew up in the early part of the twentieth century about maintaining distinctions between in/appropriate sexualities and public and private life which had become evident during the previous century. Among some, the life of the body was veiled within their accounts, while for others, the problematic nature of the body provided a focus for talk, revealing things which had – in some cases – been silenced for many years. By contrast, expectations of their relationships – particularly their emotional aspects – and the creation of empathic understanding were issues which emerged from women who courted much later, from the 1960s onward. Older women, however, were more likely to dismiss such notions, indicating that theirs was an age-cohort which simply 'got on with it'. From within these narratives, we are therefore led to ask: at what point did women begin to have expectations of emotional intimacy within their relationships, why and with what effect?

Data presented throughout this volume highlight the extent to which children and young people's acquisition of heterosexual knowledge was mystified. Older women described being *'green'* in relation to knowledge of periods and where babies came from, seeking information from friends, neighbours and work colleagues when their mothers failed to equip them with such information. Thus, we have an 85-year-old woman who did not know what sanitary products were for until she went to work in a surgical appliance factory, and a 74-year-old woman who had been told by friends that babies *'popped out of a brown line down your stomach'*. Belying the notion of the family as the appropriate source of knowledge about sexuality, the latter turned to an older neighbour for guidance since her own mother seemed not to *'have the words'* to offer a more satisfactory explanation. Any information that was forthcoming also appeared to be shrouded in mystery and accompanied by unexplained, calamitous warnings. For example, the grave warning that one must *'stay away from boys'* following the onset of puberty, the caution to avoid touching meat while menstruating (lest you made it *'go off'*), or the contradiction that you mustn't wash your hair while menstruating, but at the same time needing to keep oneself *'clean'*.

Such ignorance was not, however, specific to girl and boyhood. A middle-class participant described her wedding night, when she made her sexual debut, and the Dutch courage both partners required, she slipping up to bed before he did to avoid the embarrassment of getting undressed in front of one another. She recalls how her husband had given her a book, *The Red Light: Intimate Hygiene for Men and Women*, to help prepare her for her 'wifely duties'. Stella Gold (78) had kept a copy of this book (lest her daughters ever asked any questions, *'which they never did'*). Its principal concern was with instructing young men and women about intimate personal hygiene, the avoidance of sexually transmitted infections, the morality of liaisons within and outside marriage and 'the technique of lovemaking'. The preoccupation with the potentially 'polluting' nature of women's bodies is highlighted when the author, Rennie MacAndrew, acknowledges having been asked if *'gonorrhoea can be caused through having intercourse with a healthy woman during menstruation'.* This question, combined with what older women reveal of their 'education' regarding their changing bodies, reflects the tendency for young people at this time to be given the implicit message that the female body – at the onset of puberty – became dangerous, dirty and so polluting.

As is discussed in Chapter 7, even for women born in the 1950s and 1960s, there is the sense that what sets them apart from boys and younger girls was something to be hidden from other family members. Hence, bras and pants which had been hung up to dry on the clothes horse had to be removed before father came home to spare his embarrassment, and the sanitary products, purchased for mother, were hidden from brothers in brown paper bags. Interestingly, one woman describes how soiled sanitary towels would be wrapped in newspaper and burnt on the open fire, but *'woe betide you if you ever did it [.] when your dad was 'ome from sea!'* Laws (1990), in her work on menstruation, documents menstrual taboos and restrictions which persisted up until the 1980s and were reinforced by 'science'. Moreover, where once it was perceived that there was something magic or evil about menstrual blood, society has now become fixated by chemical imbalances wrought in women's bodies by their menstrual cycle, leading to such phenomena as 'premenstrual tension' and lack of emotional control which is said to precipitate at best clumsiness and, in extreme cases, murder.

The sequestering of aspects of women's bodies and their 'difference' are not exclusively working-class phenomena. As described in Chapter 6, a middle-class interviewee described a *faux pas* when, aged 11, she unwittingly recounted a story about tampons falling out of someone's bag, which led to her father's *'purple-faced'* exit from the dining table before the end of the meal. Here, the young female child fails to observe what Laws (1990) describes as the etiquette of silence which has been constructed around the bodily event of menstruation. Similarly, the ensuing talk – from her mother – about what should/not be discussed at the dining table reinforces the mother being cast – like Victorian woman before her – in the role of regulator of her family's sexuality, protecting fathers and sons from both their own 'baser instincts' and the realities of their daughters'/sisters' emerging sexuality.

Chapter 6 discusses how this feminised work of bodily regulation was not restricted to the household, but extended to the maintenance of the family's good name in the wider community. So, for example, Marion

Ogden's mother publicly disowned the daughter who brought shame on her family by becoming pregnant by a married man. Humphries' (1988) study of sexuality between 1900 and 1950 is littered with stories of women who became pregnant outside marriage, often while working away in domestic service; many at the hands of sons of their employers. When this kind of occurrence was discussed by older middle-class focus group participants, one woman suggested that the social and economic background of a young woman might affect her ability – or willingness – to reject advances of this nature. She recalls an elderly aunt who had worked for the nobility:

She had (approaches) made to her by the son of the house, she was one who could cope with it you see. And the father was as bad, and she dropped the soup in his lap when she was serving and he was trying to fondle her. She didn't lose her job either, she was a good worker. It went on, but you see, if you get someone who hasn't that, she was a bit older by that time, a younger person, say a 15, 16 year old, from a deprived background would be easily flattered that . . . 'Oh I've got someone that's going to help me and I'm not going to have all the misery of ( )', you know, you dream, don't you when you're (in your teens)?

An older participant in another focus group described how one of her WAAF colleagues became pregnant during the war. The social implications were harsh, even for 'nice' girls:

Well, if you became pregnant, well, then you were in a heck of a mess, weren't you? And if he wouldn't marry the girl, it was really tragic. We had one girl in the WAAF, (that's all) that I knew, and she was a very, very nice girl, she was lovely girl. And she got on with this (guy) that was supposed to be divorced, and he invited her to his home for the weekend to meet his family and then when his parents were out, he persuaded her to have sex with, and it was the first time she'd ever been with anybody, didn't want to, but then she gave in and she became pregnant. And she had to go into a mother and baby home to have this baby, and then have it adopted, and she was, she came from a very good home. Her mother was a widow, one of her brothers was a bank manager and another was something else. And I've often wondered how she went on. She was a lovely girl but, you see, she brought shame on her family.

This was not, however, the experience of all our participants. While her sister was ostracised by her mother, Marion's Ogden's good friend of 30 years or so, Bernice Parr (78), describes her own 'fall from grace' when she became pregnant, aged 17, during the war. As we note in Chapter 4, although she acknowledges that some people at that time were of the view that: ' *"Oh, she's one of them", you all got a bad name, whether it was the first time or whether you was a woman of the streets, you were all classed the same'*, she says that her own parents *were* supportive. There was never a consideration that the child should be adopted and her mother looked after the child while Bernice worked to support them. Interestingly, Bernice does not eulogise the past in the way that some of our older participants did. Instead, she reminds us how youthful experiences were mediated by external, historical factors and her narrative poignantly illustrates the weaving of historical and biographical time. She reflects upon falling in love during wartime:

> *Bernice:* ... *I thought he* [the father of her child] *was wonderful, you know.*
> *AM: Why? What was it about him?*
> *Bernice: I don't know, I can't, it's something you can't explain really, it's just a feeling that you get. Haven't you ever had it? [CHUCKLE]*
> *AM: Yeah, but, what we're interested in is how it's different, that feeling, for women of your generation to what it is for girls now?*
> *Bernice: Well, to women of our generation, you thought it was the be-all and end-all of everything. You never talked about going out, I mean, um [..] I, I, I think today's women are much better off than what we were ... How can I put it, you, er, [...] I don't know, um [..] of course, when the war came, it changed all sexual feelings and everything, you know, um, you met somebody and you thought they were wonderful and they were off, then, and you never saw them again, they were killed or something like that, you know.*
> *AM: Do you think, because of that, it made you do things that you (wouldn't normally have done)?*
> *Bernice: Well, I think it did, yeah.*
> *AM: That sense of urgency and?*
> *Bernice: Yeah, it did, yeah. Don't think about anything else except the time you was with them.*

Clearly – as Chapter 4 highlights – the Second World War is understood to have precipitated social changes which were to affect the way that people of different age-cohorts and genders were able to relate to each other – both privately within relationships, and publicly within the realm of work – and that these would be difficult to reverse in peacetime.

What we now go on to explore is how these have been responded to, embraced or rejected, reinforced or found to be destabilising of the institution of heterosexuality.

Contemporary heterosexualities: emotions, expectations and disappointments

Jamieson (1998) observes that the shift from marriage as an institution to marriage freely made on the basis of love between equals cannot be easily located in time, but that the public story of this kind of marriage comes into play after the Second World War. This is an elision which Mansfield and Collard (1988) explain in terms of the 'privatisation' of marriage, wherein institutional recognition continues to be sought. As Morgan observes: 'The public and the private, the institutional and the relational, meet in the wedding ceremony' (1991: 127). Marriage in which the major thread is love gained in currency following the Second World War but is not a phenomenon simply reducible to a romantic discourse. As Chapter 4 notes, commentators on this period highlight that companionship, complementarity, teamwork and growth were the buzzwords of this era, yet as Finch and Summerfield (1999) note, in reality a contradictory picture emerged in that 'companionate marriage' was feared to jeopardise key features of family life which were believed to be central to its stability.

Jamieson (1998) nonetheless views the post-modern family as an increasingly self-contained unit, relying less and less upon the wider kinship and support networks that had characterised pre-industrial life. The implications for women have, therefore, been quite pronounced in that they have become increasingly isolated within their relationships. Arguably, such isolation has been buttressed to some degree by the emergence of the 'pure relationship' (Giddens, 1992) and the growing emphasis on 'disclosing intimacy' (Jamieson, 1998) which focuses the attention of the couple on each other as both confidante and friend, creating expectations of empathy, communication and understanding. These are phenomena most closely associated with the post-1960s period, a time associated with rising divorce rates. Morgan (1991) notes that professionals frequently cite unrealistic expectations of modern marriage as a principal contributory factor in such increases – and he asks where these expectations arise from. Indeed, one of our participants reflects: *'I wanted to be happily married in a big bungalow with roses growing round the front. A typical happy family.'* Mansfield and Collard (1988), in their study of 60 newlywed couples reveal that the heady experience of 'falling in love' soon gives way to the cold reality that couples often seek incompatible goals in marriage. They observe: 'Most (though not all men) seek a *life in common* with their wives, a home life, a physical and psychological base; somewhere to set out from and return to' while wives sought '*a common life* with an empathetic partner . . . a close exchange of intimacy which would make them feel valued as a person not just a wife' (1988: 178–9).

While the media, Hollywood films and romantic novels appear as the key sources of couples' unrealistic expectations, our data reveal greater subtleties. Indeed, when we asked participants to reflect upon the relationships of older and younger family members, it was not uncommon for divorced women in their late forties and fifties to reflect with some sadness upon their parents' marriages. They saw these marriages as 'successful' in comparison to their own, in that they had withstood the trials and tribulations of surviving the Second World War and raising a family, to be separated only in death. When her interview was over, one woman who had been twice divorced remarked: *'They were always so in love, my mum and dad.'*

If post-1960s heterosexual relationships were premised increasingly on the practices extolled in self-help books – talking, listening, sharing your thoughts and showing your feelings – what Jamieson refers to as 'disclosing intimacy', communication between partners, became a principal expectation of women in particular. Nonetheless, studies of letters submitted to the 'problem' pages' in women's popular magazines during the 1960s and 1970s indicate increasing dissatisfaction among women with regard to their partners' capacity for mutual disclosure. The key message to emerge in the responses was that couples should tackle problems together through discussion and mutual agreement of solutions. One article specifically observed:

> Marriage is changing. These days it's more about needs and feelings than about the rules, rights and duties of being a husband and wife. This means that we expect a great deal more of the partnership in emotional terms. (Cited in Richards and Elliot, 1991: 37)

Data from participants which describe experiences during the 1960s and afterwards clearly evidence this shift. No longer a somewhat peripheral aspect of heterosexual relations, emotions, their management and their expression emerge as central to the contemporary institution of heterosexuality.

Gender, intimacy and emotional labour

Duncombe and Marsden observe that:

> there is various evidence to suggest that conflict arises because individuals' capacities to express emotion are socially regulated or 'managed' in such a way that men and women have a differing ability or willingness to think and talk in terms of 'love' and 'intimacy' and to make the emotional effort which appears (to many women at least) necessary to sustain close heterosexual relationships. (1993: 221)

Consequently, they question how far can and should men change emotionally in the ways that many women now appear to demand. While the number of male participants to whom we could put this question was relatively limited, there were nonetheless men who spoke reflexively and at length about their emotional lives. That said, many women had clear views on what is commonly referred to as 'male emotional inarticulacy' or, simply put, a failure to 'talk' (for a summary of debates around masculinities and emotion, see Williams, 2001). In the excerpt below we have a group of women aged between their late thirties and late seventies talking about precisely this issue:

Kathy: Men are a different breed, I tell you.
Elaine: They are.
Kathy: Men don't communicate like a woman.
Elaine: They don't talk, do they?
Kathy: Man's the hunter, whereas a woman supports her family through emotions.
Elaine: Yeah,
Audrey: They're emotional, aren't they?
Elaine: Well, men together at work, they don't sit and talk about, I mean they don't talk like we do,
Kathy: No.
Elaine: They might talk about football,
Audrey: Football and horseracing.
Elaine: They don't say anything. I can ask him, ask me husband if he asked one of his mates how his wife is, how the bairns are,
Elaine: 'I don't know'. He didn't think to ask, that's just what men are like.
Kathy: They're just a different breed.

While we have foregrounded a focus on emotionality among our post-1960s age-cohort, the notion of woman supporting her family 'though emotions' is not a new one, being tied into her role as mother, nurturer, carer. As Beck and Beck-Gernsheim (1995) observe, listening to her husband and his worries and mediating the family quarrels are intrinsic to the emotional work for which a woman is responsible in caring for and maintaining the relationship. However, they point out that this self-denying, 'adhesive' role traditionally occupied by women is vanishing and question: who will assume responsibility (1995: 63) as individuals become preoccupied with individualism and the project of 'the self'?

What we found, then, was that while women from among our youngest age-cohort described rejecting what they saw as unsatisfactory relationships where they either felt used for sex or experienced an absence of emotional reciprocity from their partners, their mothers' generation – while openly acknowledging their disappointments – were more inclined to persist in trying to hold their relationships and their families together. Indeed, stories of relationships formed during the 1960s and 1970s were replete with incidents involving an entire emotional continuum: in particular, the explosion of male anger in domestic violence and marital rape, which women struggled to understand, respond to and shield their families from.

While interviewees frequently associated domestic violence and marital rape with alcohol, for 59-year-old Carol Taylor, there was a different trigger. It was his discovery that she had secretly been taking the contraceptive pill that prompted Carol's first husband to rape her, leading to her third pregnancy and the birth of her youngest son. However, she draws on an emotional discourse to explain his violence, pointing out that despite being *'really in love'* with her husband and wanting to share physical intimacy with him, *'he thought sex was to have children, not for enjoyment'*. Consequently, she decided: *'I aren't having sex twice a year or something like that and getting caught with a baby every time, so I'm going to go on the pill.'* In spite of the rape (which was described as: *'he'd forced me to have sex against my will'* at that time) and the virtual absence of a physical relationship, the marriage continued for a further ten years or so, until Carol had an affair with the man who was to become her second husband. Again, we see a woman going through the motions of family life, maintaining the appearance of 'normality'.

While many of our older participants readily told the narrative of their experiences and expressed disappointment at how these compared with the expectations they had once had, it was less frequent for women to reflect critically on their own behaviour in these circumstances. Anita

Leigh (50) is a notable exception and in her account we witness the emotional damage to her self-esteem which her husband's violence precipitated. In reflecting upon the years of abuse which she experienced at the hands of her alcoholic husband, Anita felt an anger which was predominantly self-directed. She reproached herself both for having let the violence continue for as long as it did, and for having believed that she was responsible for its occurrence, castigating herself for having been a *'victim'*. For her, the emotion she recognised as 'love' had been her ultimately futile defence against his aggression:

It was always one sided, right through all our years together, it was always [.] I tried, I was so fuckin' [.] I just wouldn't let go, I really believed, because I loved [.] this, this, this love was so strong that I could make this work, I really could, it didn't matter what 'appened, I could make this work an' then, year after year after year, it just dragged me down an' dragged me down an' dragged me down an' it didn't work, it got worse and worse and worse . . . I feel so ashamed because I let it go on for so long, that's the [.] that's the only thing that upsets me, the fact that I let it go on . . . I think what it was, as well, it was my fault, all these things went wrong because of me, this is what, yeah, because 'e got me so down that everything that went wrong was my fault, you see, so it was [.] I had to try an' make things better by bein' different an', I mean, 'ow sad's that?

It was both interesting and tragic to later interview Anita's 20-year-old son, Stuart, whom she had expressed concern about, since he pointedly refused to discuss his father. She explained that any attempt to try to encourage him to discuss and deal with the events that he witnessed between his parents as a child simply caused Stuart to *'flare up'*. Indeed, despite her attempts to persuade him that *'you need to talk things through'*, Stuart simply expressed anger that *'the bastard died before I was old enough to get 'old of him'*. Unexpectedly, the tough, racist, homophobic young man that Angela had been warned about broke down and dissolved into tears when, having reluctantly talked through the confusion and anger he felt towards his late father, he asserted: *'I want to be the best fucking dad in the world'* and went on to acknowledge: *'that's the worst fear, growing up to be like my dad, you know, I don't want to be a wife-beater and a drunk'*. Both Angela *and* Stuart were quite unprepared for this unexpected display of emotion, the latter expressing embarrassment since it was uncharacteristic of him and admitting that: *'I've never told anybody about this stuff, you know, so, I think that's why I'm (scared) of it.'*

While the examples above have been of 'extreme' emotions, usually kept well-hidden within heterosexual experience, throughout this book we have also concerned ourselves with the more mundane experiences believed to characterise hegemonic heterosexuality and we conclude this chapter by presenting a case study of one of only three *couples* who agreed to participate in the study. Their story illustrates the post-war struggle to achieve emotional fulfilment with one another and their resulting frustrations.

'Love is loneliness for two'

Graham Roberts (48) and his wife, Fay (50) were interviewed separately towards the end of the study. Graham had been recruited via one of his male friends who had already taken part. We also spoke to Graham's mother and 23-year-old son and Fay eagerly volunteered to be interviewed when she was approached some weeks after Graham's interview. Angela recalls feeling slightly uncomfortable interviewing Graham in the living room while Fay and their daughter sat next door in the kitchen, separated only by a glass partition. Since they could be heard talking, it was assumed that so would they be able to hear what was said in the interview. Fay later confirmed this and, with hindsight, Graham would also have been conscious of this, yet proceeded to unburden himself nonetheless. Indeed, when invited to participate in a dissemination workshop which the project arranged for practitioners and other therapists, Graham chose to publicly acknowledge having told Angela things that he had never told either his wife or the Relate counsellors whom the couple had seen over the years. In this he echoed Stuart Leigh who had stated: *'I know it sounds daft, but you've been here what an hour and a bit, but I feel like, you know more about me than my mam, I don't tell her stuff like this at all . . . Sounds daft doesn't it, but, I've told you more in an hour about me than I've told my mam in 20 years.'* In keeping with the 'confessional turn' associated with post-modernity, we thus see the research interview constructed as 'therapy' by participants.

Married for almost 20 years, both Fay and Graham had children from previous marriages. Fay's first husband had been both violent and an alcoholic and Graham had taken custody of his two young sons, apparently enjoying subverting traditional gender roles by playing the 'stay-at-home' father – and admitting that this was something that women found attractive. While Fay grew up in a secure, close and stable family unit, Graham's childhood was marred by his own father's drunken violence and he described feeling emotionally distant from other family members. Indeed, he acknowledged only having kissed his mother once, and that this had been approximately five years ago. Even after his step-father's death, he said that he had been unable to offer his mother comfort. This emotional distance was also – by his own acknowledgement – a bone of contention within his marriage.

Graham's reflections upon his youth were marked by colourful sexual stories which created an image of a young man for whom sex was very important. Likewise, Fay also acknowledges that sex has always been important to her, even as a young woman. She says: *'I'm fairly highly-sexed, I think I must have been even then, I got very strong feelings.'* But for her, the importance lies not in the physical act, but in the *emotional exchange* which this signifies: *'I was very, very into sex, loving sex, not talking about just sex for the sake of sex.'* This contrasts with Graham's approach to sex which for him had always been a purely physical act. The following extract highlights both the depth of Graham's struggle and his sense of failure regarding his wife's needs:

Graham: ... *I started equating it with love and closeness, instead of just sex, and I stopped wanting it, because it was*

AM: *Sorry, I'm not following you. Spell that out for me a bit.*

Graham: *[COUGH] All my life, when I've had sex with a woman, it's been a purely physical thing.*

AM: *Lust?*

Graham: *Yes. It was the first time that it came to me that it was an act of closeness and love between me and her, and scared me, and I backed right off, and it became less frequent [COUGH].*

AM: *When did that start happening?*

Graham: *Quite early on, after two or three years, and even before that probably, don't think I admitted it [COUGH]... It's weird, it's like the kissing thing, I hate kissing. The feeling of somebody's lips on mine like that, just makes me go, I just literally just clam, it's too intimate, too close, and yet I'll kiss the kids, when they was little, like that.*

AM: *But it isn't about intimacy, is it?*

Graham: *Exactly, it's just that, and it's, it was coming, it was getting myself to accept that side of things, and that's very important to Fay, is the, because I don't show it like normal men in holding hands, in cuddling, um, the only physical proof of my love was sex, to her, so, I mean when that's dried up or started being erratic, then she started having a lot of problems, what was I thinking of her and all the rest of it [COUGH], and I'd go through*

> *a phase, where I'd try and be real attentive and just give her a*
> *hug for no reason.*
> AM: *Rather than having sex?*
> Graham: *Well, to try and reassure her that I still loved her, and*
> AM: *Did you have to force yourself to do that?*
> Graham: *I had to think, it wasn't spontaneous, sometimes it is, I'm getting*
> *better over the years. Fay slowly has got round me and round me*
> *and round me over the years, to open up more.*
> AM: *It sounds like it's her that's having to do a lot of the work?*
> Graham: *Oh, hundred percent.*

By Graham's own admission, his wife labours emotionally under intense pressure to address both his long-standing depression and his issues around intimacy and its absence in their relationship – and her own need for it. This struggle is not always easy for Fay to rationalise or maintain. She recounts the following words from a conversation she had with him:

> *'Do you realise, Graham, I have lived with you for longer than anybody in your life, including your mother? So everything that they've done to you, I've not, and I've shown you that you can trust me, and that I'm there for you and that I'll stand by you and I'll stick with you', I said, 'Shouldn't I be seeing some benefit from that?' So, he says, 'I'm fed-up with this and I'm putting my barriers back up'. So, I said, 'So all the crap I've took in the past is all for nothing, there's no pay-back, now I'm redundant, I'm finished?'*

Illustrating her awareness of what Duncombe and Marsden (1993) describe as the transition from the early, heady phase of romantic love to more mature and stable love, Fay's account reflects an expectation of a companionate love, rather than one which is premised upon the need to acquire intimate knowledge of self through the other. She says:

> *I wanted somebody I could be friends with. I mean, I did want the hearts and flowers, we all want the romantic bit, especially to begin with, until you realise that can't be kept up, because I realised that very quickly. But I wanted somebody who was a friend as well as a lover, somebody who loved me and who wanted me, who made me feel attractive and feel loved, and a friend at the same time that I could do things with.*

In many respects, Fay's narrative reflects a very traditional emotional division of labour within a couple. However, unlike many traditional accounts in which men are also characterised as remote fathers, Graham expressed no qualms in being able to share intimacy with his children, at least when they were young. For him, this is an *'unthreatening'* form of love. Confirming the observations of Beck and Beck-Gernsheim (1995), Graham acknowledges that his children accept and love him uncondi-tionally and that there is no fear of *'rejection'* within this kind of loving relationship. In heterosexual relationships, however, he operates on the basis of: *'I reject before I get rejected. So if I think I'm going to get rejected and lose her, I get in there first and I go all the way, and I also push, push, push to make them prove they love me, because I'm not used to receiving love.'* Nonetheless, Graham acknowledges that Fay has quite different needs and that this has been a source of conflict within their marriage, leading them to Relate counselling on more than one occasion. When asked how he expressed his love to Fay, Graham said:

> *I played, well, that was one of the problems, um, I used to play a record that I thought expressed my love. It was Meatloaf, it was 'Two Out of Three Ain't Bad', it's on the Bat Out of Hell CD, LP, and it's [COUGH], 'two out of three ain't bad, I want you, I need you, but there ain't no way I'm ever going to love you, but don't be sad, 'cause two out of three ain't bad', you see. I just thought, this is alright . . . It's been a huge bone of contention between us, because it's my failure to express love compared to hers or most normal people.*

Compared with material from among the oldest cohort where sexual ignorance and pregnancy outside marriage were key threats to hetero-sexual identity, and where the gaze of friends and neighbours led to relationships being assessed against hegemonic forms of heterosexu-ality, this couple have spent approximately 20 years engaged in what they see as a problematic experience of emotional expression/repression which, for Graham, was felt to extend to his childhood and own family background. It is the absence of intimacy and emotional engagement which threatens to undo the marriage and undermine their hetero-sexual identities. While Graham may have difficulty in expressing his emotions to his wife, his interview data and his willingness to come forward and take part in the study illustrate that this in itself was a source of emotional upheaval and a powerful focus for reflection and worry. While our evidence of this kind of inner turmoil among men is limited, it is also manifest within Stuart Leigh's narrative, indicating that this may not be a cohort-specific experience. It is also noteworthy that both men felt able to use the interview as a space in which they could express themselves emotionally in ways that they had perhaps not been able to before. While the younger man's emotional outpouring occurred spontaneously, Graham openly admits that his motivation for taking part in the study was to perhaps help other men who were struggling with the same kinds of issues that he was. Although Graham cannot be characterised as a man who is struggling to become a 'new' man in the sense of a public outpouring of emotion, he is clearly struggling with his perceived inability to engage emotionally at a level which he perceives to be 'normal'. Nonetheless, both his volunteering to take part in our study and his previous efforts to address his depression and anger are reflective of what Seidler (1998) and Williams (2001) describe as men's increasing propensity to take responsibility for their emotional lives.

Conclusion

Where once the concern was with maintaining the good name of a family within a community, avoiding shame and gossip (see Chapter 6), a shift has been observed in the period after the Second World War, whereby the couple and their success – or failure – in meeting the expectations they set out with have become the primary focus within our culture. This chapter has explored how the priorities and concerns of our participants have altered across generations, interweaving accounts of historical and biographical time, highlighting the influence of one upon the other. In spite of these changes, however, it becomes clear from the data provided by our participants that while the institution of heterosexuality may have undergone challenges from feminists and has metamorphosed over the last century, it remains dominant, pervasive and a taken-for-granted residual category within our culture.

The data presented in this and other chapters have illustrated our attempts to bring a unique historical perspective to bear on long-standing theoretical dilemmas. In drawing upon the experiences of women and men who have lived out heterosexual lives at different historical junctures over the last century or so, we have been able to illustrate how – despite its pervasiveness as an 'institution' – hegemonic heterosexuality has not been immutable. Indeed, the twentieth century bears witness to the coexistence of many forms of heterosexual identity under the larger umbrella of the institution. Some aspects have remained more visible than others, those which are least acceptable being sequestered from public view at different periods in time, and we have documented a shift in emphasis from what we have conceptualised as the regulation of the body and sexuality, to the management of unruly emotions. This shift allows us to move towards a feminist revisioning of the concept of agency, as demonstrated in Chapter 3, raising more subtle questions about the resources available to women – and men – as they seek to suture a critical lack of fit between hegemonic heterosexuality and an everyday world of stigmatised sex and illegitimate unhappiness. As Beck and Beck-Gernsheim observe: 'seventh heaven and mental torment seem to be very close neighbours in our ideal image of the loving couple. Perhaps they just live in separate storeys – tower room and torture chamber – in the same castle' (1995: 173).

10
Conclusion

This book reflects the empirical project of examining everyday hetero-sexual life from a feminist perspective. It has worked from data generated within a two-year ESRC-funded research project in order to gradually develop a position from which heterosexual lives may be viewed – with insight, with compassion and with a form of critical engagement which can empower individuals, families, communities and indeed policy-makers to address the limitations, the inequalities and the suffering which an unexamined heterosexual life can involve. Like any project of this kind, it in no way represents the last word. Rather its objective is to make strange the tried and somehow still trusted, to problematise commonsense notions of what 'being heterosexual' might mean. Its objective is therefore to open doors rather than generate any ultimate conclusions.

The book begins by outlining the personal and professional imperat-ives which inspired us: the experience of everyday conversations made up of heartfelt uncertainties as to how a heterosexual life might be led; and our awareness of the limited empirical evidence as to how gendered relationships which are thought of as 'natural' or conven-tional are constructed and practised, despite a sustained growth in sound feminist theories linking heterosexuality and patriarchy. While the narratives of homosexual and lesbian relatedness had been made available (Weeks et al., 1999; Dunne, 1999; Weeks, 2000), they alone seemed to represent the operation of personal choice and in ways which heterosexual relationships were seen not to. Weeks' data, for example, reveal non-heterosexuals describing their relationships as 'chosen' and 'created': 'I take my family [of origin] for granted, whereas my friend-ships are, to a degree, chosen, and therefore they're created' (Weeks, 2000: 217). What drove the design of our project, then, was concern that structural arguments, which treat heterosexuality as a compulsory institution that limits women's (and indeed men's) subjectivities, were in danger of mirroring the essentialising perspective of naturalised accounts of institutions such as 'marriage' and 'motherhood'. That we chose to work among the members of extended families and to explore with them the details of their everyday lives, represents our desire to think critically about a view of heterosexuality as either the outcome of patriarchal forces or 'natural drives'. Although feminist theory has at times represented the institution of heterosexuality as monolithic and inflexible in its hegemonic forms of marriage and the family, at the level of the individual these social arrangements are seen as open to change. Yet it is noteworthy that this is seen to be possible only at considerable personal and indeed social cost (Beck and Beck-Gernsheim, 1995). We have therefore embraced Jackson's suggestion that we should 'cease to theorize at an entirely abstract level and pay attention to what is known about material, embodied men and women going about the business of living their sexualities' (1999: 26). In so doing we have drawn on the invaluable resource of over three decades of feminist theorising around heterosexuality, working in a spirit of inclusivity which recognises the contribution of feminist scholars from Adrienne Rich through to Dorothy Smith, Andrea Dworkin and Sheila Jeffreys to the growing range of authors who are addressing questions around heterosexuality. Critical engagement with this work, alongside those of many other feminist scholars in Europe and the US, has therefore been a mainstay of the present project.

If the lack of a theoretical framing of heterosexuality – which makes diversity its starting point – means that its status as a 'natural', procreative relationship will transmute into a feminist perspective which reifies a particular model of heterosexuality, then scope for individual agency is likely to be seen as limited. As we have argued, an adequate theoretical foregrounding of agency does require an awareness of a wider social and structural context which includes women's inequality in the family and at work, an emphasis on penetrative sex in heterosexual relationships and the pervasiveness of male violence (Ramazanoglu, 1993; Robinson, 1997). Nonetheless, whilst taking account of these dimensions of heterosexuality, the nature and scope of our participants' agency has remained our core focus throughout this book.

This is not to say that the granting of greater weight to issues of agency is particular to this project. Nonetheless its development as a focus for social scientists of many different backgrounds has also involved a concern with the personalising of private relationships. This reflects a pervasive notion that modernity has brought about a proliferation of autonomous, lifestyle choices and sexual pluralism (Giddens, 1992). Whether these are seen to represent 'a radical democratisation of the interpersonal domain' (Weeks, 2000b: 214) or simply the breakdown of a coherent social order has been one the questions to which we have given critical attention. In the related area of family obligations, for example, Finch shows that rather than following structured rules of conduct, practical help is negotiated within families who 'work it out' as need arises (1989). We have therefore asked whether the same is true of heterosexual relationships. Has their patterning become less taken for granted within a pluralist social environment where there appears to be evidence of new family forms (Jagger and Wright, 1999)? Or, as Jackson and Scott (2004b) argue, does the assumption that modern societies have become progressively more sexually liberal founder on evidence such as the persistence of homophobia, in both the legal domain and on the streets, the trend towards extending heterosexual institutions to include people who are gay or lesbian, and the vilification of early pregnancy outside marriage and the practice of non-monogamy? In that the gathering and comparison of data from people of different age-cohorts was central to the design of our empirical work, we have been able to examine both the social history of heterosexuality alongside accounts of those who grew up and grew old during the twentieth and twenty-first centuries.

Although the 1960s were associated with the liberalisation of attitudes, increased individualism, greater freedom regarding sex, reforms on the laws governing sexual behaviour, the advent of the pill and the uncoupling of sex from marriage, we noted Weeks' argument that their impact was limited at the time. That said, these years can be seen as the harbingers of much wider transformations (Weeks, 2004: 95) – as we observed among the youngest of our three age-cohorts. Their experiences and reflections mesh with Weeks' observation that we have subsequently witnessed a 'secularisation' of sexuality as sexual values have progressively become detached from religious values. This, he suggests, has gone hand in hand with a process of 'individualisation' encouraged by the growth in world capitalism in the 1980s. Correspondingly, then, these social changes have contributed to the commodification of areas of experience previously identified as 'private life', the pornographic industry, for example, having resisted pressure from traditionalists and feminists alike (Weeks, 2004: 96). This commercialisation of leisure has also influenced patterns of courtship, and new technologies have helped reshape personal life: from sex aids to Viagra and designer drugs, so combining sexual and social experience. What these most recent social and cultural changes confirm is that what we understand as 'sexuality' is not something which exists outside history and the social and political forces of our time, but is – indeed – a historical product and one which is both culturally constructed and socially organised (Weeks 2004: 28).

How historical changes such as these inflect individual biographies, within the specific locales which make up East Yorkshire, has been one of our central concerns, and what our account reveals are the nuances introduced by differences of social class, age, gender and region. And these, as we have shown throughout the book, are not only key to the meshing of historical and biographical time but also to the entire process of exploring what had made up the heterosexual lives we were investigating. As early chapters describe, what our interviewees understood by the term 'heterosexual' provided our starting point and here 'sexual' predominated in terms of their understandings. The language through which narratives of heterosexuality were produced was therefore resourced by particular discourses around sex, romance, respectability, gender and social class. What was key to our empirical work was an understanding that not only everyday sexual practice, beliefs and attitudes, but also 'sex research' itself was the outcome of particular sets of power relationships, as constituted within contemporary white, western heterosexuality. Through working reflexively, we have therefore explored how differences based on age, gender and social class create hierarchies, distances and allegiances between the researcher and the range of individuals she is interviewing. Our detailed analysis shows that while these categories cannot be seen to exercise a predictable or mechanical influence over the relationship between researcher and interviewee, a more nuanced exploration which took account of the details of *both* their biographies showed, for example, that age and gender differences did not necessarily preclude an easy rapport. Rather, differences of social class seemed to create a greater sense of risk in disclosing information about 'sex'. During the interview itself, then, women and men sought a mode of expression which would allow them to present their account *safely* to the researcher, who herself made judgements as to the terminology within which she framed her questions. Thus, neither the acts of recollecting and narrating, nor those of questioning and listening, are neutral or abstracted moments. Rather, they represent both an extension of, and an intervention into, the biographies of interviewee and interviewer; and take place as an aspect of these individuals' ongoing life-course trajectories. We agree with Woodward (2004), therefore, that gendering, like ethnicisation, needs to be explicit and self-conscious in the reflexive research process, something both dynamic and dialogic.

What we have argued, therefore, is that within a research process where layers of difference and commonality are continuously being negotiated, data on 'sex' need to be recognised not as a transparent body of descriptive information and reflection, but rather as the outcome of a set of understandings which reflect the social identities of both parties involved in the interview. This, we have argued, aids rather than obscures our understanding of the everyday lives of the people we interviewed. For them too, that which might be taken for granted as 'sex' is a similarly emergent category of experience, one which comes into being out of the flux of relationships between parental and child generations; among same sex peers; between siblings; and between women and men who negotiate sexual relationships within the conditions of possibility afforded by the gendered institution of heterosexuality. In addition, 'interview data' are not only an aspect of the interviewee's 'social history'; rather than simply an account of it, they are also a work of imaginative reconstruction which points toward the *future* as well as the past. That which we researched as 'sex' was itself, therefore, not only reconstituted, but also subsequently played out in the imagination, in talk or, indeed, in practice, as an aspect or outcome of the social interaction we know as an 'interview'. And importantly, this holds for both the interviewee and the interviewer. There is, therefore, a dialectical relationship between the hour(s) of the interview and the life-course trajectories within which it is situated. Just as feminist methodology reminds us of the socially located nature of the practice of interviewing, so that practice itself needs to be recognised as one among the many layers of negotiation and, indeed, resistance, which make up the focus of the research process: 'sex'.

If we began with participants' own understandings of heterosexuality as a sexual category, this required us to locate those understandings within the broader body of data which the project generated. What we sought to understand was both the question of how heterosexuality was both reproduced and resisted and the issue of how gendered heterosexual subjectivities came into being. Data revealed the presence of a heterosexual imaginary (Ingraham, 1999, 2005), a repertoire of images and texts which represented an idealised combining of masculinity and femininity within the welcome confines of family life. As such, however, this imaginary cannot be seen as a blueprint for personal happiness, a culturally specific game-plan for the successful heterosexual life. Rather, it constituted that range of objectives and aspirations which individuals had grown up into – within their families and local communities, and from within the popular media of their day, from romantic fiction through self-help sex manuals, such as the writings of Marie Stopes, and the sexual self-improvement programmes offered by the contributors to *Cosmopolitan* and *Heat* magazines. Data show that these were consumed and reflected upon critically. Contradictions and tensions were evident within the heterosexual imaginary which participants sought to draw upon, partly as a result of the diversity of its sources, partly as an outcome of the ragged processes of historical change.

As regards how such representations of the heterosexual life might inform the subjectivities of those engaged with their own particular heterosexual life-course, we worked with the notion of discourses as the source of narratives through which practices might be reflected upon and particular interpretations might allow for that which we call 'experience'. At the point of working with individuals' narratives, however, it was their concern with the sexual and its contradictory carnal and romantic dimensions which concerned us, particularly the relationship between these different aspects of participants' sexual desires and practices and their gender. A careful and reflexive discussion of their uses of language, as discussed above, allowed us to trace connections between sexuality, gender, respectability and, importantly, social class. This work provided the basis for our subsequent more critical analysis of how 'sex' might relate to the institution of heterosexuality. It led us to ask the question 'what's sex got to do with it?', one which led us to consider the far more pervasive role of heterosexuality as an organising principle which informed a diversity of everyday practices which transcended the limits of the simply sexual. Moreover, in our work on the family and the home as a particular spatialised context for heterosexuality – indeed its hegemonic environment – we then examined the paradoxical tensions between family life and sexual identity, noting that generational and sexual identities can often be in tension with one another.

Throughout the book we have referred repeatedly to the notion that we can draw the unmarked category of heterosexuality into a more critical light by attending to that which fails to be easily incorporated within it. Foucault may have initiated the argument that homosexuality, conceived of as oppositional to heterosexuality, has a generative status and operates to sustain the distinctive nature of the heterosexual. This has been taken up by authors such as Butler (1990) and Hanson (1997), yet what we have argued here is that the relationship between heterosexuality and its boundaries is a potential focus for investigation which can be extended beyond homosexuality. We are drawn to this perspective on the basis not only of our participants' difficulties in articulating what it means to be heterosexual, an inarticulacy which has been noted in relation to membership of other dominant categories such as 'white', 'male' and 'able-bodied', but also in response to the weight they placed upon those aspects of their heterosexual lives which they somehow felt troubled by and which we can therefore term 'transgressive'. In the close to this book we make such 'transgressions' our primary focus and it is here that we show how historical and biographical time intersect most powerfully. While participants from among our oldest cohort described the social and emotional suffering wrought by aspects of embodied life which failed to conform to hegemonic heterosexuality, they stood in clear contrast to those from our middle and youngest cohort. What was striking was that while the bodily dimensions of sex, coupledom and parenthood were by no means as circumscribed by social stigma, emotional aspects of a heterosexual life were either repeatedly subjected to intense scrutiny or avoided, deferred or scrambled as young people sought to restrict their narratives to sexuality's more carnal dimensions.

This focus on emotional uncertainties, or indeed transgressions, among individuals who grew up from the 1960s onwards bears out the informal experiences of 'heterosexual' conversations which first alerted Jenny's interest in reflexive dimensions of the experience of heterosexual life. As a result of our empirical project we have been able to contextualise such talk in terms of the differences between age-cohorts and between the members of different generations. In drawing upon the existing body of theoretical work in this area, we have also succeeded in providing an analysis of these data which draws attention to the role and status of heterosexuality as expressed in the achievement of adulthood, the management of class-based risks and identities, the maintenance of cross-generational family relationships and, indeed, the organisation of everyday life. In that we set out to provide an empirically grounded account of how heterosexuality is reproduced and resisted within a familial context, the everyday has been our primary focus. Nonetheless, our data have revealed the diversity and heterogeneity of the everyday and we have drawn on the concepts of the mundane and the extreme to examine the complex, nuanced relationship between the ways in which the mundanity of oppressive heterosexual relationships contributes to the power and inequality which characterises them; yet, in addition, can encompass the embodied, materially grounded moments which signal profound transitions, both into and out of such relationships.

The work presented here, therefore, reflects five years of committed team-work on the part of the book's three authors. It has been a period of considerable, at times radical change in our heterosexual lives and, as we began by reporting, working with these data has sometimes been both disturbing and distressing. In that they have helped *us* to make strange the familiarity of our mundane heterosexual lives, however, it has had far-reaching personal implications, ones which, it is our hope, this account has made available to its readers.

References

Adler, S. and Brenner, J. (1992) 'Gender and Space: Lesbians and Gay Men in the City', *International Journal of Urban and Regional Research*, 16: 24–31.

Alasuutari, P. (1995) *Researching Culture: Qualitative Method and Cultural Studies*, London: Sage.

Arber, S. and Ginn, J. (1995) *Connecting Gender and Ageing*, Buckingham: Open University Press.

Bachelard, G. ([1958] 1994) *The Poetics of Space*, Boston: Beacon Press.

Beck, U. and Beck-Gernsheim, E. (1995) *The Normal Chaos of Love*, Cambridge: Polity.

Bell, D. (1992) 'Insignificant Others: Lesbian and Gay Geographies', *Area*, 23: 323–9.

Bennett, T. (2002) 'Home and Everyday Life', in T. Bennett and D. Watson (eds), *Understanding Everyday Life*, Oxford: Blackwell.

Bennett, T. and Watson, D. (eds) (2002) *Understanding Everyday Life*, Oxford: Blackwell.

Bernard, J. (2002), 'The Husband's Marriage and the Wife's Marriage', in S. Jackson and S. Scott (eds), *Gender: a Sociological Reader*, London: Routledge.

Bernardes, J. (1997) *Family Studies*, London: Routledge.

Bourdieu, P. (1977) *Outline of a Theory of Practice*, Cambridge: Cambridge University Press.

Brah, A. (1996) *Cartographies of Diaspora*, London: Routledge.

Brannen, J. (1988) 'Research Note: the Study of Sensitive Subjects: Notes on Interviewing', *Sociological Review*, 36, 3: 552–63.

Brannen, J. (1999) 'Reconsidering Children and Childhood: Sociological and Policy Perspectives', in E. Silva and C. Smart (eds), *The New Family?* London: Sage.

Brannen, J. and Nilsen, A. (2002) 'Young People's Time Perspectives: From Youth to Adulthood', *Sociology*, 36, 3: 513–37.

Brittan, A. (2001) 'Masculinities and Masculinism', in S. Whitehead and F. Barrett (eds), *The Masculinities Reader*, Cambridge: Polity.

Brunt, R. (1988) 'Love is in the Air', *Marxism Today*, February: 18–21.

Bunch, C. (1975) 'Not For Lesbians Only', *Quest: a Feminist Quarterly*, 2, 2.

Burgess, A. (1997) *Fatherhood Reclaimed: the Making of the Modern Father*, London: Random House.

Bury, M. (1995) 'Ageing, Gender and Sociological Theory', in S. Arber and J. Ginn (eds), *Connecting Gender and Ageing*, Buckingham: Open University Press.

Butler, J. (1990) *Gender Trouble: Feminism and the Subversion of Identity*, New York: Routledge.

Butler, J. (1993) *Bodies that Matter: On the Discursive Limits of 'Sex'*, London: Routledge.

Butler, J. (1997) *Excitable Speech: a Politics of the Performative*, London: Routledge.

Carabine, J. (1996) 'Heterosexuality and Social Policy', in D. Richardson (ed.), *Theorising Heterosexuality*, Buckingham: Open University Press.

190

Chaney, D. (2002) *Cultural Change and Everyday Life*, Basingstoke: Palgrave Macmillan.

Cline, S. (1993) *Women, Celibacy and Passion*, London: Optima.

Cline, S. (1998) *Couples: Scene from the Inside*, London: Little, Brown and Company.

Cohen, A. (1994) *Self Consciousness*, London: Routledge.

Cohen, A. and Rapport, N. (1995) *Questions of Consciousness*, London: Routledge.

Cokely, C. (2005) ' "Someday My Prince Will Come": Disney, the Heterosexual Imaginary and Animated Film', in C. Ingraham (ed.), *Thinking Straight: the Power, the Promise and the Paradox of Heterosexuality*, New York: Routledge.

Connell, R.W. (1987) *Gender and Power: Society, the Person and Sexual Politics*, Cambridge: Polity.

Connell, R. W. (1995) *Masculinities*, Cambridge: Polity.

Connell, R. W. (2000) *The Men and the Boys*, London: Polity.

Cotterill, P. (1992) 'Interviewing Women: Issues of Friendship, Vulnerability and Power', *Women's Studies International Forum*, 15: 593–606.

Craib, I. (1999) 'Narrative as "Bad Faith" '. Paper presented in the Social Theory seminar series. Department of Sociology, University of Warwick, 22 February.

Crang, M. and Thrift, N. (eds) (2000) *Thinking Space*, London: Routledge.

Crawford, J., Kippax, S. and Waldby, C. (1994) 'Women's Sex Talk and Men's Sex Talk: Different Worlds', *Feminism and Psychology*, 4: 571–87.

Dallos, S. and Dallos, R. (1997) *Couples, Sex and Power: the Politics of Desire*, Buckingham: Open University Press.

Davies, C. A. (1999) *Reflexive Ethnography: a Guide to Researching Selves and Others*, London: Routledge.

Davis, K. (1991) 'Critical Sociology and Gender Relations', in K. Davis, M. Leijenaar and J. Oldersma (eds), *The Gender of Power*, London: Sage.

Delphy, C. and Leonard, D. (1992) *Familiar Exploitation: a New Analysis of Marriage in Contemporary Western Societies*, Cambridge, Polity.

Duncombe, J. and Marsden, D. (1993) 'Love and Intimacy: the Gender Division of Emotion and "Emotion Work": a Neglected Aspect of Sociological Discussion of Heterosexual Relationships', *Sociology*, 27: 221–41.

Duncombe, J. and Marsden, D. (1996) 'Whose Orgasm is it Anyway: "Sex Work" in Long-term Couple Relationships', in J. Weeks and J. Holland (eds), *Sexual Cultures: Communities, Values and Intimacy*, New York: St. Martin's Press.

Dunne, G. (1999) 'A Passion for "Sameness"? Sexuality and Gender Accountability', in E. Silva and C. Smart (eds), *The New Family?* London: Sage.

Dworkin, A. (1981) *Pornography: Men Possessing Women*, London: Women's Press.

Dworkin, A. (1987) *Intercourse*, London: Arrow.

Dyer, R. (1985) 'Male Sexuality in the Media', in A. Metcalf and M. Humphries (eds), *The Sexuality of Men*, London: Pluto.

Dyer, R. (1997) *White*, London: Routledge.

Elliot, B. J. (1991) 'Demographic Trends in Domestic Life, 1945–87', in D. Clark (ed.), *Marriage, Domestic Life and Social Change*, London: Routledge.

Engels, F. (1986) *The Origin of the Family, Private Property and the State*, Harmondsworth: Penguin.

Essig, L. (2005) 'The Mermaid and the Heterosexual Imagination', in C. Ingraham (ed.), *Thinking Straight: the Power, the Promise and the Paradox of Heterosexuality*, New York: Routledge.

Fawcett, B. and Hearn, J. (2004) 'Researching Others: Epistemology, Experience, Standpoints and Participation', *International Journal of Social Research Methodology*, 7: 201–18.

Felski, R. (1999–2000) 'The Invention of Everyday Life', *New Formations*, 39: 15–31.

Finch, J. (1989) *Family Obligation and Social Change*, Cambridge: Polity Press.

Finch, J. and Summerfield, P. (1999) 'Social Reconstruction and the Emergence of the Companionate Marriage, 1945–59', in G. Allan (ed.), *The Sociology of the Family: a Reader*, Oxford: Blackwell.

Finlay, S. J. and Clarke, V. (2003) ' "A marriage of inconvenience?" Feminist Perspectives on Marriage', *Feminism & Psychology*, 14: 415–20.

Foucault, M. (1987) *The History of Sex and Sexuality: an Introduction*, London: Penguin.

Gabb, J. (2005) 'Lesbian M/Otherhood: Strategies of Familial-Linguistic Management in Lesbian Parent Families', *Sociology*, 39, 4: 585–604.

Gardiner, M. E. (2000) *Critiques of Everyday Life*, London: Routledge.

Geertz, C. (1975) *The Interpretation of Cultures*, London: Hutchinson.

Giddens, A. (1991) *Modernity and Self Identity*, Cambridge, Polity.

Giddens, A. (1992) *The Transformation of Intimacy: Sexuality, Love and Eroticism in Modern Societies*, Cambridge: Polity.

Giles, J. (1995) *Women, Identity and Private Life in Britain: 1900–50*, Basingstoke: Palgrave Macmillan.

Gilfoyle, J., Wilson, J. and Own, B. (1993) 'Sex, Organs and Audiotape: a Discourse Analytic Approach to Talking about Sex and Relationships', in S. Wilkinson and C. Kitzinger (eds), *Heterosexuality: a Feminism and Psychology Reader*, London: Sage.

Ginn, J. and Arber, S. (1995) ' "Only Connect": Gender Relations and Ageing', in S. Arber and J. Ginn (eds), *Connecting Gender and Ageing*, Buckingham: Open University Press.

Goffman, E. (1959) *The Presentation of Self in Everyday Life*, Garden City, NY: Doubleday Anchor.

Goffman, E. (1961) *Asylums*, Garden City, NY: Doubleday Anchor.

Goffman, E. (1968) *Stigma: Notes on the Management of Spoiled Identity*, Harmondsworth: Pelican.

Gurney, C. (2000) 'Transgressing Private–Public Boundaries in the Home: a Sociological Analysis of the Coital Noise Taboo', *Venereology*, 13: 39–46.

Hakim, C. (1996) *Key Issues in Women's Work: Female Heterogeneity and the Polarisation of Women's Employment*, London: Athlone Press.

Hall, S. (1996) 'Introduction: Who Needs "Identity"?' in S. Hall and P. du Gay (eds), *Questions of Cultural Identity*, London: Sage.

Hallet, C. (ed.) (1995) *Women and Social Policy*, Basingstoke: Macmillan.

Hanson, C. (1997) 'Virginia Woolf in the House of Love: Compulsory Heterosexuality in *The Years*', *Journal of Gender Studies*, 6, 1: 55–62.

Harding, S. (1987) 'Introduction: Is There a Feminist Method?' in S. Harding (ed.), *Feminism and Methodology*, Milton Keynes: Open University Press.

Hawkes, G. (1996) *A Sociology of Sex and Sexuality*, Buckingham: Open University Press.

Haywood, C. and Mac An Ghaill, M. (2003) *Men and Masculinities*, Buckingham: Open University Press.

Hendry, J. and Watson, C. W. (eds) (2001) *An Anthropology of Indirect Communication*, London: Routledge.

Highmore, B. (2002) *Everyday Life and Cultural Theory*, London: Routledge.

Hines, S. (2006) 'Intimate Transitions: Transgender Practices of Partnering and Parenting', *Sociology*, 40, 2: 353–71.

Hockey, J. and James, A. (1993) *Growing Up and Growing Old: Ageing and Dependency in the Life Course*, London: Sage.

Hockey, J. and James, A. (2003) *Social Identities across the Life Course*, Basingstoke: Palgrave Macmillan.

Hockey, J., Meah, A. and Robinson, V. (2004) 'A Heterosexual Life: Older Women and Agency within Marriage and the Family', *Journal of Gender Studies*, 13: 227–38.

Hockey, J., Robinson, V. and Meah, A. (2002) ' "For Better or Worse?": Heterosexuality Reinvented'. *Sociological Research Online*, 7, 2.

Holland, J. and Ramazanoglu, C. (1994) 'Coming to Conclusions: Power and Interpretation in Researching Young Women's Sexuality', in M. Maynard and J. Purvis (eds), *Researching Women's Lives from a Feminist Perspective*, London: Taylor & Francis.

Holland, J., Ramazanoglu, C., Sharpe, S. and Thomson, R. (1996) 'In the Same Boat? The Gendered (In) Experience of First Heterosex', in D. Richardson (ed.), *Theorising Heterosexuality*, Buckingham, Open University Press.

Holland, J., Ramazanoglu, C., Sharpe, S. and Thomson, R. (1998) *The Male in the Head: Young People, Heterosexuality and Power*, London: Tufnell.

Holland, J., Ramazanoglu, C., Sharpe, S. and Thomson, R. (2002) 'In the Same Boat?', in S. Jackson and S Scott (eds), *Gender: a Sociological Reader*, London: Routledge.

Hollway, W. (1984) 'Gender, Difference and the Production of Subjectivity', in J. Henriques, W. Hollway, C. Urwin, C. Venn and V. Walkerdine (eds), *Changing the Subject: Psychology, Social Regulation and Subjectivity*, London: Methuen.

hooks, b. (1989) *Talking Back: Thinking Feminist–Thinking Black*. London: Sheba.

Horrocks, R. (1994) *Masculinity in Crisis: Myths, Fantasies and Realities*, London: Macmillan.

Hubbard, P. (2000) 'Desire and Disgust: Mapping the Moral Contours of Heterosexuality', *Progress in Human Geography*, 24: 191–217.

Humphries, S. (1988) *A Secret World of Sex, Forbidden Fruit: the British Experience 1900–1950*, London: Sidgwick & Jackson.

Ingraham, C. (1996) 'The Heterosexual Imaginary: Feminist Sociology and Theories of Gender', in S. Seidman (ed.), *Queer Theory/Sociology*, Oxford: Blackwell.

Ingraham, C. (1999) *White Weddings: Romancing Heterosexuality in Popular Culture*, New York: Routledge.

Ingraham, C. (2002) 'The Heterosexual Imaginary', in S. Jackson and S. Scott (eds), *Gender: a Sociological Reader*, London: Routledge.

Ingraham, C. (2005) *Thinking Straight: the Power, the Promise and the Paradox of Heterosexuality*, London: Routledge.

Ingrisch, D. (1995) 'Conformity and Resistance as Women Age', in S. Arber and J. Ginn (eds), *Connecting Gender and Ageing*, Buckingham: Open University Press.

Jackson, S. (1993) 'Love and Romance as Objects of Feminist Knowledge', in M. Kennedy, C. Lubelska and V. Walsh (eds), *Making Connections: Women's Studies, Women's Movements, Women's Lives*, London: Taylor & Francis.

Jackson, S. (1996) 'Heterosexuality and Feminist Theory', in D. Richardson (ed.), *Theorising Heterosexuality*, Buckingham: Open University Press.

Jackson, S. (1997) 'Women, Marriage and Family Relationships', in V. Robinson and D. Richardson (eds), *Introducing Women's Studies: Feminist Theory and Practice*, London: Macmillan.

Jackson, S. (1998) 'Telling Stories: Memory, Narrative and Experience in Feminist Research and Theory', in K. Henwood, C. Griffin and A. Phoenix (eds), *Standpoints and Differences: Essays in the Practice of Feminist Psychology*, London: Sage.

Jackson, S. (1999) *Heterosexuality in Question*, London: Sage.

Jackson, S. (2005) 'Sexuality, Heterosexuality and Gender Hierarchy: Getting our Priorities Straight', in C. Ingraham (ed.), *Thinking Straight: the Power, the Promise and the Paradox of Heterosexuality*, New York: Routledge.

Jackson, S. (2006) 'Gender, Sexuality and Heterosexuality', *Feminist Theory*, 7, 1: 105–21.

Jackson, S. and Scott, S. (eds), (1996) *Feminism and Sexuality: a Reader*, Edinburgh: Edinburgh University Press.

Jackson, S. and Scott, S. (2004a) 'The Personal is Still Political: Heterosexuality, Feminism and Monogamy', *Feminism and Psychology*, 14, 1: 151–7.

Jackson, S. and Scott, S. (2004b) 'Sexual Antinomies in Late Modernity', *Sexualities*, 7, 2: 233–48.

Jagger, G. and Wright, C. (1999) *Changing Family Values*, London: Routledge.

James, A. (1999) 'Parents: a Children's Perspective', in A. Bainham, S. Day Sclater and M. Richards (eds), *What is a Parent? A Socio-Legal Analysis*, Oxford: Hart Publishing.

James, A., Jenks, C. and Prout, A. (1998) *Theorising Childhood*, Cambridge: Polity Press.

Jamieson, L. (1998) *Intimacy: Personal Relationships in Modern Societies*, Cambridge: Polity.

Jeffreys, S. (1993) *Anti-climax: a Feminist Perspective on the Sexual Revolution*, London: Women's Press.

Jenkins, R. (2002) *Foundations of Sociology*, Basingstoke: Palgrave Macmillan.

Jenkins, R. (2004) *Social Identity*, London: Routledge.

Johnson, P. (2005) *Love, Heterosexuality and Society*, London: Routledge.

Johnson, P. and Lawler, S. (2005) 'Coming Home to Love and Class', *Sociological Research Online*, 10, 3.

Jones, C. (1985) 'Sexual Tyranny in Mixed Sex Schools: an In-depth Study of Male Violence', in G. Weiner (ed.), *Just a Bunch of Girls*, Milton Keynes: Open University Press.

Jordanova, L. (1989) *Sexual Visions: Images of Gender in Science and Medicine between the Eighteenth and Twentieth Centuries*, Madison: University of Wisconsin Press.

Kelly, L. (1988) *Surviving Sexual Violence*, Cambridge: Polity.

Kimmel, M. S. and Messner, M. A. (2004) 'Introduction', in M. S. Kimmel and M. A. Messner (eds), *Men's Lives*, Boston: Pearson.

Kitzinger, C. and Wilkinson, S. (1993) 'Theorising Heterosexuality', in S. Wilkinson and C. Kitzinger (eds), *Heterosexuality*, London: Sage.

Land, H. (1999) 'The Changing Worlds of Work and Family', in S. Watson and L. Doyal (eds), *Engendering Social Policy*, Buckingham: Open University Press.

Laqueur, T. (1987) 'Orgasm, Generation and the Politics of Reproductive Biology', in C. Gallaher and T. Laqueur (eds), *The Making of the Modern Body: Sexuality and Society in the Nineteenth Century*, Berkeley: University of California Press.

Larkin, P. (1974) *High Windows*, London: Faber and Faber.

Latour, B. (1993) *We Have Never Been Modern*, London: Harvester Wheatsheaf.

Lawler, S. (2002) 'Mobs and Monsters: *Independent* Man Meets Paulsgrove Woman', *Feminist Theory*, 3, 1: 103–14.

Lawler, S. (2005) 'Disgusted Subjects: the Making of Middle-class Identities', *Sociological Review*, 53, 3.

Laws, S. (1990) *Issues of Blood: the Politics of Menstruation*, Basingstoke: Macmillan.

Lee, D. (1997) 'Interviewing Men: Vulnerabilities and Dilemmas', *Women's Studies International Forum*, 20: 553–64.

Lees, S. (1993) *Sugar and Spice: Sexuality and Adolescent Girls*, London: Penguin.

Lefebvre, H. (1991) *The Critique of Everyday Life*, Volume 1, London: Verso. First published in France, 1947.

Lewallen, A. (1988) '*Lace*: Pornography for Women?' in L. Gamman and M. Marshment (eds), *The Female Gaze*, London: Women's Press.

Lewis, J. and Kiernan, K. (1996) 'The Boundaries between Marriage, Nonmarriage and Parenthood: Changes in Behaviour and Policy in Postwar Britain', *Journal of Family History*, 20, 3: 372–87.

Lonsdale, S. (1990) *Women and Disability*, Basingstoke: Macmillan.

Lupton, D. (1998) *The Emotional Self*, London: Sage.

McMahon, A. (1999) *Taking Care of Men: Sexual Politics in the Public Mind*, Cambridge: Cambridge University Press.

McNulty, A. (2003) *Using the Biographical-Narrative Interpretive Method to Explore 'Teenage Pregnancy'*, Gender Research Forum, University of Teeside, May.

McNulty, A. (2004) 'Stories of Sex, Relationships and "Teenage Pregnancy" ', paper given at Northern Primary Care Research Network

McRobbie, A. (1991) *Feminism and Youth Culture: from 'Jackie' to 'Just Seventeen'*, Basingstoke: Macmillan.

MacAndrew, R. (undated) *The Red Light: Intimate Hygiene for Men and Women*, London: Wales Publishing Co.

Macionis, J. and Plummer, K. (2002) *Sociology: a Global Introduction*, Essex: Pearson Education.

Mackay, H. (1997) *Consumption and Everyday Life*, London: Sage.

MacKinnon, C. A. (1982) 'Feminism, Marxism, Method and the State: Agenda for Theory', *Signs*, 7, 3: 515–44.

MacKinnon, C. A. (1996) 'Feminism, Marxism, Method and the State: Agenda for Theory', in S. Jackson and S. Scott (eds), *Contemporary Feminist Theories*, Edinburgh: Edinburgh University Press.

MacLean, M. and Groves, D. (eds) (1991) *Women's Issues in Social Policy*, London: Routledge.

Madigan, R. and Munro, M. (1999) ' "The more we are together": Domestic Space, Gender and Privacy', in T. Chapman and J. Hockey (eds), *Ideal Homes? Social Change and Domestic Life*, London: Routledge.

Malone, K. and Cleary, R. (2002) '(De)Sexing the Family: Theorizing the Social Science of Lesbian Families', *Feminist Theory*, 3, 3: 271–94.

Mann, K. and Roseneil, S. (1999) 'The Poor Choices of Lone Mothers', in V. Robinson and D. Richardson (eds), *Introducing Women's Studies: Feminist Theory and Practice*, London: Macmillan.

Mansfield, P. and Collard, J. (1988) *The Beginning of the Rest of Your Life? A Portrait of Newly-Wed Marriage*, London: Macmillan.

Marsden, D. (2004) 'The Changing Experience of Researching Family and Intimate Relationships', *International Journal of Social Research Methodology*, 7: 65–71.

Marshment, M. (1997) 'The Picture is Political: Representations of Women in Contemporary Popular Culture', in V. Robinson and D. Richardson (eds), *Introducing Women's Studies: Feminist Theory and Practice*, London: Macmillan.

Martin, E. (1987) *The Woman in the Body*, Cambridge: Cambridge University Press.

Mason, J. (1996) *Qualitative Researching*, London: Sage.

Mason, J. (2002) 'Qualitative Interviewing: Asking, Listening and Interpreting', in T. May (ed.), *Qualitative Research in Action*, London: Sage.

Mauthner, N. and Doucet, A. (2003) 'Reflexive Accounts and Accounts of Reflexivity in Qualitative Data Analysis', *Sociology*, 37: 413–32.

Maynard, M. (1994) 'Methods, Practice and Epistemology: the Debate About Feminism and Research', in M. Maynard and J. Purvis (eds), *Researching Women's Lives from a Feminist Perspective*, London: Taylor & Francis.

Maynard, M. and Purvis, J. (eds) (1995) *(Hetero)sexual Politics*, London: Taylor & Francis.

Maynard, M. and Winn, J. (1997) 'Women, Violence and Male Power', in V. Robinson and D. Richardson (eds), *Introducing Women's Studies: Feminist Theory and Practice*, London: Macmillan.

Meadows, M. (1997) 'Exploring the Invisible: Listening to Mid-life Women About Heterosexual Sex', *Women's Studies International Forum*, 20: 145–52.

Meah, A. (2001) 'Reflecting upon a Feminist Research Processs: a Study of Gatekeeping in an HIV/AIDS Organisation in Durban' (unpublished PhD thesis, University of Manchester).

Meah, A., Hockey, J. and Robinson, V. (2004) 'Narrating Heterosexual Identities: Recollections, Omissions and Contradictions', in D. Robinson, C. Horrocks, N. Kelly and B. Roberts (eds), *Narrative, Memory and Identity: Theoretical & Methodological Issues*, Huddersfield: University of Huddersfield Press.

Middleton, P. (1992) *The Inward Gaze: Masculinity, Subjectivity and Modern Culture*, London: Routledge.

Mies, M. (1983) 'Towards a Methodology for Feminist Research', in G. Bowles and R. Duelli-Klein (eds), *Theories of Women's Studies*, London, Routledge & Kegan Paul.

Miller, V. (2002) 'Intimacy and the Production of Space', paper presented at the Emotional Geographies International Conference, University of Lancaster.

Mishra, R. (1981) *Society and Social Policy*, London: Macmillan.

Misztal, B.A. (2003) *Theories of Social Remembering*, Buckingham: Open University Press.

Moraga, C. and Anzaldua, G. (1981) *This Bridge Called My Back: Writings by Radical Women of Colour*, Watertown, Mass.: Persephone Press.

Morgan, D. (1991) 'Ideologies of Marriage and Family Life', in D. Clark (ed.), *Marriage, Domestic Life and Social Change: Writings for Jacqueline Burgoyne (1944–88)*, London: Routledge.

Morgan, D. (1996) *Family Connections*, Cambridge: Polity.

Morgan, D. (1999) 'Risk and Family Practices: Accounting for Change and Fluidity in Family Life', in E. Silva and C. Smart (eds), *The New Family?* London: Sage.

Morris, J. (1991) *Pride Against Prejudice: Transforming Attitudes to Disability*. London: Women's Press.

Morrison, B. (2002) 'Why do we do it?', *Guardian*, 14 October.

Murphy, R. (1987) *The Body Silent*, New York: Henry Holt.

Namaste, K. (1996), 'Genderbashing: Perceived Transgressions of Normative Sex-Gender Relations in Public Spaces', *Environment and Planning D: Society and Space*, 14: 221–40.

National Statistics Online (ONS) (2006a), accessed 7 February 2006.

National Statistics Online (ONS) (2006b), accessed 18 May 2006.

Nettleton, S. and Watson, J. (1998) *The Body in Everyday Life*, London: Routledge.

Oakley, A. (1981) 'Interviewing Women: a Contradiction in Terms', in H. Roberts (ed.), *Doing Feminist Research*, London: Routledge & Kegan Paul.

Painter, J. (2000) 'Pierre Bourdieu', in M. Crang and N. Thrift (eds), *Thinking Space*, London: Routledge.

Penelope, J. (1994) *Out of the Class Closet: Lesbians Speak*, Freedom, CA: The Crossing Press.

Petersen, A. (1998) *Unmasking the Masculine: 'Men' and 'Identity' in a Sceptical Age*, London: Sage.

Plummer, K. (1995) *Telling Sexual Stories: Power, Change and Social Worlds*, London: Routledge.

Purwar, N. (1997) 'Reflecting Upon Interviewing Women MPs', *Sociological Research Online*, 2, 1.

Ramazanoglu, C. (1993) 'Love and the Politics of Heterosexuality', in S. Wilkinson and C. Kitzinger (eds), *Heterosexuality: a Feminism and Psychology Reader*, London: Sage.

Rapport, N. (1993) *Diverse Worldviews in an English Village*, Edinburgh: Edinburgh University Press.

Rich, A. (1980) 'Compulsory Heterosexuality and Lesbian Existence', *Signs*, 5: 631–60.

Richards, M. and Elliot, B. J. (1991) 'Sex and Marriage in the 1960s and 1970s', in D. Clark (ed.), *Marriage, Domestic Life and Social Change: Writings for Jacqueline Burgoyne (1944–88)*, London: Routledge.

Richardson, D. (1996) 'Heterosexuality and Social Theory', in D. Richardson (ed.), *Theorising Heterosexuality*, Buckingham: Open University Press.

Richardson, D. (1997) 'Sexuality and Feminism', in V. Robinson and D. Richardson (eds), *Introducing Women's Studies: Feminist Theory and Practice*, London: Macmillan.

Richardson, D. (2000) *Rethinking Sexuality*, London: Sage.

Richardson, D. (2004) 'Locating Sexualities: From Here to Normality', *Sexualities*, 7, 4: 391–411.

Richardson, D., McLaughlin, J. and Casey, M. (eds) (2006) *Feminist and Queer Intersections: Sexualities, Cultures and Identities*, London: Palgrave Macmillan.

Robinson, V. (1993) 'Heterosexuality: Beginnings and Connections', in S. Wilkinson and C. Kitzinger (eds), *Heterosexuality*, London: Sage.

Robinson, V. (1996) 'Heterosexuality and Masculinity: Theorising Male Power or the Male Wounded Psyche?' in D. Richardson (ed.), *Theorising Heterosexuality*, Buckingham: Open University Press.

Robinson, V. (1997) 'My Baby Just Cares For Me: Feminism, Heterosexuality and Non-Monogamy', *Journal of Gender Studies*, 6, 2: 143–57.

Robinson, V. (2003) 'Problematic Proposals: Marriage and Cohabitation', *Feminism & Psychology*, 14, 4: 437–41.

Robinson, V. (2004) 'Taking Risks: Identity, Masculinities and Rock Climbing', in B. Wheaton (ed.), *Understanding Lifestyle Sports: Consumption, Identity and Difference*, London: Routledge.

Robinson, V. (forthcoming, 2008) *A Different Kind of Hard: Masculinities, the Everyday and Rock Climbing*, Oxford: Berg.

Robinson, V., Hockey, J. and Meah, A. (2004) ' "What I did . . . on my mother's settee": Spatialising Heterosexuality', *Gender, Place & Culture*, 11: 417–35.

Rosa, B. (1994) 'Anti-Monogamy: a Radical Challenge to Compulsory Heterosexuality', in G. Griffin et al. (eds), *Stirring It: Challenges for Feminism*, London: Taylor & Francis.

Rosen, S (1968) *Plato's Symposium*, New Haven, CT: Yale University Press.

Rutherford, J. (1992) *Predicaments in Masculinity*, London: Routledge.

Schutz, A. ([1932] 1972) *Phenomenology of the Social World*, London: Heinemann.

Schutz, A. (1973) 'Common-sense and Scientific Interpretation of Human Action', in A. Schutz (ed.), *Collected Papers: the Problem of Social Reality*, The Hague: Martin Nijhoff.

Scott, S. (2004) Plenary Address, British Sociological Association Annual Conference, University of York.

Seidler, V. (1989) *Rediscovering Masculinity: Reason, Language and Sexuality*, London: Routledge.

Seidler, V. (ed.), (1992) *Men, Sex and Relationships: Writings From Achilles Heel*, London: Routledge.

Seidler, V. (1998) 'Masculinity, Violence and Emotional Life', in G. Bendelow and S. J. Williams (eds), *Emotions in Social Life: Critical Themes and Contemporary Issues*, London: Routledge.

Seidman, S. (2005) 'From Polluted Homosexual to the Normal Gay: Changing Patterns of Sexual Regulation in America', in C. Ingraham (ed.), *Thinking Straight: New Work in Critical Heterosexuality Studies*, New York: Routledge.

Seller, A. (1994) 'Should the Feminist Philosopher Stay at Home?' in K. Lennon and M. Whitford (eds), *Knowing the Difference*, London: Routledge.

Shipman, B. and Smart, C. (2007) ' "It's made a huge difference": Recognition, Rights and the Personal Significance of Civil Partnerships', *Sociological Research Online*, 12, 1.

Silva, E. and Bennett, T. (eds) (2004) *Contemporary Culture and Everyday Life*, Durham: Sociology Press.

Silva, E. and Smart, C. (1999) 'The "New" Practices and Politics of Family Life', in E. Silva and C. Smart (eds), *The New Family?* London: Sage.

Simpson, B. (1998) *Changing Families*, Oxford: Berg.

Skeggs, B. (1997) *Formations of Class and Gender: Becoming Respectable*, London: Sage.

Smart, C. (1996) 'Collusion, Collaboration and Confession: Moving Beyond the Heterosexuality Debate', in D. Richardson (ed.), *Theorising Heterosexuality*, Buckingham: Open University Press.

Smart, C. (2006) 'Beyond Individualisation: Redrawing the Field of Personal Life', presentation given at the launch of the Morgan Centre for the Study of Relationships and Family Life, University of Manchester, 12 May.

Smith, D. (1987) *The Everyday World as Problematic: a Feminist Sociology*, Milton Keynes: Open University Press.

Smith, D. (1990) *Texts, Facts and Femininity*, London: Routledge.

Spring Rice, M. (1939) *Working Class Wives: Their Health and Conditions*, Harmondsworth: Pelican.

Stacey, J. (1988) 'Can There Be a Feminist Ethnography?' *Women's Studies International Forum*, 11: 21–7.

Stacey, J. (1994) 'Imagining a Feminist Ethnography: a Response to Elizabeth E. Wheatley', *Women's Studies International Forum*, 17: 417–19.

Stanley, L. (1995) *Sex Surveyed 1949–1994: From Mass-Observation's 'Little Kinsey' to the National Survey and the Hite Reports*, London: Taylor & Francis.

Stanley, L. (1997) 'Methodology Matters!' in V. Robinson and D. Richardson (eds), *Introducing Women's Studies: Feminist Theory and Practice*, London: Macmillan.

Steedman, C. (1986) *Landscape for a Good Woman: the Story of Two Lives*, London: Virago.

Stopes, M. (1962) *Married Love: a New Contribution to the Solution of Sexual Difficulties*, London: Hogarth.

Strathern, M. (1987) 'The Limits of Auto-ethnography', in A. Jackson (ed.), *Anthropology at Home*, London: Tavistock.

Swingewood, A. (1991) *A Short History of Sociological Thought*, Basingstoke: Macmillan.

Taylor, Y. (2005a) 'The Gap and How to Mind It: Intersections of Class and Sexuality', *Sociological Research Online*, 10, 3.

Taylor, Y. (2005b) 'What Now? Working-class Lesbians' Post-school Transitions', *Youth and Policy*, 87: 29–43.

Taylor, Y. (forthcoming, 2007) *Working Class Lesbian Life: Classed Outsiders*, Basingstoke: Palgrave Macmillan.

Thomson, R. and Scott, S. (1990) *Researching Sexuality in the Light of AIDS: Historical and Methodological Issues*, London: Tufnell.

Valentine, G. (1993) 'Hetero-sexing Space: Lesbian Perceptions and Experiences of Everyday Spaces', *Environment and Planning D: Society and Space*, 9: 395–413.

VanEvery, J. (1995) *Heterosexual Women Changing the Family: Refusing to be a 'Wife'!* London: Taylor & Francis.

VanEvery, J. (1996) 'Heterosexuality and Domestic Life', in D. Richardson (ed.), *Theorising Heterosexuality*, Buckingham: Open University Press.

Walby, S. (1990) *Theorising Patriarchy*, Oxford: Blackwell.

Walker, A. (1983) 'Social Policy, Social Administration and the Social Construction of Social Policy', in M. Looney, D. Boswell and J. Clark (eds), *Social Policy and Social Welfare*, Buckingham: Open University Press.

Walkowitz, J. (1980) 'The Makings of an Outcast Group: Prostitutes and Working Women in Nineteenth Century Plymouth and Southampton', in M. Vicinus (ed.), *A Widening Sphere: Changing Roles of Victorian Women*, London: Methuen.

Weeks, J. (1989) *Sex, Politics and Society: the Regulation of Sexuality Since 1800*, London: Longman.

Weeks, J. (2000) *Making Sexual History*, Cambridge: Polity.

Weeks, J. (2004) *Sexuality*, London: Routledge.

Weeks, J., Donovan, C. and Heaphy, B. (1999) 'Everyday Experiments: Narratives of Non-heterosexual Relationships', in E. Silva and C. Smart (eds), *The New Family?* London: Sage.

Wheatley, E. (1994) 'How Can We Engender Ethnography with a Feminist Imagination? A Rejoinder to Judith Stacey', *Women's Studies International Forum*, 17: 403–16.

Whitehead, S. M. (2002) *Men and Masculinities*, Cambridge: Polity.

Whyte, S. R. and Ingstad, B. (1995) 'Disability and Culture: an Overview', in B. Ingstad and S. M. Reynolds (eds), *Disability and Culture*, Berkeley: University of California Press.

Wight, D. (1994) 'Boys' Thoughts and Talk About Sex in a Working Class Locality of Glasgow', *Sociological Review*, 42: 703–37.

Wight, D. (1996) 'Beyond the Predatory Male: the Diversity of Young Glaswegian Men's Discourses to Describe Heterosexual Relationships', in L. Adkins and V. Merchant (eds), *Sexualising the Social: Power and the Organisation of Sexuality*, London: Macmillan.

Wilden, A. (1987) *The Rules are No Game: the Strategy of Communication*, London: Routledge & Kegan Paul.

Wilkinson, S. and Kitzinger, C. (1993) *Heterosexuality: a Feminism and Psychology Reader*, London: Sage.

Williams, S. J. (2001) *Emotion and Social Theory: Corporeal Reflections on the (Ir)Rational*, London: Sage.

Wittig, M. (1992) *The Straight Mind and Other Essays*, Brighton: Harvester Wheatsheaf.

Woodward, K. (2004) 'Outside In: Researching Masculinities', paper presented at the University of Newcastle, Department of Sociology, April.

Wray, S. (2003) 'Women Growing Older: Agency, Ethnicity and Culture', *Sociology*, 37: 511–28.

Subject Index

Author Index